RISK ANALYSIS IN THEORY AND PRACTICE

RISK ANALYSIS IN THEORY AND PRACTICE

JEAN-PAUL CHAVAS

ELSEVIER
BUTTERWORTH
HEINEMANN

AMSTERDAM • BOSTON • HEIDELBERG • LONDON
NEW YORK • OXFORD • PARIS • SAN DIEGO
SAN FRANCISCO • SINGAPORE • SYDNEY • TOKYO

Elsevier Academic Press
525 B Street, Suite 1900, San Diego, California 92101-4495, USA
84 Theobald's Road, London WC1X 8RR, UK

This book is printed on acid-free paper. ∞

Library of Congress Cataloging-in-Publication Data
Chavas, Jean-Paul.
Risk analysis in theory and practice / Jean-Paul Chavas.
    p.cm.
  Includes bibliographical references and index.
  ISBN 0-12-170621-4 (alk. paper)
  1. Risk–Econometric models. 2. Uncertainty–Econometric models. 3. Decision
making–Econometric models. 4. Risk–Econometric models–Problems, exercises,
etc. I. Title.

HB615.C59 2004
330'.01'5195–dc22   2004404524

British Library Cataloguing in Publication Data
A catalogue record for this book is available from the British Library

ISBN: 0-12-170621-4

For all information on all Academic Press publications
visit our Web site at www.academicpress.com

Printed in the United States of America

04 05 06 07 08 8 7 6 5 4 3 2 1

To Eloisa, Nicole, and Daniel

Contents

Chapter 1

Introduction

The economics of risk has been a fascinating area of inquiry for at least two reasons. First, there is hardly any situation where economic decisions are made with perfect certainty. The sources of uncertainty are multiple and pervasive. They include price risk, income risk, weather risk, health risk, etc. As a result, both private and public decisions under risk are of considerable interest. This is true in positive analysis (where we want to understand human behavior), as well as in normative analysis (where we want to make recommendations about particular management or policy decisions). Second, over the last few decades, significant progress has been made in understanding human behavior under uncertainty. As a result, we have now a somewhat refined framework to analyze decision-making under risk. The objective of this book is to present this analytical framework and to illustrate how it can be used in the investigation of economic behavior under uncertainty. It is aimed at any audience interested in the economics of private and public decision-making under risk.

In a sense, the economics of risk is a difficult subject; it involves understanding human decisions in the absence of perfect information. How do we make decisions when we do not know some of the events affecting us? The complexities of our uncertain world certainly make this difficult. In addition, we do not understand how well the human brain processes information. As a result, proposing an analytical framework to represent what we do not know seems to be an impossible task. In spite of these difficulties, much progress has been made. First, probability theory is the cornerstone of *risk assessment*. This allows us to measure risk in a fashion that can be communicated among decision makers or researchers. Second, *risk preferences* are now better understood. This provides useful insights into the economic rationality of decision-making under uncertainty. Third, over the last decades, good insights have been developed about the *value of information*. This helps us to better understand the role of information and risk in private as well as public decision-making.

This book provides a systematic treatment of these issues. It provides a mix of conceptual analyses and applied problems. The discussion of conceptual issues is motivated by two factors. First, theoretical developments help frame the structure supporting the empirical analysis of risk behavior. Given the complexity of the factors affecting risk allocation, this structure is extremely valuable. It helps organize information that allows us to gain new and useful insights into the economics of risk. Indeed, without theory, any empirical analysis of decision-making under risk would be severely constrained and likely remain quite primitive. Second, establishing strong linkages between theory and applied work helps assess the strengths and limitations of the theory. This can help motivate the needs for refinements in our theory, which can contribute to improvements in our understanding of risk behavior.

The book also covers many applications to decision-making under risk. Often, applications to risk analysis can appear challenging. Again, this reflects in large part the complexity of the factors affecting economic behavior under risk. A very important aspect of this book involves the examples presented at the end of the chapters. To benefit significantly from the book, each reader is strongly encouraged to go through these examples. They illustrate how risk analysis is conducted empirically. And they provide a great way to fully understand the motivation and interpretation of applied risk analyses. As such, the examples are an integral part of the book. Many examples involve numerical problems related to risk management. In simple cases, these problems can be solved numerically by hand. But most often, they are complex enough that they should be solved using a computer. For that purpose, computer solutions to selected homework problems from the book are available at the following Web site: http://www.aae.wisc.edu/chavas/risk.htm

All computer applications on the Web site involve the use of Microsoft Excel. Since Excel is available to anyone with a computer, the computer applications presented are readily accessible. In general, the computer applications can be run with only minimal knowledge about computers or Excel. For example, the data and Excel programming are already coded in all the applications presented on the Web site. This means that the problems can be solved with minimal effort. This makes the applications readily available to a wide audience. However, this also means that each Excel file has been customized for each problem. If the investigator wants to solve a different problem, he/she will need to modify the data and/or Excel code. While this will typically require some knowledge of Excel programming, often the templates provided can serve as a useful guide to make this task relatively simple.

The book assumes that the reader is familiar with calculus and probabilities. A quick review of probability and statistics is presented in Appendix A. And an overview of some calculus and of optimization methods is presented in Appendix B. The measurement of risk is presented in Chapter 2. It reviews how probability theory provides a framework to assess how individuals perceive uncertainty. Chapter 3 presents the expected utility model. It is the most common model used in the analysis of decision-making under uncertainty. The nature of individual risk preferences is discussed in Chapter 4, where the concept of risk aversion is defined and evaluated. Chapters 5 and 6 review some basic tools used in applied risk analysis. Chapter 5 presents stochastic dominance analysis, which involves the ranking of risky prospects when individual risk preferences are not precisely known. Chapter 6 focuses on the mean-variance analysis commonly used in applied work and evaluates conditions for its validity. Chapter 7 reviews some of the difficulties associated with modeling risk behavior. It evaluates the limitations of the expected utility model and discusses how alternative models can help us better understand decision-making under risk. Chapter 8 develops an analysis of production decisions under risk. The effects of price and production risk on supply decisions are evaluated. The role of diversification and of hedging strategies is discussed. Chapter 9 presents portfolio selection and its implications for asset pricing. The analysis of dynamic decisions under risk is developed in Chapter 10. The role of learning and of the value of information is evaluated in detail. Chapter 11 presents a general analysis of the efficiency of resource allocation under uncertainty. It stresses the role of transaction costs and of the value of information. It discusses and evaluates how markets, contracts, and policy design can affect the efficiency of risk allocation. Chapter 12 presents some applications focusing on risk sharing, insurance, and contract design under asymmetric information. Finally, Chapter 13 evaluates the economics of market stabilization, providing insights into the role of government policies in market economies under uncertainty.

This book is the product of many years of inquiry into the economics of risk. It has been stimulated by significant interactions I had with many people who have contributed to its development, including Rulon Pope, Richard Just, Matt Holt, and many others. The book has grown out of a class I taught on the economics of risk at the University of Wisconsin. My students have helped me in many ways with their questions, inquiries, and suggestions. The book would not have been possible without this exceptional environment. In addition to my family, I want to thank my colleagues at the University of Wisconsin and elsewhere for the quality of the scientific atmosphere that I have enjoyed for the last twenty years. Without their support, I would not have been able to complete this book.

Jean-Paul Chavas

Chapter 2

The Measurement of Risk

We define risk as representing any situation where some events are not known with certainty. This means that the prospects for risk are prevalent. In fact, it is hard to consider any situation where risk does not play a role. Risk can relate to weather outcomes (e.g., whether it will rain tomorrow), health outcomes (e.g., whether you will catch the flu tomorrow), time allocation outcomes (e.g., whether you will get a new job next year), market outcomes (e.g., whether the price of wheat will rise next week), or monetary outcomes (e.g., whether you will win the lottery tomorrow). It can also relate to events that are relatively rare (e.g., whether an earthquake will occur next month in a particular location, or whether a volcano will erupt next year). The list of risky events is thus extremely long. First, this creates a significant challenge to measure risky events. Indeed, how can we measure what we do not know for sure? Second, given that the number of risky events is very large, is it realistic to think that risk can be measured? In this chapter, we address these questions. We review the progress that has been made evaluating risk. In particular, we review how probability theory provides a formal representation of risk, which greatly contributes to the measurement of risk events. We also reflect on the challenges associated with risk assessment.

Before we proceed, it will be useful to clarify the meaning of two terms: *risk* and *uncertainty*. Are these two terms equivalent? Or do they mean something different? There is no clear consensus. There are at least two schools of thought on this issue. One school of thought argues that risk and uncertainty are not equivalent. One way to distinguish between the two relies on the ability to make probability assessments. Then, risk corresponds to events that can be associated with given probabilities; and uncertainty corresponds to events for which probability assessments are not possible. This suggests that risky events are easier to evaluate, while uncertain events are more difficult to assess. For example, getting "tails" as the outcome of flipping a coin is a risky event (its probability is commonly assessed to be 0.5), but the occurrence of an earthquake in a particular location is an uncertain event. This seems intuitive. However, is it always easy to separate risky events from uncertain events? That depends in large part on the meaning of a probability. The problem is that there is not a clear consensus about the existence and interpretation of a probability. We will briefly review this debate. While the debate has generated useful insights on the complexity of risk assessment, it has not yet stimulated much empirical analysis. As a result, we will not draw a sharp distinction between risk and uncertainty. In other words, the reader should know that the terms *risk* and *uncertainty* are used interchangeably throughout the book. It implicitly assumes that individuals can always assess (either objectively or subjectively) the relative likelihood of uncertain events, and that such assessment can be represented in terms of probabilities.

DEFINITION

We define a risky event to be *any event that is not known for sure ahead of time*. This gives some hints about the basic characteristics of risk. First, it rules out sure events (e.g., events that already occurred and have been observed). Second, it suggests that time is a fundamental characteristic of risk. Indeed, allowing for learning, some events that are not known today may become known tomorrow (e.g., rainfall in a particular location). This stresses the temporal dimension of risk.

The prevalence of risky events means that there are lots of things that are not known at the current time. On one hand, this stresses the importance of assessing these risky outcomes in making decisions under uncertainty. On the other hand, this raises a serious issue: How do individuals deal with the extensive uncertainty found in their environment? Attempting to rationalize risky events can come in conflict with the scientific belief, where *any* event can be explained in a cause–effect framework. In this context, one could argue that the scientific belief denies the existence of risk. If so, why are there risky events?

Three main factors contribute to the existence and prevalence of risky events. First, risk exists because of our *inability to control and/or measure* precisely some causal factors of events. A good example (commonly used in teaching probability) is the outcome of flipping a coin. Ask a physicist or an engineer if there is anything that is not understood in the process of flipping a coin. The answer is no. The laws of physics that govern the path followed by the coin are well understood. So, why is the outcome not known ahead of time? The answer is that a coin is never flipped exactly the same way twice. As a result, as long as the coin trajectory is long enough, it is hard to predict how it will land. What creates the uncertainty here is the fact that the initial conditions for the coin trajectory are not precisely controlled. It is this lack of control that makes the coin-flipping outcome appear as a risky event. A second example is the pseudo-random number generator commonly found nowadays in calculators. It generates numbers that are difficult to predict. But how can a calculator create uncertainty? It cannot. All it does is go through a deterministic process. But this process has a special characteristic: It is a *chaotic process* that is sensitive to initial conditions. It means that some small change in initial conditions generates diverging paths and different long-term trajectories. Here, the initial conditions are given by the fraction of a second at which you push the *random number generator* button on the calculator. Each time you push the button, you likely pick a different *seed* and start the chaotic process at a different point, thus generating a different outcome. In this case, it is our inability to control precisely our use of a calculator that makes the outcome appear as a risky event. A final example is the weather. Again, the weather is difficult to predict because it is the outcome of a chaotic process. This holds even if the laws of thermodynamics generating weather patterns are well understood. Indeed, in a chaotic process, any imprecise assessment of the initial conditions is sufficient to imply long-term unpredictability. It is our inability to measure all current weather conditions everywhere that generates some uncertainty about tomorrow's weather.

Second, risk exists because of our *limited ability to process information*. A good example is the outcome of playing a chess game. A chess game involves well-defined rules and given initial conditions. As such, there is no uncertainty about the game. And there are only three possible outcomes: A given player can win, lose, or draw. So why is the outcome of a chess game uncertain? Because there is no known playing strategy that can guarantee a win. Even the largest computer cannot find such a strategy. Interestingly, even large computers using sophisticated programs have a difficult time winning against the best chess players in the world. This indicates that the human brain has an amazing power at processing information compared to computers. But it is the brain's limited power that prevents anyone from devising a strategy that would guarantee a win. It is precisely the reason why playing chess is interesting: One cannot be sure which player is going to win ahead of time. This is a good example to the extent that chess is a simple game with restricted moves and few outcomes. In that sense, playing chess is less complex than most human decision-making. This stresses the importance of information processing in the choice of decision rules. The analysis of decision rules under some limited ability to process information has been called *bounded rationality*. As just noted, the outcome of a chess game is uncertain precisely because the players have a limited ability to process information about the payoff of all available strategies (otherwise, the outcome of the game would be known with the identification of the first mover). Once we realize that no one is able to process all the information available about our human environment, it becomes clear that risky events are very common.

Third, even if the human brain can obtain and process a large amount of information, this does not mean that such information will be used. Indeed, obtaining and processing information is typically costly. The *cost of information* can take many forms. It can involve a monetary cost (e.g., purchasing a newspaper or paying for consulting services) as well as nonmonetary cost (e.g., the opportunity cost of time spent learning). Given that human learning is time consuming and that time is a scarce resource, it becomes relevant to decide what each individual should learn. Given bounded rationality, no one can be expected to know a lot about everything. This suggests a strong incentive for individuals to specialize in areas where they can develop special expertise (e.g., plumber specializing in plumbing, medical doctors specializing in medical care, etc.). The social benefits of specialization can be quite significant and generate large improvements in productivity (e.g., the case of the industrial revolution). If information is costly, this suggests that obtaining and processing information is not always worth it. Intuitively, information should be obtained only if its benefits are greater than its cost. Otherwise, it may make sense not to collect and/or process information. These are the issues addressed in Chapter 10 on the economics of information. But if some information is not being used because of its cost, this also means that there is greater uncertainty about our environment. In other words, costly information contributes to the prevalence of risky events.

So there are many reasons why there is imperfect information about many events. Whatever the reasons, all risky events have a unique characteristic: They are not known for sure ahead of time. This means that there is always more than one possibility that can occur. This common feature has been captured by a unified theory that has attempted to put some structure on risky events. This is the theory of probability. The scientific community has advanced *probability theory* as a formal structure that can describe and represent risky events. A review of probability theory is presented in Appendix A. Given the prevalence of risk, probability theory has been widely adopted and used. We will make extensive use of it throughout this book. We will also briefly reflect about some of its limitations.

Note that it is possible that one person knows something that is unknown to another person. This suggests that imperfect knowledge is typically individual specific (as you might suspect, this has created a large debate about the exact interpretation of probabilities). It is also possible for individuals to learn over time. This means that imperfect knowledge is situation and time specific. As a result, we define "imperfect knowledge" as any situation where, at a given time, an individual does not have perfect information about the occurrences in his/her physical and socioeconomic environment.

In the context of probabilities, any event A has a probability $Pr(A)$, such that $0 \leq Pr(A) \leq 1$. This includes as a special case sure events, where $Pr(A) = 1$. Since risky events and sure events are defined to be mutually exclusive, it follows that *risky events are characterized by* $Pr(A) < 1$. A common example is the outcome of flipping a coin. Even if this is the outcome of a deterministic process (as discussed previously), it behaves *as if* it were a risky event. All it takes for a risky event is that its outcome is not known for sure ahead of time. As discussed above, a particular event may or may not be risky depending on the ability to measure it, the ability to control it, the ability to obtain and process information, and the cost of information.

In general, in a particular situation, denote the set of all possible outcomes by S. The set S is called the *sample space*. Particular elements A_1, A_2, A_3, ..., of the set S represent particular events. The statement $A_i \subset A_j$ reads "A_i is a subset of A_j" and means that all elementary events that are in A_i are also in A_j. The set $(A_i \cup A_j)$ represents the union of A_i and A_j, that is the set of elementary events in S that occur *either* in A_i or in A_j. The set $(A_i \cap A_j)$ represents the intersection of A_i and A_j, that is the set of elementary events in S that occur in *both* A_i and A_j. Two events A_i and A_j are said to be disjoint if they have no point in common, that is if $(A_i \cap A_j) = \varnothing$, where $\varnothing$ denotes the empty set). Then, for a given sample space S, a *probability distribution Pr* is a function satisfying the following properties:

1. $Pr(A_i) \geq 0$ for all events A_i in S.
2. $Pr(S) = 1$.
3. If A_1, A_2, A_3, ..., are disjoint events, then
   $Pr(A_1 \cup A_2 \cup A_3 \ldots) = \sum_i Pr(A_i)$.

In the case where risky events are measured by real numbers, this generates random variables. A *random variable X* is a function that takes a specific real value $X(s)$ at each point s in the sample space S. Then, the *distribution function* of the random variable X is the function F satisfying $F(t) = Pr(X \leq t)$. Thus, the distribution function measures the probability that X will be less than or equal to t. See Appendix A for more details.

As you might suspect, the rather loose characterization of risky events has generated some disagreement about the exact meaning of a probability. In general, a probability can be interpreted to measure anything that we don't know for sure. But knowledge can be subjective and vary across individuals. This has led to alternative interpretations of probabilities.

First, a probability can be interpreted as measuring the *relative frequency* of an event. This is very intuitive. For example, if a coin is flipped many times, the outcomes tend to be *heads* 50 percent of the time and *tails* the other 50 percent of the time. As a result, we say that the probability of obtaining *heads* at any particular toss is 0.5, and the probability of obtaining *tails* is 0.5. This is the relative frequency interpretation of probabilities. It is quite intuitive for events that are repeatable (e.g., coin flipping). In this case, repeating the underlying experiment many times and observing the associated outcomes provide a basis for assessing the probabilities of particular events. As long as the experimental conditions do not change, this generates sample information that can be used to estimate the probability of each event. This is the standard approach used in *classical statistics*.

But not all risky events are repeatable. Some events are observed very rarely (e.g., the impact of a comet hitting earth) and others are observed under changing conditions (e.g., a meltdown in a nuclear power plant). In such cases, it is difficult to acquire sample information that would allow us to assess the probability of the corresponding events. In addition, it is quite possible to see different individuals disagree about the probability of some event. This can happen for two reasons. First, individuals typically have specialized knowledge. As a result, we expect risk assessment provided by "experts" to be more reliable than the one provided by "nonexperts." For example, information about a health status tends to be more reliable when coming from a medical doctor than from your neighbor. In some cases, it means that the opinion of experts is consulted before making an important decision (e.g., court decisions). But in other cases, decisions are made without such information. This may be because experts are not available or the cost of consulting them is deemed too high. Then the information used in human decision-making would be limited. This is a situation where the assessment of the probability of risky events may vary greatly across individuals. Second, even if experts are consulted, they sometimes disagree. This is the reason why some patients decide to obtain a second opinion before proceeding with a possibly life-threatening treatment. Again, disagreements among experts about risky events would generate situations where the assessment of probabilities would vary across individuals.

These arguments indicate that the probability assessment of risky events is often personal and subjective. They are subjective in the sense that they may be based on limited sample information (e.g., the case on nonrepeatable events). And they are personal in the sense that they can vary across individuals (e.g., the assessed probability that the home team will win a game can depend on whether the individual is a sports fan or not). In this context, the relative frequency interpretation of probability appears inadequate. As an alternative, this has stimulated the *subjective interpretation* of probabilities. A probability is then seen as a subjective and personal evaluation of the *relative likelihood* of an event reflecting the individual's own information and belief. This is the approach used in *Bayesian statistics*. Here, the concept of relative likelihood seems broad enough to cover both nonrepeatable events and individual variability in beliefs. But is it reasonable to assume that subjective probabilities exist?

THE EXISTENCE OF PROBABILITY DISTRIBUTIONS

In this section, we present arguments supporting the existence of subjective probabilities. They are based on the concept of (subjective) *relative likelihood*. For a given sample space S, we will use the following notation:

$A <_L B$: event B is more likely than event A.

$A \leq_L B$: event B is at least as likely as event A.

$A \sim_L B$: events A and B are equally likely.

We consider the following assumptions:

As1: For any two events A and B, exactly one of the following holds:

$$A <_L B, \ A \sim_L B, \ B <_L A.$$

As2: If $A_1 \cap A_2 = \varnothing = B_1 \cap B_2$ *and* $A_i \leq_L B_i$, $i = 1, 2$, then

$$(A_1 \cup A_2) \leq_L (B_1 \cup B_2).$$

If in addition, either $A_1 <_L B_1$ *or* $A_2 <_L B_2$, then

$$(A_1 \cup A_2) <_L (B_1 \cup B_2).$$

As3: For any event A, $\varnothing \leq_L A$. In addition, $\varnothing <_L S$.

As4: If $A_1 \supset A_2 \supset \ldots$ is a decreasing sequence of events and if $B \leq_L A_i$, $i = 1, 2, \ldots$, then

$$B \leq_L (A_1 \cap A_2 \cap A_3 \ldots).$$

As5: There exists a random variable X uniformly distributed in the interval $[0, 1]$, i.e., where X satisfies

$[x \in (a_1,\ b_1)] \leq_L [x \in (a_2,\ b_2)]$ if and only if $(b_1 - a_1)(b_2 - a_2)$
for any sub-interval $\{(a_i,\ b_i):\ 0 \leq a_i \leq b_i \leq 1,\ i = 1,\ 2\}$.

Proposition 1: Under assumptions As1–As5, for any event A, there exists a unique probability function $Pr(A)$ satisfying

$$A \sim_L G[0,\ Pr(A)]$$

where $G[a,\ b]$ is the event that a uniformly distributed random variable lies in the interval (a, b). Also, $Pr(A) \leq Pr(B)$ if $A \leq_L B$ for any two events A and B.

For a proof, see Savage, or DeGroot (p. 77). Proposition 1 establishes that, under some regularity conditions, the concept of relative likelihood is sufficient to imply the existence of a subjective probability distribution for any risky event. This suggests that probability theory can be applied broadly in any analysis of risky situations. This is the type of argument that has contributed to making probability theory the basic building block of statistics and the analysis of decision-making under risk. For that reason, we will rely extensively on probability theory throughout this book.

Proposition 1 is also useful in another way. It identifies five assumptions that are needed to validate the existence of probabilities. It means that, if probabilities failed to represent risky events, it must be because at least one of these assumptions is not valid. Assumptions As3, As4, and As5 are usually noncontroversial. For example, As3 simply eliminates some trivial situations. But assumptions As1 and As2 can be challenged. They imply that an individual can always rank the relative likelihood of risky events in a consistent manner. For example, there may be situations of bounded rationality where relative likelihood rankings by an individual are not consistent with probability rankings. In this case, probability theory can fail to provide an accurate representation of (subjective) risk exposure. There has been a fair amount of empirical evidence (collected mainly by psychologists) pointing out these inconsistencies. It has stimulated some research on alternative representations of risk. This includes the theory of "fuzzy sets" and "ambiguity theory." *Fuzzy sets* theory is based on the premise that individuals may not be able to distinguish precisely between alternative prospects (*see* Zadeh 1987; Zimmermann 1985; Smithson 1987). *Ambiguity* theory considers the case where individuals may not be able to assign unique probabilities to some risky events (*see* Ellsberg 1961; Schmeidler 1989; Mukerji 1998). However, while this stresses potential shortcomings of probabilities, it is fair to say that, at this point, no single alternative theory has been widely adopted in risk assessment. On that basis, we will rely extensively on probability theory throughout the book.

ELICITATIONS OF PROBABILITIES

Consider the case where Assumptions As1–As5 hold. From Proposition 1, this means that probabilities provide a comprehensive way of assessing the relative likelihood of risky situations. This will prove useful in risk analysis, but only if probabilities can be empirically estimated. This raises a number of questions. Given some risky events represented by a probability distribution, how can we estimate this probability distribution? Or in the case where the risky outcomes are measured with numbers, how can we estimate the associated distribution function?

CASE OF REPEATABLE EVENTS

In the case of repeatable events, repeated experiments can generate *sample information*. This sample information can be used to assess the probability distribution (or the distribution function) of risky events. In general, there are different ways of conducting these experiments, each experiment providing different information. Of course, no experiment can provide information about everything that is unknown. For example, studying a math textbook can help students learn about math and prepare for a math test, but it will not help them learn about history (or prepare for a history test). Thus, once we identify the uncertain events we want to know better, which experiment should be performed? The *theory of experimental design* addresses the issue of choosing an experiment so as to maximize the amount of desired information. The sample information generated can then be used to learn about specific risky events.

Assume that sample information has been collected from repeated applications of an experiment about some risky prospects. The *classical approach to statistics* focuses on the analysis of this sample information. The sample information can be used in at least three ways. First, it can be used to assess directly the probability distribution (or distribution function) of the risky events. An example is the plotting of the distribution function based on the sample observations of a random variable (e.g., the outcome of rolling a die; or price changes, assuming that their distribution is stable over time). This simply involves plotting the proportion of sample observations that are less than some given value t as a function of t. Then drawing a curve through the points gives a sample estimate of the distribution function. Since this can be done without making any a priori assumption about the shape of the distribution function, this is called the *nonparametric approach*. The sample distribution function being typically erratic, it is often smoothed to improve its statistical properties. This is the basis of *nonparametric statistics*.

Second, we may want to assume that the probability distribution belongs to a class of parametric functions. An example is the class of normal distribution in the case of continuous random variables (which involves two sets of parameters: means and variances/covariances). Then, the sample information can be used to estimate the parameters of the distribution function. This is the basis of *parametric statistics*. A common approach is to evaluate the likelihood function of the sample and to choose the parameters that maximize the sample likelihood function. This is the *maximum likelihood method*. It generates parameter estimates that have desirable statistical properties when the sample is relatively large. However, this method requires a priori knowledge about the parametric class of the probability distribution.

Third, when we are not sure of the exact properties of the distribution function, it is still possible to obtain some summary statistics from the sample information. In the context of random variables, this can be done by estimating *sample moments* of the distribution: sample mean, sample variance, sample skewness, sample kurtosis, etc. The mean provides a simple measure of central tendency for a random variable. The variance measures the dispersion around its mean. The only requirement for this approach is that the sample moments remain finite. A common example is the *least squares method in regression analysis*, which estimates the *regression line* measuring the mean value of the dependent variable for given values of the explanatory variables. Again, this does not require a priori knowledge about the exact form of the distribution function.

Case of Nonrepeatable Events

However, there are a number of risky events that are not repeatable. This applies to rare events as well as to events that occur under conditions that are difficult to measure and control. In this case, it is problematical to generate sample information that would shed light on such risky prospects. In the absence of sample information, Proposition 1 indicates that subjective probabilities can still provide a complete characterization of the risk. Then, we need to rely on subjective probability judgments. Since such judgments often vary across individuals (as discussed previously), it means a need for individual assessments of probabilities. This can be done by conducting individual interviews about risky prospects, relying on the concept of relative likelihood (from Proposition 1). There are at least two approaches to the interview: using reference lotteries and using the fractile method. They are briefly discussed next.

Using Reference Lotteries

Consider the case of an individual facing risky prospects represented by mutually exclusive events A_1, A_2, ... Parts of the interview involve the prospect of paying the individual a desirable prize $\$Y > 0$ if particular events occur. For each event A_i, $i = 1, 2, \ldots$, design the individual interview along the following iterative scheme:

Step 1: Start with some initial guess p_{ij} as a rough estimate of $Pr(A_i)$, $j = 1$.

Step 2: Consider the game G_{i0}: give the individual $\$Y > 0$ if A_i occurs, $\$0$ otherwise.

Step 3: Consider the game G_{ij}: give the individual $\$Y > 0$ with probability p_{ij}.

Step 4: Ask the individual if he/she prefers game G_{i0} over game G_{ij}.
If he/she prefers game G_{i0}, choose $p_{i, j+1}$ smaller than p_{ij}. Then, with $j = j + 1$, go to step 3.
If he/she prefers game G_{ij}, choose $p_{i, j+1}$ larger than p_{ij}. Then, with $j = j + 1$, go to step 3.
If he/she is indifferent between game G_{i0} and game G_{ij}, then $p_{ij} = Pr(A_i)$.

Step 4 relies on the implicit (and intuitive) assumption that the individual is better off when facing a higher probability of gaining $\$Y$. The above procedure is relatively simple to implement when the number of events is small. It is general and can be used to obtain an estimate of the individual subjective probability of any risky event. However, it can become tedious when the number of risky prospects becomes large. As stated, it also assumes that the individual is familiar with the concept of probabilities. If not, step 3 needs to be modified. For example, if $(100p_{ij})$ is an integer, then game G_{ij} in step 3 could be defined as follows: give $\$Y$ to the individual when a red marble is drawn at random from a bag containing $(100p_{ij})$ red marbles and $[100(1 - p_{ij})]$ white marbles.

The Fractile Method

The fractile method can be applied to the assessment of probabilities for random variables. More specifically, for an individual facing a continuous random variable X (e.g., price, income), it involves the estimation of the subjective distribution function $Pr(X \leq z_i)$ for selected values of z_i. Design the individual interview along the following iterative scheme:

Step 1: Find the value $z_{.5}$ such that the two events $(x \leq z_{.5})$ and $(x \geq z_{.5})$ are evaluated by the individual to be equally likely: $(x \leq z_{.5}) \sim_L (x \geq z_{.5})$.

Step 2: Find the value $z_{.25}$ such that the two events $(x \le z_{.25})$ and $(z_{.25} \le x \le z_{.5})$ are evaluated by the individual to be equally likely: $(x \le z_{.25}) \sim_L (z_{.25} \le x \le z_{.5})$.

Step 3: Find the value $z_{.75}$ such that the two events $(x \ge z_{.75})$ and $(z_{.5} \le x \le z_{.75})$ are evaluated by the individual to be equally likely: $(x \ge z_{.75}) \sim_L (z_{.5} \le x \le z_{.75})$.

Same for $z_{.125}$, $z_{.375}$, $z_{.625}$, $z_{.875}$, etc . . . .

Plot the points $i = Pr(x \le z_i)$ as a function of z, and draw a curve through them. This gives an estimate of the distribution function for x.

This procedure is general and applicable to the estimation of the personal subjective distribution function of any continuous random variable. At each step, uncovering the value z_i can be assessed through indirect questioning. For example, in step 1, several values may be tried before uncovering the value $z_{.5}$ that satisfies $(x \le z_{.5}) \sim_L (x \ge z_{.5})$.

BAYESIAN ANALYSIS

Bayesian analysis relies on both *sample information* and *prior information* about uncertain prospects. This is expressed in *Bayes theorem*, which combines prior information and sample information to generate *posterior probabilities* of risky events (see Appendix A). When the prior information is sample-based, this gives a way to update probabilities in the light of new sample information. More generally, it allows for the prior information to be subjective. Then, Bayesian analysis provides a formal representation of human learning, as an individual would update his/her subjective beliefs after receiving new information.

There are two main ways of implementing Bayesian analysis. First, if the posterior probabilities have a known parametric form, then parameter estimates can be obtained by *maximizing the posterior probability function*. This has the advantage of providing a complete characterization of the posterior distribution. Second, we can rely on *posterior moments*: posterior mean, variance, etc. This is the scheme implemented by the Kalman filter. It generates estimates of posterior moments that incorporate the new sample information. It has the advantage of not requiring precise knowledge of the posterior probability function.

Note that a long-standing debate has raged between classical statisticians and Bayesian statisticians. Classical statistics tends to rely exclusively on sample information and to neglect prior information. This neglect is often justified on the grounds that prior information is often difficult to evaluate and communicate (especially if it varies significantly among individuals). Bayesian statisticians have stressed that prior information is always present and that neglecting it involves a significant loss of information. In general, the scientific community has leaned in favor of classical statistics, in large part because the great variability of individual beliefs is difficult to assess empirically.

While Bayesian analysis can provide a formal representation of human learning, it is relevant to ask: How realistic is it? The general answer is that Bayes' rule appears to provide only a crude representation of how humans process information. Psychologists have documented the process of human learning. There are situations where people do not update their prior beliefs quite as much as predicted by Bayes' theorem (e.g., the case of conservative beliefs that are not changed in the face of new information). Alternatively, people sometimes neglect their prior beliefs in the face of new information.

In general, human learning is quite complex. While the ability of the brain to process information is truly amazing, the functioning of the brain is still poorly understood. The way the brain stores information is of special interest. On one hand, the brain has a *short-term memory* that exhibits limited capacity and quick decay. On the other hand, the brain has a *long-term memory* that exhibits nearly limitless capacity and slow decay, but is highly selective. If the information stored by the brain is decaying, then *memory loss* suggests that new information (sample information) may tend to carry more weight than the old information (prior information). But actions can be taken to slow down the decay process of information stock (e.g., reviewing). This indicates that trying to remember something can be costly.

In addition, the *learning process is costly*. Obtaining and processing information typically involves the use of money, time, resources, etc. In general, *education and experience* can reduce learning cost. This stresses the role of human capital in economic decisions and resource allocation under uncertainty. Under costly information, some information may not be worth obtaining, processing, or remembering. Under *bounded rationality*, people may not be able to obtain or process some information. And if prior probability judgments are revised in light of additional evidence, individuals may not update them according to Bayes' theorem.

Finally, *new information is carried out by signals* (e.g., written words, language, etc.). These signals are not perfect (e.g., they may have different meanings for different people). The nature of signals can influence the way information is processed by individuals. This is called *framing bias*. In general, this suggests that some framing bias is likely to be present in the subjective elicitation of individual information.

All these arguments point out the complexities of the learning process. As a result, we should keep in mind that any model of learning and behavior under risk is likely to be a somewhat unsatisfactory representation of the real world. Does that invalidate Bayesian analysis? It depends on what we are trying to accomplish. If we want to obtain an accurate representation of human learning, then Bayesian analysis may be seen as unsatisfactory. On the other hand, if we think that Proposition 1 applies, then Bayes' theorem provides a convenient rationalization of probability updating in the face of new information.

PROBLEMS

Note: An asterisk (*) indicates that the problem has an accompanying Excel file on the web page http://www.aae.wisc.edu/chavas/risk.htm.

*1. Think of a fixed site outside the building which you are in at this moment. Let X be the temperature at that site at noon tomorrow. Choose a number x_1 such that

$$Pr(X < x_1) = Pr(X > x_1) = 1/2.$$

Next, choose a number x_2 such that

$$Pr(X < x_2) = Pr(x_2 < X < x_1) = 1/4.$$

Finally, choose numbers x_3 and x_4 ($x_3 < x_1 < x_4$) such that

$$Pr(X < x_3) + Pr(X > x_4) = Pr(x_3 < X < x_1) = Pr(x_1 < X < x_4) = 1/3.$$

    a. Using the values of x_1 and x_2 that you have chosen and a table of the standard normal distribution, find the unique normal distribution for X that satisfies your answers (x_1, x_2).

    b. Assuming that X has the normal distribution established in $a/$, find from the tables the values which x_3 and x_4 must have. Compare these values with the values you have chosen. Decide whether or not your distribution for X can be represented approximately by a normal distribution.

*2. The joint probability function of two random variables X and Y is given in the following table:

Probability	$Y = 5$	$Y = 6$	$Y = 7$	$Y = 8$
$X = 1$	0.01	0.18	0.24	0.06
$X = 2$	0.06	0.09	0.12	0.03
$X = 3$	0.02	0.03	0.04	0.12

    a. Determine the marginal probability functions of X and Y.
    b. Are X and Y independent? Why or why not?
    c. What is the conditional probability function of X, given $Y = 7$?
    d. What is the expected value of Y, given $X = 3$?
    e. What is the expected value of Y? of X?

f. What is the variance of X? The variance of Y? The covariance between X and Y? The correlation between X and Y?

*3. You face a decision problem involving three states of nature with prior probabilities

$$Pr(a_1) = .15, \ Pr(a_2) = .30, \ and \ Pr(a_3) = .55.$$

To gain further information, you consult an expert who gives you a forecast (z) with conditional probabilities:

$$Pr(z|a_1) = 0.30; \ Pr(z|a_2) = 0.50; \ Pr(z|a_3) = 0.10.$$

If you are a Bayesian learner, what probabilities do you want to use in your decision?

Chapter 3

The Expected Utility Model

Given the existence of risky events, how do individuals make decisions under risk? First, they must evaluate the risk itself. As seen in Chapter 2, probability assessments provide a way of characterizing the nature and extent of individual risk exposure. In this chapter, we will assume the risk has been assessed and that the corresponding probabilities have been estimated. The next issue is, given an assessment of risk exposure, which decision should the individual make? This is a nontrivial issue. Indeed, human decision-making under uncertainty can be extremely complex for at least two reasons. First, the number of risky events facing an individual is typically quite large. Second, the way information is processed to make decisions under risk can be quite complicated.

Given these complexities, we will start with simple hypotheses about decision-making under risk. As you might expect, while simple models have the advantage of being empirically tractable, they may provide unrealistic representations of human decision-making. This identifies some trade-off between empirical tractability and realism. The analysis presented in this chapter will be limited in scope. We consider only the case of uncertain monetary rewards, and we focus our attention on the expected utility model developed by von Neumann and Morgenstern in the mid 1940s. It has become the dominant model used to represent decision-making under uncertainty. Further extensions and generalizations will be explored in later chapters.

THE ST. PETERSBURG PARADOX

Before considering the expected utility model, we will consider a very simple model of decision-making under risk. In a situation involving monetary rewards, a simple measure of individual payoff is the mean (also called the *average*, or the *expected value*) of the reward. Treating the reward as a random variable with a given subjective probability distribution, its expected value measures the central tendency of its distribution. Consider the (intuitive) assumption where individuals are made better off when receiving higher monetary rewards. This suggests considering the following hypothesis: decision-making maximizes *expected reward*. This provides a simple model of decision-making under uncertainty. It has the advantage of being empirically tractable. For example, consider an individual facing uncertainty represented by mutually exclusive states, e_1, e_2, e_3, . . ., and receiving the monetary reward $a(e_s, d)$ under state e_s when making decision d. If the probability of facing the s-th state under decision d is $Pr(e_s, d)$, then the expected reward under decision d is $E(a(d)) = \sum_s Pr(e_s, d) \cdot a(e_s, d)$. Note that this allows the decision d to influence both the reward $a(e_s, d)$ and the probability that the individual faces the s-th state. Then, the maximization of expected reward means that the individual would choose d so as to maximize $E(a(d))$. This can be implemented easily. First, evaluate $E(a(d)) = \sum_s Pr(e_s, d) \cdot a(e_s, d)$ for different choices d; and second, make the decision d that gives the highest value for $E(a(d))$. However, this implicitly neglects the potential role played by the variability of rewards (e.g., as measured by its variance). Is this realistic? In other words, do people behave in the way consistent with the maximization of expected rewards?

To address this question, consider the following game. Flip a coin repeatedly until a head is obtained for the first time and receive the reward $\$(2^n)$ if the first head is obtained on the nth toss. This is a simple game. What is the maximum amount of money you would be willing to pay to play this game? As you might suspect, no individual is willing to invest all his/her wealth just to play this game. Yet, the probability of a head at any coin toss being $\frac{1}{2}$, the expected value of the reward is

$$E(\text{reward}) = \sum_{n \geq 1} 2^n (1/2)^n = 1 + 1 + \ldots = \infty.$$

Thus, if individuals behaved in a way consistent with the maximization of expected rewards, their willingness to play the game would be infinite. The fact that this is not the case indicates that people *typically do not behave so as to maximize the expected value of rewards*. This has been called the "St. Petersburg paradox." Although it is really not a paradox, it is of historical significance. Bernoulli first mentioned it in the eighteenth century in his discussion of decision-making under uncertainty. (St. Petersburg was a center for gambling in Europe at that time.) It provides empirical evidence that the maximization of expected rewards is really too simple and does not provide a good representation of decision-making under risk.

THE EXPECTED UTILITY HYPOTHESIS

If individuals do not maximize expected rewards, how do they behave under risk? Intuitively, this suggests that they are concerned with more than just the mean or expected value of the reward. This means that we need a model that takes into consideration the dispersion of the rewards around the mean. A convenient way to do this is to assume that individuals make decisions on the basis of the *expected utility of rewards*.

Consider an individual making decisions facing risky monetary rewards represented by the random variable a. Each decision affects the probability distribution of the monetary payoff. Let $a(d_i)$ be the random reward when decision d_i is made, $i = 1, 2, 3, \ldots$. The individual has to decide among the risky prospects $a_1 \equiv a(d_1)$, $a_2 \equiv a(d_2)$, $a_3 \equiv a(d_3), \ldots$. The first issue is to record the individual preferences among those prospects. Concerning the choice between a_1 and a_2, this is denoted as follows:

$a_1 \sim^* a_2$ denotes indifference between a_1 and a_2,

$a_1 \geq^* a_2$ denotes that a_2 is not preferred to a_1,

$a_1 >^* a_2$ denotes that a_1 is preferred to a_2.

At this point, this involves only statements about preferences among risky choices. This can be used to describe actual behavior. For example, one would observe an individual choosing a_1 over a_2 when his/her preferences satisfy $a_1 \geq^* a_2$. But if we also want to predict behavior or make recommendations about particular decisions, we need some formal framework to represent the decision-making process under risk.

> **expected utility hypothesis**: A decision-maker has risk preferences represented by a utility function $U(a)$, and he/she makes decisions so as to maximize expected utility $EU(a)$, where E is the expectation operator based on the subjective probability distribution of a.

The expected utility hypothesis states that individual decision-making under uncertainty is always consistent with the maximization of $EU(a)$. In the case where "a" is a discrete random variable taking values $a(e_i)$ under state e_i, where $a(e_i)$ occurs with probability $Pr(a(e_i))$, $i = 1, 2, \ldots$, the individual's expected utility is given by $EU(a) = \sum_{i \geq 1} U(a(e_i))Pr(a(e_i))$. And in the case where "a" is a continuous random variable with distribution function $F(a)$, then $EU(a) = \int U(a)dF(a)$. This provides a convenient way of assessing expected utility. As such, the expected utility model provides a convenient basis for risk analysis. But is the *expected utility hypothesis* a reasonable representation of individual behavior under risk? And how do we know that the utility function $U(a)$ exists?

THE EXISTENCE OF THE UTILITY FUNCTION

Once the probabilities of the risky prospects have been assessed, the expected utility model requires us to know the individual risk preferences, as represented by the utility function $U(a)$. But how do we know that a utility function $U(a)$ will summarize all the risk information relevant to making individual decisions under uncertainty? To address this issue, we want to find conditions under which human behavior would always be consistent with the expected utility hypothesis. These conditions involve the following assumptions on individual preferences among risky prospects.

Assumption A1 (ordering and transitivity)

- For any random variables a_1 and a_2, exactly one of the following must hold:

$$a_1 >^* a_2, \ a_2 >^* a_1, \ or \ a_1 \sim^* a_2.$$

- If $a_1 \geq^* a_2$ *and* $a_2 \geq^* a_3$, then $a_1 \geq^* a_3$. (transitivity)

Assumption A2 (independence)
For any random variables a_1, a_2, a_3, and any α $(0 < \alpha < 1)$, then $a_1 \leq^* a_2$ if and only if

$$[\alpha \ a_1 + (1 - \alpha)a_3] \leq^* [\alpha \ a_2 + (1 - \alpha)a_3].$$

(the preferences between a_1 and a_2 are independent of a_3)

Assumption A3 (continuity)
For any random variables a_1, a_2, a_3 where $a_1 <^* a_3 <^* a_2$, there exist numbers α and β, $0 < \alpha < 1$, $0 < \beta < 1$, such that

$$a_3 <^* [\alpha \ a_2 + (1 - \alpha)a_1] \text{ and } a_3 >^* [\beta a_2 + (1 - \beta)a_1].$$

(a sufficiently small change in probabilities will not reverse a strict preference)

Assumption A4
For any risky prospects a_1, a_2 satisfying $Pr[a_1 \leq r : a_1 \leq^* r] = Pr[a_2 \geq r : a_2 \geq^* r] = 1$ for some sure reward r, then $a_2 \geq^* a_1$.

Assumption A5

- For any number r, there exist two sequences of numbers $s_1 \geq^* s_2 \geq^* \ldots$ and $t_1 \leq^* t_2 \leq^* \ldots$ satisfying $s_m \leq^* r$ and $r \leq^* t_n$ for some m and n.
- For any risky prospects a_1 and a_2, if there exists an integer m_0 such that $[a_1$ conditional on $a_1 \geq s_m : a_1 \geq^* s_m] \geq^* a_2$ for every $m \geq m_0$, then $a_1 \geq^* a_2$. And if there exists an integer n_0 such that $[a_1$ conditional $a_1 \leq t_n : a_1 \leq^* t_n] \leq^* a_2$ for every $n \geq n_0$, then $a_1 \leq^* a_2$.

expected utility theorem: Under assumptions A1–A5, for any risky prospects a_1 and a_2, there exists a utility function $U(a)$ representing individual risk preferences such that

$$a_1 \geq^* a_2 \text{ if and only if } EU(a_1) \geq EU(a_2),$$

where $U(a)$ is defined up to a positive linear transformation.

See von Neumann and Morgenstern, or De Groot (p. 113–114) for a proof. This states that under Assumptions A1–A5, the expected utility hypothesis provides an accurate characterization of behavior under risk. This gives axiomatic support for the expected utility model. It means that under Assumptions A1–A5, observing which decision an individual makes is equivalent to solving the maximization problem: Max $EU(a)$. As such, the expected utility model can be used in positive economic analysis, trying to explain (and predict) human behavior under risk. In addition, if both the probability distribution of "a" and the individual risk preferences $U(\cdot)$ are known, then the expected utility model can be used in normative economic analysis, making recommendations about which decision an individual should make. Exploring these issues will be the subject of the following chapters.

It is important to note that the expected utility model is *linear in the probabilities*. To illustrate, consider the case where "a" is a discrete random variable. Then, the expected utility is given by $EU(a) = \sum_i Pr(a^i) U(a^i)$, which is indeed linear in the probabilities $Pr(a^i)$. But where does this linearity come from? From the expected utility theorem, it must be associated with the assumptions made. A closer examination of these assumptions indicates that the linearity in the probability follows from the *independence assumption* (A2).

The expected utility theorem provides some basis for evaluating the empirical validity of the expected utility model. Indeed, it gives necessary and sufficient conditions (Assumptions A1–A5) for Max $EU(a)$ to be consistent with human behavior. This means that, if the expected utility model is observed to be inconsistent with observed behavior, it must be because some of the Assumptions A1–A5 are not satisfied. This can provide useful insights about the search for more refined models of decision-making under risk. In this context, which of the five assumptions may be most questionable? Assumptions A4–A5 are rather technical. They are made to guarantee that $EU(\cdot)$ is measurable. As such, they have not been the subject of much debate. This leaves Assumptions A1, A2, and A3. Each of these three assumptions has been investigated. The ordering Assumption A1 has been questioned on the grounds that decision-makers may not always be able to rank risky alternatives in a consistent manner. As noted above, the independence Assumption A2 means that preferences are linear in the probabilities. Thus, Assumption A2 may not hold if individual preferences exhibit significant interactions between probabilities. In other words, finding evidence that preferences are nonlinear in the probabilities is equivalent to questioning the validity of the independence Assumption A2. Finally, the continuity Assumption A3 may not apply if decision rules involve threshold levels (e.g., subsistence levels) that must be met under all circumstances. These arguments provide some insights about potential weaknesses of the expected utility model (Machina, 1984). They also point to possible directions for developing more complex models of decision-making under risk. We will examine these issues in more detail in Chapter 7.

Finally, the expected utility theorem states that the utility function $u(a)$ is defined up to a *positive linear transformation*. This means that, if $U(a)$ is a utility function for a particular individual, then so is $W(a) = \alpha + \beta U(a)$ for any scalar α and any scalar $\beta > 0$.

> **Proof:** Start from the equivalence between $a_1 \geq^* a_2$ and $EU(a_1) \geq EU(a_2)$ stated in the expected utility theorem. But, given $\beta > 0$, $EU(a_1) \geq EU(a_2)$ is equivalent to $\alpha + \beta EU(a_1) \geq \alpha + \beta EU(a_2)$, which is equivalent to $EW(a_1) \geq EW(a_2)$. Thus, $a_1 \geq^* a_2$ if and only if $EW(a_1) \geq EW(a_2)$, meaning that $W(\cdot)$ and $U(\cdot)$ provide equivalent representations of individual risk preferences.

This means that the utility function $U(a)$ is not unique. Without affecting the individual preference ranking, $U(a)$ can be shifted by changing its intercept and/or by multiplying its slope by a positive constant. This special characteristic will be exploited below.

DIRECT ELICITATION OF PREFERENCES

While the expected utility theorem provides a basis for modeling behavior under risk, how can it be used empirically? Its empirical tractability would improve significantly if it were possible to measure the individual risk preferences $U(\cdot)$. Then, following a probability assessment of the random variable "a," the evaluation of $EU(a)$ would be straightforward and provide a basis for an analysis (either positive or normative) of behavior under risk. We discuss below methods that can be used to estimate the utility function $U(a)$ of a decision-maker.

CASE OF MONETARY REWARDS

Focusing on the case of monetary rewards, we start with the situation where "a" is a scalar random variable. It will be convenient to consider the situation where the random variable "a" is bounded, with $a_L \leq a \leq a_U$, and where $U(a)$ is a strictly increasing function (meaning that a higher reward makes the decision-maker better off). Then, under the expected utility model, the utility function $U(a)$ of an individual can be assessed from the individual's answers to a questionnaire.

Questionnaire Design

Ask the individual to answer the following questions:

1. Find the reward a_1 obtained with certainty, which is regarded by the person as equivalent to the lottery:

    $\{a_L$ with probability $1/2$; a_U with probability $1/2\}$.

2. Find the reward a_2 obtained with certainty, which is regarded as being equivalent to the lottery:

    $\{a_1$ with probability $1/2$; a_U with probability $1/2\}$.

3. Find the reward a_3 obtained with certainty, which is regarded as being equivalent to the lottery:

    $\{a_1$ with probability $1/2$; a_L with probability $1/2\}$.

4. etc.

Finding $U(a)$ from the Questionnaire Results

Since the utility function $U(a)$ is defined up to a positive linear transformation, without a loss of generality, we can always choose $U(a_L) = 0$ and $U(a_U) = 1$.

From question 1, we have $a_1 \sim^* [a_L$ with probability $1/2$; a_U with probability $1/2]$. Under the expected utility model, this implies that $U(a_1) = \frac{1}{2}U(a_L) + \frac{1}{2}U(a_U) = 0.5$. From question 2, we have $a_2 \sim^* [a_1$ with probability $\frac{1}{2}$ a_U with probability $\frac{1}{2}]$. Under the expected utility model, this means that $U(a_2) = \frac{1}{2}U(a_1) + \frac{1}{2}U(a_U) = 0.75$. From question 3, we have $a_3 \sim^* [a_1$ with probability $\frac{1}{2}$; a_L with probability $\frac{1}{2}]$. Under the expected utility model, this implies that $U(a_3) = \frac{1}{2}U(a_1) + \frac{1}{2}U(a_L) = 0.25$. And so on. Then, plot $U(a)$ as a function of "a," and draw a line through the points. This gives an estimate of the utility function of the individual $U(a)$.

Note that additional questions can be asked to validate the approach. To illustrate, add the following question to the above questionnaire: Find the reward A obtained with certainty and regarded as being equivalent to the lottery $\{a_2$ with probability $\frac{1}{2}$; a_3 with probability $\frac{1}{2}\}$. Under the expected utility model, this implies that $U(A) = \frac{1}{2}U(a_2) + \frac{1}{2}U(a_3) = 0.5$. Thus, $U(A) = U(a_1) = \frac{1}{2}$. Assuming that $U(a)$ is strictly increasing in a, this implies that $A = a_1$. If A indeed equals a_1, this validates the preference elicitation procedure just described. However, what if $A \neq a_1$? This can be interpreted as evidence that the expected utility model is inconsistent with the individual ranking of risky prospects. It shows how the expected utility model can be subject to empirical testing.

MULTIDIMENSIONAL CASE

So far, we have focused our attention on monetary rewards, where "a" is a scalar random variable. This is relevant in the evaluation of risky income. However, there are situations where the uncertainty is not directly linked with monetary returns (e.g., the case of health risk). Under such scenarios, the decision-maker may worry about multiple sources of uncertainty. If each source of uncertainty is represented by a random variable, then the risk assessment involves a vector of random variables $x = (x_1, x_2, \ldots)$. For example, x_1 can represent uncertain income, x_2 uncertain health status, etc. The expected utility model can be extended in this multivariate framework. Then, $U(x_1, x_2, \ldots)$ being the utility function of the decision-maker representing his/her risk preferences, consider that individual decisions are made in a way consistent with the maximization of expected utility, Max $EU(x_1, x_2, \ldots)$, where E is the expectation with respect to the subjective probability distribution of the random vector $(x_1, x_2, \ldots)$.

In this multivariate case, the questionnaire procedure discussed above (under a single random variable) can be used by changing one variable at a time, the other variables being held constant. This can be easily implemented to estimate the individual utility function $U(x)$ as long as the number of variables is small (e.g., 2 or 3). However, this gets complicated for dimensions greater than two or three.

Yet, there is a simple way of assessing an individual multivariate utility function $U(x_1, x_2, \ldots)$ when the utility function is *additive* and takes the particular form

$$U(x_1, x_2, \ldots) = \sum_i k_i U_i(x_i), \; 0 \le U_i(x_i) \le 1, \; 0 \le k_i \le 1, \; \sum_i k_i = 1.$$

This can be done as follows. Let $x_i^+ =$ most preferred level of x_i with $U_i(x_i^+) = 1$, and $x_i^- =$ least preferred level of x_i with $U_i(x_i^-) = 0$, for all $i = 1, 2, \ldots$. First, under additivity, the questionnaire presented above can be used to estimate each $U_i(x_i)$, $i = 1, 2, \ldots$.

Second, consider the following procedure to estimate k_i, $i = 1, 2, \ldots$. Using a questionnaire, find the probability p_1 such that the person is indifferent between $\{(x_1^+, x_2^-, x_3^-, \ldots)$ with certainty$\}$ and $\{(x_1^+, x_2^+, x_3^+, \ldots)$ with probability p_1; $(x_1^-, x_2^-, x_3^-, \ldots)$ with probability $(1 - p_1)\}$. Under the expected utility hypothesis, this implies

$$U(x_1{}^+,x_2{}^-,x_3{}^-,\dots) = p_1\,U(x_1{}^+,x_2{}^+,x_3{}^+,\dots)+(1-p_1)U(x_1{}^-,x_2{}^-,x_3{}^-,\dots)$$

or

$$k_1 = p_1[k_1 + k_2 + \dots] + (1 - p_1)[0]$$

or

$$k_1 = p_1.$$

Then, repeat this procedure with p_2, p_3, ... to estimate k_2, k_3,.... This provides a framework to estimate the individual utility function $U(x) = \sum_i k_i U(x_i)$. This is particularly convenient to assess risk preferences when individuals face multiple sources of uncertainty. However, it should be kept in mind that it is rather restrictive in the sense that the additivity assumption neglects possible preference interactions among the random variables.

PROBLEMS

Note: An asterisk (*) indicates that the problem has an accompanying Excel file on the Web page http://www.aae.wisc.edu/chavas/risk.htm.

*1. A farmer's utility function for money gains and losses is approximately represented by $U(X) = 2X - 0.01X^2, (X \le 100)$, where X denotes farm profit (in thousands of dollars). (The farmer is currently wondering hour much to spend on fertilizer for his 1000 ha farm.) Pertinent information is shown in the following payoff matrix of possible dollar profits per hectare.

*2. If you were offered a choice between bet A and bet B, which one would you choose?

    Bet A : You win $1,000,000 for sure.
    Bet B : You win $5,000,000 with probability 0.10.

Type of Season	Probability	Spend $4/ha	Spend $8/ha	Spend $12/ha	Spend $16/ha
			Profit ($/ha)		
poor	0.1	−8	−12	−16	−20
fair	0.2	−2	−8	−12	−16
good	0.5	2	4	6	8
excellent	0.2	12	20	24	26

a. How much should the farmer spend on fertilizer?
b. Given the optimal decision, what would the farmer be willing to pay to eliminate all risk and just receive the expected profit?

You win $1,000,000 with probability 0.89.
You win $0 with probability 0.01.
Now choose between bet C and bet D:
    Bet C: You win $1,000,000 with probability 0.11.
         You win $0 with probability 0.89.
    Bet D: You win $5,000,000 with probability 0.10.
         You win $0 with probability 0.90.
Assume that the expected utility hypothesis holds.

   a. Prove that if you choose bet A, you should also choose C.
   b. Prove that if you choose bet B, you should also choose bet D. (Note: Empirical observations violating the results in a. or b. have been called *Allais paradox*).
   c. Comment on the role of expected utility as a means of analyzing consistent choices under risk.

*3. A construction company does subcontracting on government contracts. The construction company's utility function is approximately represented by $U(X) = 2X - 0.01X^2, (X \leq 100)$, X being income (in thousands of dollars).

   a. Suppose the company is considering bidding on a contract. Preparation of a bid would cost $8,000, and this would be lost if the bid failed. If the bid succeeded, the company would make $40,000 gain. The company judges the chance of a successful bid as 0.3. What should it do?
   b. What chance of a successful bid would make the company indifferent between bidding and not bidding for the contract?

Chapter 4

The Nature of Risk Preferences

Chapter 2 developed the arguments that risk can be assessed using probability measures, i.e., that the relevant probabilities can be estimated empirically using sample information and/or subjective assessments. In this chapter, we assume that the probabilities of risky events have been estimated. Chapter 3 developed a formal theory of decision-making under risk: the expected utility model. In the expected utility model, each decision-maker has a utility function representing his/her risk preferences. In this chapter, we examine the nature of risk preferences. For simplicity, we focus our attention on the case of risky monetary rewards. In this context, we establish formal relationships between the properties of the utility function and risk preferences. This will provide some useful insights in the empirical analysis of risk behavior.

MATHEMATICAL PRELIMINARIES

First, we present some mathematical results that will prove useful in our analysis. A key concept is the concavity (or convexity) of a function. A function $U(a)$ is said to be a concave function, if for any α, $0 < \alpha < 1$, and any two points a_1 and a_2,

$$U(\alpha a_1 + (1 - \alpha)a_2) \geq \alpha U(a_1) + (1 - \alpha)U(a_2).$$

And $U(a)$ is a convex function, if for any α, $0 < \alpha < 1$, and any two points a_1 and a_2,

$$U(\alpha a_1 + (1 - \alpha)a_2) \leq \alpha U(a_1) + (1 - \alpha)U(a_2).$$

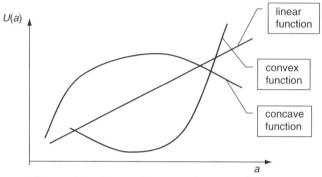

Figure 4.1 Convex, linear, and concave functions

These definitions apply to a general function $U(a)$, whether it is differentiable or not. However, if we also know that the function $U(a)$ is twice continuously differentiable, then

- $U(a)$ is concave if and only if $\partial^2 U/\partial a^2 \leq 0$ for all a.
- $U(a)$ is convex if and only if $\partial^2 U/\partial a^2 \geq 0$ for all a.

This is illustrated in Figure 4.1.
Next, we state an important property of concave (convex) functions.

Jensen's Inequality:

If $U(a)$ *is a* $\left\{ \begin{array}{c} \text{concave} \\ \text{linear} \\ \text{convex} \end{array} \right\}$ function of the random variable "a", then

$$U[E(a)] \left\{ \begin{array}{c} \leq \\ = \\ \geq \end{array} \right\} EU(a), \text{ where } E \text{ is the expectation operator.}$$

This is illustrated in Figure 4.2 for a concave function in the context of a discrete random variable taking two possible values: a_1 which occurs with probability p_1, and a_2 which occurs with probability $p_2 = (1 - p_1)$, where $E(a) = p_1 a_1 + p_2 a_2$, and $EU(a) = p_1 U(a_1) + p_2 U(a_2)$.

THE RISK PREMIUM

Consider the case of a decision-maker facing an uncertain monetary reward, as represented by the random variable "a." Let w denote the

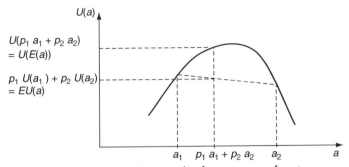

Figure 4.2 Jensen's inequality for a concave function

decision-maker's initial wealth. Thus, his/her terminal wealth is $(w + a)$. Throughout, we will assume that the initial wealth w is known with certainty. Under the expected utility model, let his/her risk preferences be represented by the utility function $U(w + a)$. We will assume that $U(w + a)$ is a strictly increasing function of $(w + a)$. This is intuitive. It simply states that the decision-maker is made better off by an increase in his/her terminal wealth $(w + a)$.

The first question we address is how to measure the monetary value of risk? This can be done by using *income compensation tests*. They involve finding the change in sure income that would make the decision-maker indifferent to a change in risk exposure. There are many ways of defining such compensation tests. Here, we discuss three monetary valuations of risk.

The Selling Price of Risk

The selling price of risk, R_s, is defined as the sure amount of money a decision-maker would be willing to receive to eliminate (sell) the risk "a" if he/she had it. More specifically, it is the sure amount of money R_s that makes him/her indifferent between facing the risky prospect $\{w + a\}$ versus facing the sure prospect $\{w + R_s\}$. In other words, R_s is the monetary amount satisfying the indifference relationship:

$$\{w + R_s\} \sim^* \{w + a\}.$$

Under the expected utility model, this implies that R_s is the solution to the implicit equation

$$U(w + R_s) = EU(w + a).$$

THE ASKING PRICE (BID PRICE) OF RISK

The bid price of risk, R_b, is defined as the sure amount of money a decision-maker would be willing to pay to obtain (buy) the risk "a." More specifically, it is the sure amount of money R_d that makes him/her indifferent between facing the sure prospect $\{w\}$ versus facing the sure prospect $\{w + a - R_b\}$. In other words, R_b is the monetary amount satisfying the indifference relationship:

$$\{w\} \sim^* \{w + a - R_b\}.$$

Under the expected utility model, this implies that R_b is the solution to the implicit equation

$$U(w) = EU(w + a - R_b).$$

Note that $R_b = R_s$ in the "absence of income effects," where preferences satisfy $U(w + a) = w + V(a)$ for all w and a. However, if $U(w + a) \neq w + V(a)$, then preferences exhibit "income effects." In the presence of income or wealth effects, then $R_b \neq R_s$ and the bid price and the selling price of risk differ from each other. The effects of wealth on the valuation of risk will be further examined below.

THE RISK PREMIUM

The risk premium, R, is defined as the sure amount of money a decision-maker would be willing to receive to become indifferent between receiving the risky return "a" versus receiving the sure amount $[E(a)-R]$, where $E(a)$ is the expected value of "a." In other words, R is the monetary amount satisfying the indifference relationship:

$$\{w + a\} \sim^* \{w + E(a) - R\}.$$

Under the expected utility model, this implies that R is the solution to the implicit equation

$$EU(w + a) = U(w + E(a) - R).$$

Given that $U(w + a)$ is a strictly increasing function, its inverse function always exists. Denote the inverse function by U^{-1}, where $U(w) = u$ is equivalent to $w = U^{-1}(u)$. It follows that $U^{-1}(EU(w+a)) = w + E(a) - R$. Thus, the risk premium R can always be written as

$$R = w + E(a) - U^{-1}(EU(w + a)).$$

In general, the risk premium R is a function of w and of the probability distribution of "a." The properties of the risk premium are further examined in the following paragraphs.

From the definition of the risk premium and given that $U(\cdot)$ is an increasing function, note that maximizing $EU(w + a)$ is equivalent to maximizing the nonrandom expression $[w + E(a) - R]$. As a result, $[w + E(a) - R]$ has been called the *certainty equivalent* of $EU(\cdot)$. It is a sure money metric measure of utility. This provides a nice and intuitive interpretation of the risk premium: R measures the *shadow cost of private risk bearing*. It is a cost since it appears as a reduction in expected terminal wealth, $w + E(a)$. And it is a shadow cost in the sense that it involves a hypothetical income compensation test. An alternative interpretation is that the risk premium R measures the individual's *willingness to insure*. Given these intuitive interpretations, we will rely extensively on the risk premium in our analysis of decision-making under uncertainty.

RISK AVERSION

Given the definition of the risk premium R, what can we say about its sign? In general, it can be negative, zero, or positive, depending on the nature of individual risk preferences. Interpreting the risk premium as the cost of private risk bearing leads to the following definition of risk aversion:

$$\text{A decision-maker is said to be} \begin{Bmatrix} \text{risk averse} \\ \text{risk neutral} \\ \text{risk lover} \end{Bmatrix} \text{if the risk premium}$$

$$R \text{ is} \begin{Bmatrix} \text{positive } (R > 0) \\ \text{zero } (R = 0) \\ \text{negative } (R < 0) \end{Bmatrix}.$$

Intuitively, a decision-maker is *risk averse* if he/she is willing to pay a positive amount of money (as measured by a positive risk premium: $R > 0$) to eliminate risk (by replacing the random variable "a" by its mean). This positive willingness-to-pay means that he/she is made worse off by risk exposure, thus the term "risk averse." Alternatively, a decision-maker is a *risk lover* if he/she must be compensated ($R < 0$) when his/her risk exposure is eliminated. This means that he/she likes risk (thus the term *risk lover*) and is made worse off when risk is removed. Finally, a decision-maker is *risk neutral* if he/she is made neither better off nor worse off when his/her risk exposure is modified.

Thus, the sign of the risk premium can be used to classify decision-makers into three categories, according to their risk preferences. By definition of the risk premium under the expected utility model, we have

$$EU(w + a) = U(w + E(a) - R).$$

Assume that the utility function $U(w + a)$ is twice continuously differentiable. To analyze the properties of the risk premium, consider taking a second order Taylor series expansion of $U(w + a)$ in the neighborhood of $[w + E(a)]$. This gives

$$U(w + a) \approx U(w + E(a)) + U' \cdot [a - E(a)] + 0.5U'' \cdot [a - E(a)]^2,$$

where $U' = \partial U / \partial w$ denotes the first derivative of the utility function, and $U'' = \partial^2 U / \partial w^2$ denotes the second derivative, each evaluated at $(w + E(a))$. Taking expectation, it follows that

$$EU(w + a) \approx EU(w + E(a)) + U' \cdot E[a - E(a)] + 0.5U'' \cdot E[a - E(a)]^2,$$
$$\approx EU(w + E(a)) + 0.5U'' \cdot \text{Var}(a),$$

since $E[a - E(a)] = 0$ and $\text{Var}(a) \equiv E[a - E(a)]^2$ is the variance of "a."

Next, consider taking a first order Taylor series expansion of $EU(w + a - R)$ with respect to R in the neighborhood of $[w + E(a) - R]$. Note that, at $[w + E(a) - R]$, $R = 0$ (by definition of the risk premium). This gives

$$U(w + E(a) - R) \approx U(w + E(a)) - U' \cdot R.$$

Substituting these two results in the definition of the risk premium yields

$$U(w + E(a)) + 0.5U'' \text{ Var}(a) \approx U(w + E(a)) - U'R.$$

Given $U' > 0$, this implies

$$\boldsymbol{R \approx -0.5(U''/U')\text{Var}(a)}.$$

This is an important result. It shows that, *in the neighborhood of the riskless case*, the *risk premium R is proportional to the variance of risk*, Var(a). The coefficient of proportionality is the term $[-0.5(U''/U')]$. In other words, $[-0.5(U''/U') \cdot \text{Var}(a)]$ is a *local measure of the risk premium R*. It is "local" or "in the small" to the extent that the Taylor series approximations used in the derivation are valid in general only in the neighborhood of the point of approximation.

The above result suggests that the term $(-U''/U')$ will play an important role in risk analysis. For this reason, define $r \equiv -U''/U'$ as the *Arrow–Pratt coefficient of absolute risk aversion*. Then, the risk premium R can be approximated "in the small" as

$$R \approx (r/2) \cdot \text{Var}(a).$$

Note that $\text{Var}(a) > 0$ for all nondegenerate random variables. Thus, "in the small," the sign of the risk premium R is always the same as the sign of $r \equiv -U''/U'$. This local result provides the first important linkages between the specification of the utility function and the nature of risk preferences. Given $U' > 0$, they are:

- *risk averse* behavior ($R > 0$) corresponds to $r > 0$ and $U'' < 0$, i.e., a *concave* utility function.
- *risk neutral* behavior ($R = 0$) corresponds to $r = 0$ and $U'' = 0$, i.e., a *linear* utility function.
- *risk loving* behavior ($R > 0$) corresponds to $r < 0$ and $U'' > 0$, i.e., a *convex* utility function.

This raises an important question. While these results were derived "locally," can they provide useful insights into the global properties of risk preferences? The answer is affirmative. To see it, note that the above statements also hold *globally*. This follows from Jensen's inequality, given $U' > 0$ and the definition of the risk premium R. In other words, risk neutrality is globally equivalent to a linear utility function. And risk aversion (risk loving behavior) is globally equivalent to a concave (convex) utility function. This is illustrated in Figure 4.3 for a risk averse decision-maker ($U'' < 0$) in the context of a discrete random variable taking two possible values: a_1 which occurs with probability p_1, and a_2 which occurs with probability $p_2 = (1 - p_1)$, where $E(a) = p_1 a_1 + p_2 a_2$, and $EU(a) = p_1 U(a_1) + p_2 U(a_2)$.

It is an empirical issue to determine whether individual risk preferences exhibit risk aversion, risk neutrality, or risk loving behavior. In general, risk preferences can vary greatly across individuals. For example, observing gambling behavior can be interpreted as evidence of risk loving behavior.

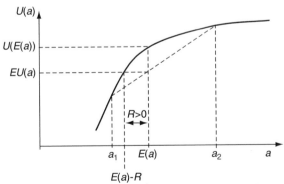

Figure 4.3 Utility for a risk-averse decision-maker

However, there is empirical evidence that *most decision-makers are often risk averse*. First, risk aversion is consistent with the fact that most individuals try to limit their risk exposure (e.g., as illustrated in the St. Petersburg paradox). Second, the presence of active insurance markets can be interpreted as indirect evidence that risk aversion is common. Finally, direct elicitation of risk preferences has documented the prevalence of risk aversion among most decision-makers. For this reason, our discussion will focus in large part on the case of risk aversion. In this case, given $U' > 0$, risk aversion imposes a restriction on the sign of the second derivative of the utility function: $U'' < 0$. This means that a *risk-averse individual has risk references represented by a utility function that exhibits decreasing marginal utility with respect to wealth or income.*

In addition, note that, by definition, $r = -U''/U' = -\partial \ln(U')/\partial w$. Integrating, this yields $\int r = -\ln(U') + c$, or $U' = e^c\, e^{-\int r}$, where c is a constant of integration. But this implies that

$$U(\cdot) = e^c \int e^{-\int r} + k,$$

where k is another constant of integration. Since $U(\cdot)$ is defined up to a positive linear transformation, we can always choose $k = 0$ (fixing the intercept) and $c = 0$ (fixing the slope). It follows that the utility function $U(\cdot)$ *can always be expressed exactly as* $U(\cdot) = \int e^{-\int r}$. In other words, the Arrow–Pratt coefficient of absolute risk aversion $r = -U''/U'$ (when evaluated at all relevant points) provides all the information needed to recover the global properties of the underlying preference function $U(\cdot)$. This gives us a hint that the properties of the Arrow–Pratt coefficient of absolute risk aversion $r = -U''/U'$ will provide useful information on the nature of risk preferences.

CONSTANT ABSOLUTE RISK AVERSION (CARA)

A special class of risk preferences is associated with the case where the absolute risk aversion $r \equiv -U''/U'$ is constant.

Risk preferences exhibit *constant absolute risk aversion* (CARA) when $r \equiv -U''/U'$ is a constant for all w.

We have seen that the utility function can be always be written as $U(\cdot) = \int e^{-\int r}$. Under CARA and given $U' > 0$, this gives us the class of CARA utility functions:

- $r > 0$ (risk aversion) corresponds to the utility function $U = -e^{-r \cdot (w+a)}$
- $r = 0$ (risk neutrality) corresponds to the utility function $U = w + a$
- $r < 0$ (risk loving) corresponds to the utility function $U = e^{-r \cdot (w+a)}$

This shows that risk neutrality is a special case of CARA with $r = 0$. Again, this corresponds to a linear utility function. Perhaps more importantly, it identifies the special properties of the exponential utility function in risk analysis and their close linkages with CARA preferences.

Note that $e^{-r \cdot (w+a)} = e^{-rw} e^{-ra}$ when $r \neq 0$. This means that, under CARA, the expected utility EU is proportional to $E(e^{-ra})$ for any w (with a coefficient of proportionality that is negative (positive) when $r > 0$ ($r < 0$)). It follows that changing initial wealth w does not affect economic decisions. And a similar result applies when $r = 0$. Thus, in general, *CARA risk preferences imply "zero wealth effects."* This result applies whether the decision-maker is risk averse, risk neutral, or risk loving. It also shows that, under the expected utility model, an exponential utility function implies the absence of wealth effects. It means that, while specifying an exponential utility function may be convenient in risk analysis, it does impose a priori restrictions on economic behavior.

To illustrate, consider the case of a risk-averse decision-maker exhibiting CARA, with utility function $U(a) = -e^{-r \cdot (w+a)}$, $r > 0$. By definition of the risk premium R, $E[-e^{-r \cdot (w+a)}] = -e^{-r \cdot (w+E(a)-R)}$. But this equation can be alternatively written as $E[-e^{-ra}] = -e^{-r \cdot (E(a)-R)}$. This shows that risk premium R does not depend on w. Under CARA, a similar result would apply under risk neutrality ($r = 0$) or risk-loving behavior ($r < 0$). Thus, *CARA implies that the risk premium R is independent of initial wealth w.* If we interpret the risk premium as measuring the willingness to insure, this means that, *under CARA, a change in initial wealth does not affect the individual's willingness to insure.* This shows the behavioral restrictions implied by CARA risk preferences in general, and by the exponential utility function in particular.

Another notable property is the nature of the risk premium R under CARA preferences when the random variable "a" is normally distributed. To see that, consider a risk averse decision maker exhibiting CARA (with $U(a) = -e^{-r \cdot (w+a)}$, $r > 0$, where "a" is normally distributed with mean A and variance V. Under normality, the expected utility becomes

$$E[-e^{-r \cdot (w+a)}] = (2\pi V)^{-1/2} e^{-rw} \int [-e^{-ra} e^{-(a-A)^2/2V}]\, da,$$

$$= (2\pi V)^{-1/2} e^{-rw} \int [-e^{-[(a-A+rV)^2 - r^2 V^2 + 2rAV]/2V}]\, da,$$

$$= e^{-rw} [-e^{(r^2 V - 2rA)/2}] \int (2\pi V)^{-1/2} [-e^{-[(a-A+rV)^2]/2V}]\, da,$$

$$= e^{-rw} [-e^{-r \cdot [A-(r/2)V]}],$$

which is an increasing function of $[A - (r/2) \cdot V]$. It follows that maximizing $EU(\cdot)$ is equivalent to maximizing $[A - (r/2)V]$. This means that

$[w + A - (r/2)V]$ is the *certainty equivalent*. Since the certainty equivalent can be written in general as $[w + E(a) - R]$, this means that $R = (r/2)V$, i.e. that $[(r/2)V]$ is a *global* measure of the risk premium. This has two implications. First, under CARA and normality, the local approximation to the risk premium we derived above ($R \approx (r/2)V$) is exact and globally valid. Second, an additive mean-variance analysis (with $[w + A -(r/2)V]$ as certainty equivalent) can be justified globally under CARA and normality. This form is particularly convenient in empirical risk analysis. However, we should keep in mind that it holds under rather restrictive conditions.

DECREASING (OR INCREASING) ABSOLUTE RISK AVERSION

While CARA preferences may be convenient, its implied "zero wealth effects" appear restrictive. This suggests a need to investigate departures from constant absolute risk aversion. Consider the general properties of the risk premium $R(w, \cdot)$ as initial wealth w changes.

Definition: Risk preferences exhibits decreasing (constant, increasing) absolute risk aversion if the risk premium $R(w, \cdot)$ is a decreasing (constant, increasing) function of initial wealth w.

We have just seen that, under constant absolute risk aversion (CARA), the risk premium is independent of initial wealth w. The definition considers two departures from CARA: decreasing absolute risk aversion (DARA) where the risk premium R decreases with initial wealth w; and increasing absolute risk aversion (IARA) where the risk premium increases with w. Under DARA, an increase in initial wealth tends to reduce the individual's willingness to insure (as measured by the risk premium R). This means that, under DARA, private wealth accumulation and insurance motives are *substitutes*, as wealthy individuals have less incentive to insure. Alternatively, under IARA, an increase in initial wealth would increase the individual's willingness to insure (as measured by the risk premium R). Thus, under IARA, private wealth accumulation and insurance motives behave as *complements*. In general, it is an empirical issue to determine whether individual risk preferences exhibit CARA, DARA, or IARA. However, there are intuitive arguments in favor of decreasing absolute risk aversion: individuals may exhibit DARA (where private wealth accumulation and insurance motives are substitutes) when their private wealth accumulation improves their ability to manage private risk exposure. There is also empirical evidence suggesting that (besides being risk averse) *most individuals exhibit DARA risk preferences*.

This suggests a need to develop linkages between the nature of risk preferences and the specification of the utility function $U(w + a)$.

Proposition 1: Consider two decision makers facing the terminal wealth $(w + a)$, each with utility function $U_1(w + a)$ and $U_2(w + a)$. Let $r_i = -U_i''/U_i'$, and R_i = the risk premium for individual i, $i = 1, 2$. Then, the following statements are equivalent:

- $R_1(w) \begin{Bmatrix} < \\ = \\ > \end{Bmatrix} R_2(w)$ *for all* w.

- $r_1(w) \begin{Bmatrix} < \\ = \\ > \end{Bmatrix} r_2(w)$ *for all* w.

Proof: By definition of the risk premium, $U_i[w + E(a) - R] = EU_i[w + a]$ implies that

$$R_i = w + E(a) - U_i^{-1} EU_i(w + a)$$

or

$$R_1 - R_2 = U_2^{-1} EU_2(w + a) - U_1^{-1} EU_1(w + a).$$

Let $t = U_2(w + a)$, or $(w + a) = U_2^{-1}(t)$. It follows that

$$R_1 - R_2 = U_2^{-1} E(t) - U_1^{-1} EU_1(U_2^{-1}(t)). \tag{1}$$

Note that

$$\partial[U_1(U_2^{-1}(t))]/\partial t = U_1'(U_2^{-1}(t))/[U_2'(U_2^{-1}(t))]$$
$$= e^{\ln(U_1'/U_2')} = \text{an increasing function of } [\ln(U_1'/U_2')].$$

Also, $\partial \ln(U_1'/U_2')/\partial w = [U_1''/U_2' - U_2'' U_1'/(U_2')^2]/(U_1'/U_2') = r_2 - r_1$.

This implies that $r_2 \begin{Bmatrix} \leq \\ = \\ \geq \end{Bmatrix} r_1$ when $\partial[U_1[U_2^{-1}(t)]]/\partial t \begin{Bmatrix} \text{decreases} \\ \text{does not change} \\ \text{increases} \end{Bmatrix}$

with t, i.e., when $U_1(U_2^{-1}(t))$ is $\begin{Bmatrix} \text{concave} \\ \text{linear} \\ \text{convex} \end{Bmatrix}$ in t. By Jensen's inequality,

$$r_2 \begin{Bmatrix} \leq \\ = \\ \geq \end{Bmatrix} r_1 \text{ when } EU_1(U_2^{-1}(t)) \begin{Bmatrix} \leq \\ = \\ \geq \end{Bmatrix} U_1(U_2^{-1}(E(t))).$$

From (1), this implies that

$$R_1 - R_2 \left\{ \begin{array}{c} \leq \\ = \\ \geq \end{array} \right\} U_2^{-1} E(t) - U_1^{-1} U_1 (U_2^{-1}(E(t))) = 0 \; as \; r_2 \left\{ \begin{array}{c} \geq \\ = \\ \leq \end{array} \right\} r_1.$$

After choosing $U_i(w) = U(w_i)$, Proposition 1 generates the following result:

Proposition 2: The following two statements are equivalent:

- $R(w)$ is an increasing (constant, decreasing) function of w for all w.
- $r(w)$ is an increasing (constant, decreasing) function of w for all w.

Proposition 2 links the properties of the risk premium $R(w)$ to the properties of the Arrow–Pratt absolute risk aversion coefficient $r(w)$ as initial wealth w changes. It includes as a special case the CARA results obtained above: When r is constant, the risk premium is independent of initial wealth w. It also provides new results when the risk premium $R(w)$ varies with wealth. In particular, under decreasing absolute risk aversion (DARA, where $R(w)$ is a decreasing function of w), it shows that $r(w) = -U''/U'$ is also a decreasing function of w. Let $U''' = \partial^3 U/\partial w^3$ denote the third derivative of the utility function with respect to wealth. It follows that, under DARA, $\partial r/\partial w = -U'''/U' + (U''/U')^2 \leq 0$. This implies that $U'''/U' \geq (U''/U')^2 \geq 0$. Given $U' > 0$, it follows that $U''' \geq 0$ *under DARA*. In other words, DARA preferences impose restrictions on the sign of the third derivative of the utility function: $U''' \geq 0$. Given $U' > 0$, this means that a risk averse individual exhibiting DARA would have a utility function satisfying $U'' < 0$ and $U''' \geq 0$. This is illustrated in Figure 4.4. The implications of the sign of U''' will be further discussed below.

This has interesting implications for the specification of the utility function. In general, from the Taylor series, a polynomial function is expected to provide a good approximation to any differentiable utility function in some relevant neighborhood. A polynomial function of degree n can be linear (when $n = 1$), quadratic (when $n = 2$), cubic (when $n = 3$), etc. The question is, what degree would make the polynomial of $U(w + a)$ a good approximation in risk analysis? We know that a linear utility function implies risk neutrality. Thus, if we are interested in investigating risk aversion, a polynomial of degree one is overly restrictive. Next, consider a *quadratic utility function* (i.e., a polynomial of degree two):

$$U(w + a) = \alpha + \beta(w + a) + 0.5\gamma(w + a)^2,$$

where (α, β, γ) are parameters. Such a quadratic utility function provides a second order approximation to any differentiable utility function. It satisfies $U' = \beta + \gamma(w + a)$, and $U'' = \gamma$. Thus, $U' > 0$ requires that $\beta + \gamma(w + a) > 0$.

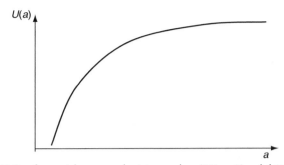

Figure 4.4 Utility for a risk-averse decision-maker ($U'' < 0$) exhibiting DARA (implying $U''' > 0$)

For given parameters (β, γ), this imposes some restrictions on the range of wealth ($w + a$). Yet, the quadratic utility function can exhibit risk aversion (when $\gamma < 0$), risk neutrality (when $\gamma = 0$), or risk-loving behavior (when $\gamma > 0$). As such, it appears reasonably flexible for risk analysis. In addition, under the expected utility model, note that $EU(w + a) = \alpha + \beta E(w + a)$ $+ 0.5\gamma E(w + a)^2 = \alpha + \beta E(w + a) + 0.5\gamma[(E(w + a))^2 + \text{Var}(a)]$. This implies that, under a quadratic utility function, expected utility can always be written as $EU(x) = f[E(w + a), \text{Var}(a)]$. In other words, quadratic utility functions can be used to justify a (nonlinear) *mean-variance analysis*. Thus, quadratic utility functions have two attractive properties: (1) they allow for risk averse, risk neutral, or risk loving behavior (depending on the sign of γ); and (2) they can justify mean-variance analysis, which may be particularly convenient in applied work. However, quadratic utility functions remain somewhat restrictive: they imply that $U''' = 0$. But we have just seen that DARA preferences imply $U''' \geq 0$. It follows that *quadratic utility functions cannot exhibit strictly decreasing absolute risk aversion*. And in the case of departure from risk neutrality, they necessarily imply increasing absolute risk aversion (IARA, where the risk premium $R(w)$ increases with initial wealth w). This inability to exhibit DARA preferences under risk aversion stresses that quadratic utility functions do impose a priori restrictions on risk behavior. In other words, a polynomial utility of degree two cannot be seen as fully flexible in risk analysis. This suggests that, if one wants to investigate the effects of initial wealth on the individual willingness to insure, a quadratic utility function would be inappropriate. Within the class of polynomial functions, a cubic utility function would be needed for that purpose.

To the extent that DARA preferences are common, it may be of interest to identify utility functions that are consistent with DARA.

Examples include:

- $U(w + a) = (\alpha + w + a)^\beta$,

where (α, β) are parameters, $(\alpha + w + a) > 0$, and $0 < \beta < 1$.

- $U(w) = \ln(\alpha + w + a)$,

where α is a parameter, and $(\alpha + w + a) > 0$.

Finally, note that Kimball investigated further the implications of the third derivatives of the utility function U'''. He linked such properties to the concept of "precaution."

RELATIVE RISK AVERSION

Under the expected utility model, we have assumed that the decision-maker makes decisions so as to maximize the expected utility of terminal wealth, $w + a$, where w is known initial wealth and "a" is a random variable representing risky income. Here, it will be convenient to denote terminal wealth by $x \equiv w + a$. Since "a" is a random variable, it follows that x is also a random variable. Then, expected utility can be written as $EU(w + a) \equiv EU(x)$.

In this context, the risk premium R can be defined as the decision-maker's willingness to pay to replace the random wealth x by its expected value $E(x)$. We have argued that it is a monetary measure of the cost of private risk bearing. As such, it will depend on the units of measurements for wealth or income (e.g., cents versus dollars, or Euros versus dollars). It would be useful to consider measuring the cost of risk in a way that does not depend on the units of measurements. One obvious way is to measure it as a proportion of the individual's wealth. This motivates the following definition.

The *relative risk premium* $\overline{R}$ is the proportion of terminal wealth x a decision-maker is willing to pay to make him indifferent between facing the risky terminal wealth x versus receiving $[(1 - \overline{R})E(x)]$.

This means that the relative risk premium $\overline{R}$ must satisfy the indifference relationship

$$x \sim^* [(1 - \overline{R})E(x)].$$

Under the expected utility model, this implies that $\overline{R}$ is the implicit solution to the equation

$$EU(x) = U[(1 - \overline{R})E(x)]. \tag{2}$$

How does the relative risk premium $\overline{R}$ relate to the absolute risk premium R? Since R satisfies $EU(x) = U(E(x) - R)$, this implies the following relationship between R and $\overline{R}$:

$$\overline{R} = R/E(x).$$

This is an intuitive result: the relative risk premium $\overline{R}$ equals the ratio of the absolute risk premium to expected terminal wealth. Being a proportion, $\overline{R}$ is independent of the units of monetary measurements.

What are the properties of the relative risk premium $\overline{R}$? Since $\overline{R}$ is a proportion, it would be useful to know how it varies with a proportional change in terminal wealth x. Of course, this would depend on the nature of the individual risk preferences. This suggests the following definition:

A decision-maker is said to exhibit increasing (constant, decreasing) relative risk aversion if $\overline{R}$ is an increasing (constant, decreasing) function of a proportional increase in terminal wealth x.

This identifies three types of risk behavior: constant relative risk aversion (CRRA) where the relative risk premium is independent of a proportional change in wealth; increasing relative risk aversion (IRRA) where the relative risk premium increases with a proportional rise in wealth; and decreasing relative risk aversion (DRRA) where the relative risk premium declines with a proportional increase in terminal wealth. Which type of risk behavior seems more common among decision-makers? The empirical evidence on this issue is mixed. As a result, it remains largely an empirical issue to determine whether a particular individual exhibits CRRA, IRRA, or DRRA.

Define $\overline{x} = x/E(x)$ as a measure of "relative risk," with $\text{Var}(x) = [E(x)]^2 \text{Var}(\overline{x})$. Also, given $x = w + a$, note that $E(x) = w + E(a)$, and $\text{Var}(x) = \text{Var}(a)$. In the neighborhood of $(w + E(a))$, we derived above the local approximation for the absolute risk premium R: $R \approx -0.5 (U''/U') \cdot \text{Var}(a)$, where U' and U'' are evaluated at $(w + E(a))$. It follows that the relative risk premium $\overline{R}$ can also be approximated locally as follows:

$$\overline{R} = R/E(x) \approx -0.5 U''/U' \ \text{Var}(x)/E(x)$$
$$\approx -0.5 (U''/U') \ E(x) \ \text{Var}(\overline{x}).$$

In the neighborhood of the point $E(x) = w + E(a)$, this suggests that a local measure of the relative risk premium is given by

$$\overline{R} \approx 0.5 \, \overline{r} \text{Var}(\overline{x})$$

where $\overline{r} \equiv [-(U''/U')x]$ is the *Arrow–Pratt coefficient of relative risk aversion*. It shows that the relative risk premium can be approximated "in the small" to be proportional to the variance of the relative risk $\text{Var}(\overline{x})$, with $(0.5\overline{r})$ as coefficient of proportionality. Note that, given $x > 0$, the relative risk aversion coefficient can also be written as $\overline{r} = -(\partial U'/\partial x) \cdot (x/U')$ $= -\partial \ln(U')/\partial \ln(x)$. It is the negative of the elasticity of the marginal utility of wealth U' with respect to wealth, measuring the proportional decrease in marginal utility due to one percent increase in x. Being an elasticity, the relative risk aversion coefficient $\bar{r}$ is independent of the units of measurement. (This contrasts with the absolute risk aversion coefficient r, which always depends on the units of monetary measurements). This suggests that the relative absolute risk aversion coefficient $\bar{r}$ can provide an attractive way of comparing risk preferences across individuals when the units of measurements change (e.g., international comparisons involving different currencies).

As noted above, the approximation $\bar{R} \approx 0.5\bar{r}\text{Var}(\bar{x})$ is in general valid only in the neighborhood of the point $E(x)$. However, as seen in propositions 1 and 2, we might suspect that such local results provide useful information about the global characterization of risk preferences. Such linkages parallel the results stated in propositions 1 and 2. They are presented in the following proposition (see Pratt for a proof).

Proposition 3: The following two statements are equivalent:

- $\bar{r}(x)$ is an increasing (constant, decreasing) function of x for all x.
- $\bar{R}$ is an increasing (constant, decreasing) function of x for all x.

Proposition 3 establishes useful linkages between the properties of relative risk aversion and the specification of the utility function $U(x)$. To see that, consider the case of constant relative risk aversion (CRRA), where the relative risk premium $\bar{R}$ is independent of a proportional change in initial wealth x. Proposition 3 states that this corresponds to the situation where the relative risk aversion coefficient $\bar{r}(x)$ is also independent of x. Assuming that $x > 0$ and treating $\bar{r}$ as a constant, this generates the following CRRA utility functions

- $U(x) = x^{1-\bar{r}}$ for $\bar{r} < 1$
- $U(x) = \ln(x)$, corresponding to $\bar{r} = 1$
- $U(x) = -x^{1-\bar{r}}$ for $\bar{r} > 1$.

It shows that a logarithmic utility function $\ln(x)$ implies CRRA, with a relative risk aversion coefficient equal to 1. More generally, the class of power utility functions $[\text{sign}(1 - \bar{r}) \cdot x^{1-\bar{r}}]$ exhibits CRRA.

In addition, since $\bar{r} = rx$, we have $\partial\bar{r}/x = r + x(\partial r/\partial x)$. From proposition 3, CRRA is equivalent to $\partial\bar{r}/\partial x = 0$ for all x. Thus, CRRA implies that $[x(\partial r/\partial x)] = -r$. Under risk aversion ($r > 0$) and given $x > 0$, this means that $(\partial r/\partial x) < 0$, which corresponds to decreasing absolute risk aversion (DARA). This shows that, under risk aversion and positive wealth, *CRRA always implies DARA*. More generally, it can be easily shown that, under risk aversion and positive wealth, nonincreasing relative risk aversion (i.e., CRRA or DRRA) implies DARA. However, a DARA utility function can exhibit constant relative risk aversion (CRRA), decreasing relative risk aversion (DRRA) or increasing relative risk aversion (IRRA).

Finally, does there exist a utility function that can nest both CARA and CRRA as special cases? The following hyperbolic utility function does that

$$U(x) = [\alpha + \beta x/(1 - \gamma)]^\gamma,$$

where (α, β, γ) are parameters, and $[\alpha x + \beta(1 - \gamma)] > 0$. The associated absolute risk aversion coefficient is $r = -U''/U' = \beta/[\alpha + \beta x/(1 - \gamma)]$, and the relative risk aversion coefficient is $\bar{r} = rx = \beta x/[\alpha + \beta x/(1 - \gamma)]$. Then, choosing $\gamma = -\infty$ yields CARA preferences with $r = \beta/\alpha$. And choosing $\alpha = 0$ yields CRRA preferences with $\bar{r} = (1 - \gamma)$.

PARTIAL RELATIVE RISK AVERSION

We have just discussed risk aversion relative to terminal wealth $x = w + a$. However, risk aversion can also be defined relative to other monetary measures. For example, it can be expressed relative to monetary income "a." This generates a different measure of relative risk aversion. Menezes and Hanson (1970) called it "partial relative risk aversion."

Define the *partial relative risk premium* $R = R/E(a)$, where R is the absolute risk premium defined above. R is a measure of the willingness to pay for insurance as *a proportion of the expected payoff $E(a)$*. Define the relative risk $\alpha = a/E(a)$, with $Var(a) = Var(\alpha)[E(a)]^2$. From the local measure of the risk premium R, it follows that $R = R/E(a) \approx -0.5(U''/U')$ $Var(a)/E(a) = -0.5(U''/U')E(a)Var(\alpha)$. Then, *in the neighborhood of* $[w+E(a)]$, the following local approximation to the partial relative risk premium holds:

$$R \approx 0.5r Var(\alpha),$$

where $r = [-(U''/U')a]$ is the *partial relative risk aversion coefficient*. In a way parallel to Propositions 2 and 3, we obtain the following result (*see* Menezes and Hanson for a proof, 1970).

Proposition 4: The following two statements are equivalent:

- R is an increasing (constant, decreasing) function of a proportional increase in "a" for all w.
- r is an increasing (constant, decreasing) function of "a" for all w.

Proposition 4 identifies three types of risk behavior: constant partial relative risk aversion (CPRRA) where the partial relative risk premium is independent of a proportional change in "a"; increasing partial relative risk aversion (IPRRA) where the partial relative risk premium increases with a proportional rise in "*a*"; and decreasing partial relative risk aversion (DPRRA) where the partial relative risk premium declines with a proportional increase in "*a*." For example, under increasing partial relative risk aversion (IPRRA), a proportional increase in "*a*" would generate an increase in the partial relative risk premium $R = R/E(a)$, i.e., a more than proportional increase in the risk premium R. Proposition 4 also provides linkages between risk behavior and the properties of the utility function $U(w+a)$ (through the partial relative risk aversion coefficient r).

PREFERENCES WITH RESPECT TO MOMENTS

Our analysis was developed so far without making a priori assumptions about the probability distribution of terminal wealth x. As such, it has been very general, as it applies to any amount or type of monetary risk exposure, and thus to any situation where a decision-maker faces an uncertain monetary payoff. However, understanding risk behavior also requires understanding the extent of risk exposure. This means knowing the probability distribution of the random variable x facing decision-makers. Often, it is convenient to represent the probability distribution of x by some sufficient statistics, i.e., statistics that summarize all the relevant information about the risky prospects. Then, a change in risk exposure can be translated in changes in these sufficient statistics (e.g., the mean and variance for normal distributions). However, the sufficient statistics are specific to each probability distribution. Is it possible to summarize the relevant information about risk in a generic fashion, i.e., in a way that would apply to all probability distributions? One possible approach is to rely on the moments of the distribution. As long as they exist (e.g., that they are finite), the moments of the random variable x provide a generic way to assess individual risk exposure. Note that we already discussed expressing risk aversion in terms of its implications for the mean and variance of "*a*." Here, we explore extending this analysis to the first r central moments, where r can be greater than 2. Recall that the mean is the first central moment, the variance the second central moment, while the third central moment reflects skewness, and the fourth central moment measures kurtosis (see the Appendix). Estimating the first 2, 3, or 4 central moments (assuming that they exist) of a random variable is a standard practice in applied statistics. This suggests a need to refine the linkages between the first r moments of the random variable x and the valuation of risk. While there is no guarantee that the first r central moments are sufficient statistics for the underlying probability distribution (since this depends on the distribution itself), this can provide a convenient way to address the valuation of risk empirically (Antle 1983).

With $x = w + a$, consider the utility function of a decision-maker $U(x)$ representing his/her risk preferences. Assume that the utility function $U(x)$ is continuously differentiable up to order r. A r-th order Taylor series expansion of $U(x)$ evaluated at $E(x)$ gives

$$U(x) \approx U(E(x)) + \sum_{i=1}^{r} [1/(i!)] \cdot U^i \cdot [x - E(x)]^i,$$

where $U^i \equiv \partial^i U / \partial x^i$ is the i-th derivative of the utility function evaluated at $E(x)$, $i = 1, \ldots, r$. Taking the expectation and assuming that the first r central moments exist, this gives

$$EU(x) \approx U(E(x)) + \sum_{i=1}^{r} [1/(i!)] \cdot U^i \cdot E[x - E(x)]^i$$

$$\approx U(E(x)) + \sum_{i=1}^{r} [1/(i!)] \cdot U^i \cdot M_i$$

where $M_i \equiv E[x - E(x)]^i$ is the i-th central moment of x, $i = 1, \ldots, r$. Recall that, in the neighborhood of $E(x)$, $EU(x) = U(E(x) - R)$ can also be approximated as $EU(x) \approx U(E(x)) - (\partial U / \partial x) \cdot R$, where R is the risk premium. Noting that $M_1 = 0$, this yields the following local approximation (in the neighborhood of $E(x)$)

$$R \approx \sum_{i=2}^{r} -[1/(i!)] \cdot (U^i / U^1) \cdot M_i$$

$$\approx \sum_{i=2}^{r} R_i \cdot M_i \qquad (3)$$

where $R_i = -[1/(i!)](U^i / U^1)$ is a measure of the marginal contribution of the i-th moment of x to the risk premium R. When $r = 2$, this gives

$$R \approx R_2 \cdot \mathrm{Var}(x) = -0.5 \cdot (U^i / U^1) \cdot \mathrm{Var}(x),$$

where $M_2 = \mathrm{Var}(x)$ is the variance of x, and $R_2 = -0.5 U'' / U' = r/2$, r being the Arrow–Pratt absolute risk aversion coefficient. This reduces to the Arrow–Pratt analysis presented previously.

More generally, when $r > 2$, expression (3) gives a local approximation to the risk premium R as a linear function of the first r moments of the distribution of terminal wealth x. For example, it shows the effect of the third central moment M_3 on the risk premium R. Here M_3 measures the skewness of distribution of x, and $R_3 = -1/6(U''' / U')$. Note that skewness to the left ($M_3 < 0$) is associated with "downside risk" exposure, while skewness to the right ($M_3 > 0$) means "upside risk" exposure. In this context, a decrease in

M_3, implies an increase in downside risk. Define *downside risk aversion* as corresponding to a positive willingness to pay to avoid downside risk (Menezes et al., "Increasing Downside Risk," 1980). The above result indicates that downside risk aversion corresponds to $R_3 < 0$ or $U''' > 0$, implying that a rise in downside risk (a decrease in M_3) would tend to increase the willingness to pay for risk (as measured by the risk premium R). But we have shown that $U'''' \geq 0$ under DARA. It follows that *DARA preferences in general imply "downside risk aversion."* Thus, if DARA characterizes the risk preferences of many people, this implies that most people are also *averse to downside risk*. This is consistent with the observation that insurance markets are most active against downside risk exposure.

Finally, we have shown that maximizing $EU(x)$ is equivalent to maximizing the *certainty equivalent* $[E(x) - R]$, where R is the risk premium. Since expression (3) provides a local approximation to the risk premium R, it follows that, as long as the first r moments exist, the objective function of a decision-maker can always be approximated by

$$[E(x) - \sum_{i=2}^{r} R_i \cdot M_i].$$

This general formulation offers two attractive characteristics. First, it does not require a full specification of the utility function $U(x)$. As such, it can be convenient to use in empirical analysis. Second, it allows going beyond a simple mean-variance analysis (e.g., by including skewness, kurtosis, etc.) in the investigation of risk behavior. This may be particularly useful in the analysis of "downside risk" exposure. However, it should be kept in mind that expression (3) is in general valid only in the neighborhood of the point $E(x)$.

PROBLEMS

Note: An asterisk (*) indicates that the problem has an accompanying Excel file on the Web page http://www.aae.wisc.edu/chavas/risk.htm.

*1. Consider a decision-maker facing an initial wealth $w = 20$, and an uncertain income that can take the following values: $a_1 = -10$ with $Pr(a_1) = 0.2, a_2 = 0$ with $Pr(a_2) = 0.3$, $a_3 = 10$ with $Pr(a_3) = 0.3$, and $a_4 = 20$ with $Pr(a_4) = 0.2$. (All monetary measures are expressed in \$1,000.) The decision-maker has risk preferences represented by the utility function $U(w + a) = -e^{-0.1 \cdot (w+a)}$.
   a. Find the risk premium and the certainty equivalent.
   b. How do the risk premium and the certainty equivalent change if initial wealth increases from 20 to 30?

c. How do the risk premium and the certainty equivalent change if the probabilities become $Pr(a_1) = 0.3$, $Pr(a_2) = 0.2$, $Pr(a_3) = 0.2$, and $Pr(a_4) = 0.3$?

d. How do the risk premium and the certainty equivalent change if the probabilities become $Pr(a_1) = 0.3$, $Pr(a_2) = 0.2$, $Pr(a_3) = 0.3$, and $Pr(a_4) = 0.2$?

*2. Same questions, but with the utility function $U(w + a) = \ln(w + a)$. Interpret your results.

*3. Same questions, but with the utility function $U(w + a) = -1/(w + a)$. Interpret your results.

Chapter 5

Stochastic Dominance

Chapter 4 presented an analysis of risk behavior under general risk preferences under the expected utility model. This provides some guidance for empirical risk analysis. However, applying this approach to decision-making under uncertainty requires having good information about two items: (1) the extent of risk exposure (as measured by the probability distribution of terminal wealth x), and (2) the risk preferences of the decision-maker (as represented by his/her utility function $U(x)$). Often, it is easier to obtain sample information about the probability distribution of x than about individual risk preferences. This raises the question, is it possible to conduct risk analysis without precise information about risk preferences? The answer is yes. This is the issue addressed in stochastic dominance. Stochastic dominance provides a framework to rank choices among alternative risky strategies when preferences are not precisely known (Whitmore and Findlay 1978). It seeks the elimination of "inferior choices" without strong a priori information about risk preferences.

To present the arguments, consider a decision-maker with a risk preference function $U(x)$, $L \leq x \leq M$, and facing a choice between two risky prospects represented by the probability functions $f(x)$ and $g(x)$. The associated distribution functions are

$$F(x) = \int_{L}^{x} f(y)dy,$$

and

$$G(x) = \int_L^M g(y)dy.$$

Under the expected utility model, $f(x) \geq^* g(x)$ if and only if $E_f U(x) \geq E_g U(x)$, where E_f *and* E_g are expectation operators based on the probability function $f(x)$ and $g(x)$, respectively. Since $E_f U(x) - E_g U(x) = \int_L^M U(x)[f(x) - g(x)]dx$, this can be written as

$$f(x) \geq^* g(x) \text{ if and only if } \int_L^M U(x)[f(x) - g(x)]dx \geq 0,$$

where $f(x) \geq^* g(x)$ means that the probability function $f(x)$ is preferred to $g(x)$. Thus, knowing the sign of the term $[\int_L^M U(x)[f(x) - g(x)]dx]$ is a necessary and sufficient condition to decide that the probability function $f(x)$ is preferred to $g(x)$. The essence of stochastic dominance is to evaluate the sign of this expression with a minimum amount of information about the utility function $U(x)$.

SOME MATHEMATICAL DERIVATIONS

Checking the sign of the term $[\int_L^M U(x)[f(x) - g(x)]dx]$ is an exercise in using integration by parts. The key mathematical results are presented in this section. Define

$$D_1(x) = G(x) - F(x),$$
$$D_2(x) = \int_L^x D_1(y)dy,$$

and

$$D_3(x) = \int_L^x D_2(y)dy.$$

Using integration by parts, we have

$$E_f(x) - E_g(x) = \int_L^M x[f(x) - g(x)]dx,$$

$$= [x(F(x) - G(x))]\Big|_L^M - \int_L^M [F(x) - G(x)]dx,$$

$$= \int_L^M [G(x) - F(x)]dx, = \int_L^M D_1(x)dx = D_2(M). \tag{1}$$

Also, using integration by parts, we obtain

$$E_f U(x) - E_g U(x) \equiv \int_L^M U(x)[f(x) - g(x)]dx$$

$$= [U(x)(F(x) - G(x))]|_L^M - \int_L^M U'(x)[F(x) - G(x)]dx,$$

$$= \int_L^M U'(x)[G(x) - F(x)]dx,$$

$$= \int_L^M U'(x)D_1(x)dx, \tag{2}$$

$$= [U'(x)\int_L^x D_1(y)dy]|_L^M - \int_L^M U''(x)\int_L^x D_1(y)dydx,$$

$$= [U'(M)\int_L^M D_1(y)dy] - \int_L^M U''(x)\int_L^x D_1(y)dydx,$$

$$= U'(M)D_2(M) - \int_L^M U''(x)D_2(x)dx, \tag{3}$$

$$= U'(M)[E_f(x) - E_g(x)] - \int_L^M U''(x)D_2(x)dx, \text{ using (1),}$$

$$= U'(M)[E_f(x) - E_g(x)] - [U''(x)\int_L^x D_2(y)dy]|_L^M + \int_L^M U'''(x)\int_L^x D_2(y)dydx,$$

$$= U'(M)[E_f(x) - E_g(x)] - U''(M)D_3(M) + \int_L^M U''''(x)D_3(x)dx. \tag{4}$$

Equations (2), (3), and (4) provide equivalent formulations for $[E_f U(x) - E_g U(x)]$. But choosing between $f(x)$ and $g(x)$ is equivalent to finding the sign of $[E_f U(x) - E_g U(x)]$. It follows that establishing the sign of equation (2), (3), or (4) is sufficient information to decide between $f(x)$ and $g(x)$. This provides the basis for stochastic dominance analysis, as discussed next.

DEFINITIONS

Choosing between the probability functions $f(x)$ and $g(x)$ typically depends on risk preferences. The question is, how much (or how little) do we need to know about risk preferences before we can decide whether or not $f(x)$ is a better choice (compared to $g(x)$)? We will focus on three classes of preference functions:

- Let U_1 denote the class of utility functions $U(x)$ satisfying $U'(x) > 0$ for all x.
- Let U_2 denote the class of utility functions $U(x) \in U_1$ satisfying $U''(x) < 0$ for all x.
- Let U_3 denote the class of utility functions $U(x) \in U_2$ satisfying $U'''(x) > 0$ for all x.

The class U_1 is quite general; it simply assumes that the marginal utility of income is positive. This is quite intuitive. It states that increasing income to any particular individual makes him/her better off. This only requires that preferences are *nonsatiated* with respect to income, so that an individual can always find some way of spending his/her income so as to increase his/her utility. Since this does not impose any restriction on the second derivative U'', this allows for risk loving ($U'' > 0$), risk neutral behavior ($U'' = 0$), or risk averse behavior ($U'' < 0$).

The class U_2 is a little more restrictive. It further restricts the class U_1 (with $U' > 0$) by considering only *risk-averse decision-makers* (with $U'' < 0$). To the extent that most decision-makers may be risk averse, this still appears rather general. Clearly, if a utility function belongs to the class U_2, it also belongs to the class U_1. However, all utility functions belonging to the class U_1 do not necessarily belong to the class U_2 (e.g., the case of risk loving preferences).

The class U_3 is the most restrictive of the three classes. It further restricts the class U_2 of risk averse decision-makers (with $U' > 0$ *and* $U'' < 0$) by focusing only on the utility functions exhibiting $U''' > 0$. We have seen that DARA (decreasing absolute risk aversion) preferences imply that $U''' > 0$. Thus, the class U_3 includes all decision makers that are risk averse and exhibit DARA. Clearly, if a utility function belongs to the class U_3, it also belongs to the class U_2 and U_1. However, there are utility functions that belong to the class U_2 but that do not belong to the class U_3 (e.g., the case of risk averse preferences exhibiting $U''' < 0$).

IMPLICATIONS

Under the expected utility model, we know that $f(x)$ is preferred to $g(x)$ (written as $f(x) \geq^* g(x)$) if and only if $E_f U(x) - E_g U(x) \equiv [\int_L^M U(x)$

$[f(x) - g(x)]dx] \geq 0$. Using the above mathematical derivations, we obtain the following stochastic dominance results. They provide relative ranking of probability distributions without precise information about the risk preferences of the decision-maker.

FIRST-ORDER STOCHASTIC DOMINANCE

Equation (2) states that $E_f U(x) \geq E_g U(x)$ if and only if $[\int_L^M U'(x) D_1(x)dx] \geq 0$. Under the expected utility model, having $U' > 0$ gives:

Proposition 1: (first-order stochastic dominance)

$f(x) \geq^* g(x)$ for all $U(x) \in U_1$ if and only if

$D_1(x) \equiv G(x) - F(x) \geq 0$ for all x.

Proposition 1 states that $D_1(x) \equiv G(x) - F(x) \geq 0$ for all x is a sufficient condition to conclude that $f(x)$ is (at least weakly) preferred to $g(x)$ for all decision-makers that are nonsatiated in income (i.e., with $U' > 0$). This is illustrated in Figure 5.1. It shows that, given $U' > 0$, if the distribution function $F(x)$ is *to the right* of the distribution function $G(x)$ so that they *do not cross*, then we know $f(x)$ is a better choice than $g(x)$.

> **Discrete Implementation**: Consider the case of choosing between two probability functions $f(x)$ and $g(x)$, where the random variable x can take n possible values, $x_1, \ldots, x_n$. To evaluate first-order stochastic dominance, calculate $D_1(x_r) = G(x_r) - F(x_r) = \Sigma_x[g(x_i) - f(x_i)]$: $x_i \leq x_r]$, for all x_r, $r = 1, 2, \ldots, n$. If $D_1(x_r) \geq 0$ for all r, then we can conclude that *choosing $f(x)$ is at least as good as $g(x)$ for all $U(x) \in U_1$* (i.e., for all preferences exhibiting nonsatiation).

SECOND-ORDER STOCHASTIC DOMINANCE

Equation (3) states that $E_f U(x) \geq E_g U(x)$ if and only if $[U'(M)D_2(M) - \int_L^M U''(x)D_2(x)dx] \geq 0$. Under the expected utility model, having $U' > 0$ and $U'' < 0$ gives:

Proposition 2: (second-order stochastic dominance)

$f(x) \geq^* g(x)$ *for all* $U(x) \in U_2$ *if and only if* $D_2(x)$

$$\equiv \int_L^x D_1(y)dy \geq 0 \text{ for all } x.$$

Proposition 2 states that $D_2(x) \equiv \int_L^x D_1(y)dy \equiv \int_L^x [G(y) - F(y)]dy \geq 0$ for all x is a sufficient condition to conclude that $f(x)$ is (at least weakly)

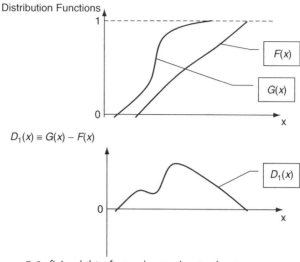

Figure 5.1 $f(x)$ exhibits first-order stochastic dominance over $g(x)$

preferred to $g(x)$ for all risk averse decision makers (with $U'' < 0$) that are nonsatiated in income (with $U' > 0$). This is illustrated in Figure 5.2. It shows that, given $U' > 0$ and $U'' < 0$, if *the area under $G(x)$ and to the left of x remains greater than the area under $F(x)$ and to the left of x for all x*, then we know that $f(x)$ is a better choice than $g(x)$. Note that this allows the two distribution functions $F(x)$ and $G(x)$ to *cross each other* (once or even several times). However, it implies that the distribution function $F(x)$ cannot start to the left of $G(x)$. And if the two distribution functions $F(x)$ and $G(x)$ cross each other, the area between them where $G(x)$ is to the right of $F(x)$ must be relatively small such that $[\int_L^x [G(y) - F(y)]dy]$ remains nonnegative.

> **Discrete Implementation**: Consider the case of choosing between two probability functions $f(x)$ and $g(x)$, where the random variable x can take n possible values, $x_1, \ldots, x_n$. To evaluate second-order stochastic dominance, calculate $D_2(x_r) = \Sigma_x[D_1(x_{i-1})][x_i - x_{i-1}] : x_i \leq x_r$, which is a piece-wise linear continuous function of x. If $D_2(x_r) \geq 0$ for all r, then we can conclude that *choosing $f(x)$ is at least as good as $g(x)$ for all $U(x) \in U_2$* (i.e., for all preferences exhibiting nonsatiation and risk aversion).

As noted above, second-order stochastic dominance allows the two distribution functions $F(x)$ and $G(x)$ to cross each other. In the special case when we know that they *cross but only once*, we can obtain some additional results. Consider the situation where $D_1(x) > 0$ for "small values" of x (so

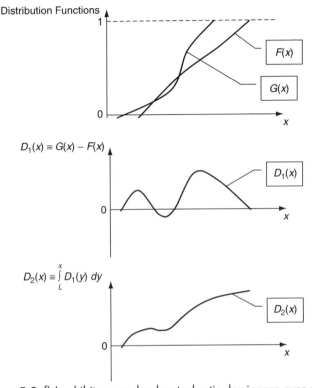

Figure 5.2 *f(x)* exhibits second-order stochastic dominance over *g(x)*

that $F(x)$ starts to the right of $G(x)$), and where $F(x)$ and $G(x)$ cross only once. Then, there exists a value x_0 such that

$$D_1(x) \equiv G(x) - F(x) > 0 \text{ for any } x, \ L \le x \le x_0,$$
$$D_1(x) \equiv G(x) - F(x) \le 0 \text{ for any } x, \ x_0 \le x \le M,$$
$$< 0 \text{ for at least some } x.$$

It follows that $D_2(x) \ge 0$ *for all* $x \le x_0$, and $D_2(x) \ge D_2(M) \equiv E_f(x) - E_g(x)$ from (1). This implies that, in the case of single crossing, $f(x) \ge^* g(x)$ *for all* $U(x) \in U_2$ if $D_2(x) \ge 0$ *for all* $x < x_0$ *and* $E_f(x) \ge E_g(x)$. Thus, under single crossing, if $D_2(x) \ge 0$ *for all* $x < x_0$ and $E_f(x) \ge E_g(x)$, then $f(x)$ is (at least weakly) preferred to $g(x)$ for all utility functions $U(x) \in U_2$ (i.e., where $U' > 0$ and $U'' < 0$).

An interesting special case involves *normal distributions*. Under normal distributions, single crossing and $D_2(x) > (\ge)0$ for $x < x_0$ correspond to $V_f(x) < (\le)V_g(x)$. Thus, under normal distributions, $\text{Var}_f(x) < \text{Var}_g(x)$

and $E_f(x) \geq E_g(x)$ imply that $f(x)$ is preferred to $g(x)$ for all utility functions $U(x) \in U_2$ (i.e. all nonsatiated, risk-averse decision-makers). Similarly, $\text{Var}_f(x) \leq \text{Var}_g(x)$ *and* $E_f(x) > E_g(x)$ imply that $f(x)$ is preferred to $g(x)$ for all $U(x) \in U_2$. This identifies the (E, V) efficiency set under risk aversion (where E = expected value, V = Variance): a risk-averse decision-maker prefers a higher expected return and a lower variance of returns.

THIRD-ORDER STOCHASTIC DOMINANCE

Equation (4) states that $E_f U(x) \geq E_g U(x)$ if and only if $[U'(M)[E_f(x) - E_g(x)] - U''(M)D_3(M) + \int_L^M U'''(x)D_3(x)dx] \geq 0$. Under the expected utility model, having $U' > 0$, $U'' < 0$, and $U''' > 0$ gives:

Proposition 3: (third-order stochastic dominance)

$$f(x) \geq {}^*g(x) \text{ for all } U(x) \in U_3 \text{ if and only if}$$

- $D_3(x) \geq 0$ for all x, and
- $E_f(x) \geq E_g(x)$.

Proposition 3 states that $E_f(x) \geq E_g(x)$ *and* $D_3(x) \equiv \int_L^x D_2(y)dy \geq 0$ for all x are sufficient conditions to conclude that $f(x)$ is (at least weakly) preferred to $g(x)$ for all risk preferences satisfying $U' > 0$ (i.e., nonsatiated), $U'' < 0$ (i.e., risk averse) and $U''' > 0$ (e.g., exhibiting decreasing absolute risk aversion, DARA). This is illustrated in Figure 5.3. Note that $E_f(x) \geq E_g(x)$ is equivalent to $D_2(M) \geq 0$ from (1). Given $U' > 0$, $U'' < 0$, and $U''' > 0$, Figure 5.3 shows that $D_2(M) \geq 0$ *and* $D_3(x) \equiv \int_L^x D_2(y)dy \geq 0$ for all x guarantee that $f(x)$ is (at least weakly) preferred to $g(x)$. Again, it allows crossing of the distribution functions $F(x)$ and $G(x)$. And it can apply even if $D_2(x)$ is not always positive (i.e., where second-degree stochastic dominance fails). However, it still requires that the distribution function $F(x)$ starts to the right of $G(x)$. And it requires that $D_2(M) \geq 0$.

> **Discrete Implementation**: Consider the case of choosing between two probability functions $f(x)$ and $g(x)$, where the random variable x can take n possible values, $x_1, \ldots, x_n$. To evaluate third-order stochastic dominance, calculate $D_3(x_r) = \Sigma_x\{(1/2)[D_2(x_i) + D_2(x_{i-1})][x_i - x_{i-1}]$: $x_i \leq x_r\}$, which is a piece-wise quadratic continuous function of x. If

- $D_3(x_r) \geq 0$ for all x_r and all x where $D_2(x) = 0$, and
- $E_f(x) \geq E_g(x)$, (or equivalently $D_2(M) \geq 0$ from (1)),
  then we can conclude that $f(x)$ is (*at least weakly*) *preferred to* $g(x)$ *for all* $U(x) \in U_3$ (i.e., for all preferences where $U' > 0$, $U'' < 0$, *and* $U''' > 0$).

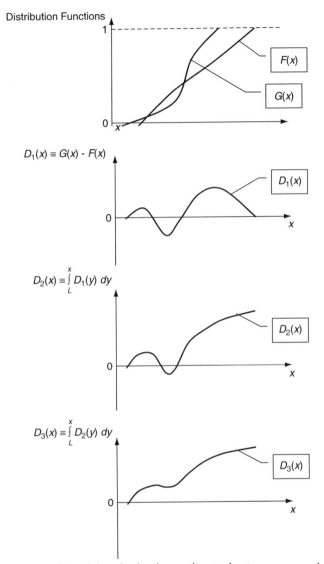

Figure 5.3 $f(x)$ exhibits third-order stochastic dominance over $g(x)$

STOCHASTIC DOMINANCE WITH RESPECT TO A FUNCTION

When two distribution functions can be ranked according to first-, second-, or third-order stochastic dominance, then we have information on which distribution would be chosen by decision-makers under weak assumptions about their risk preferences. This can be quite useful to eliminate inferior choices without precise knowledge of risk preferences. However, there are situations where distributions cannot be ranked easily. For example, if a distribution exhibits high average return but a significant exposure to downside risk, it will fail to satisfy the stochastic dominance criteria discussed above. The reason is that all criteria require that the distribution function of the preferred choice must start to the right of other distribution functions, meaning that the preferred choice must involve less downside risk exposure. This is intuitive; first-, second-, or third-order stochastic dominance allows for extreme aversion to downside risk. It means that a decision-maker could possibly decide to avoid risky prospects offering greater downside risk exposure even if such prospects generate high average returns. Note that this can apply to technological adoption under uncertainty. While new technologies often generate higher expected return, their adoption can be slow if they also increase downside risk exposure. In such situations, first-, second-, or third-order stochastic dominance analysis will not help. Of course, if we had perfect information about risk preferences, then comparing expected utilities across prospects would identify the preferred choice. But, given the empirical difficulties assessing individual risk preferences, it remains of interest to evaluate risky prospects under refined but incomplete information about risk preferences. Meyer's stochastic dominance with respect to a function provides such an approach (Meyer 1977).

DEFINITION

Let $U_f \equiv U[r_L(x), r_M(x)]$ denote a class of utility functions $U(x)$ satisfying

- $r_L(x) \leq -U''(x)/U'(x) \leq r_M(x)$ for all x, and
- $U'(x) > 0$ for all x.

Here, $r_L(x)$ *and* $r_M(x)$ are respectively a lower bound and upper bound on the Arrow–Pratt absolute risk aversion coefficient $-U''/U'$ representing the individual risk preferences at point x. The bounds $r_L(x)$ and $r_M(x)$ are to be interpreted as a priori information about individual risk preferences.

This includes several interesting special cases. First, given $U' > 0$, if $r_L(x) = -\infty$ and $r_M(x) = \infty$ for all x, then $U_f = U_1$, which reduces to the class of risk preferences analyzed above in first-order stochastic dominance. Second, given $U' > 0$, if $r_L(x) = 0$ and $r_M(x) = \infty$ for all x, then $U_f = U_2$, which is the class of risk averse preferences (with $U'' < 0$) analyzed above in second-order stochastic dominance. Third, if $r_L(x) = r_M(x) = r(x)$ for all x, then we obtain the case of precise knowledge about risk preferences (where $U(x) = \int e^{-\int r}$). The situation of interest here is when we have additional information about risk preferences that go beyond the one used in first-, second-, or third-order stochastic dominance and but falls short of perfect knowledge.

SOME DERIVATIONS

Using equation (2), we have shown that $E_f U(x) - E_g U(x) \equiv \int_L^M U(x) [f(x) - g(x)]dx = \int_L^M U'(x)[G(x) - F(x)]dx \geq 0$ if and only if $f(x) \geq {}^* g(x)$. Under the expected utility model, this generates the following result:

$$f(x) \geq {}^* g(x) \text{ if } [\text{Min}_{U \in U_f} \int_L^M U'(x)[G(x) - F(x)]dx] \geq 0.$$

This involves finding the minimum of an integral and checking that the minimum is nonnegative. To find this minimum, note that $U = \int e^{-\int r}$, where $r(x) = -U''(x)/U'(x)$ is the Arrow–Pratt absolute risk aversion coefficient. The minimization problem can then be written as

$$\text{Min}_r \left[\int_L^M U'(x)[G(x) - F(x)] \, dx : U''(x) = -r(x)U'(x), \ r_L(x) \leq r(x) \leq r_M(x) \right].$$

The corresponding Lagrangean is

$$L = \int_L^M (U'(x)[G(x) - F(x)] + \lambda(x)[-r(x)U'(x) - U''(x)])dx,$$

where $\lambda(x)$ is the Lagrange multiplier (also called *costate variable in optimal control*) under state x. Integrating by parts gives

$$L = \int_L^M (U'(x)[G(x) - F(x) - \lambda(x)r(x)])dx - [\lambda(x)U'(x)]|_L^M + \int_L^M \lambda'(x)U'(x)dx.$$

The first-order conditions to the minimization problem are

$$\partial L/\partial U' = G(x) - F(x) - \lambda(x)r(x) + \lambda'(x) = 0 \text{ for } x < M \quad (5a)$$

$$= -\lambda_M \qquad\qquad\qquad = 0 \text{ for } x = M. \quad (5b)$$

and since L is linear in r,

$$\partial L/\partial r = -\lambda(x)U'(x) \leq 0 \text{ when } r^* = r_M(x) \quad (6a)$$

$$\geq 0 \text{ when } r^* = r_L(x), \quad (6b)$$

where r^* denotes the optimal solution for r.

Note that

$$d(\lambda U')/dx = \lambda U'' + \lambda' U'$$
$$= \lambda U'' + [F - G + \lambda r]U', \text{ from (5a)}, \quad (7)$$
$$= [F - G]U', \text{ since } U'' = -rU'.$$

It follows that $\int_x^M [d(\lambda U')/dx]dx = [\lambda U']|_x^M,$

$$= -\lambda U', \text{ since } \lambda_M = 0 \text{ from (5b)},$$

$$= \int_x^M [F(x) - G(x)]U'(x)dx, \text{ from (7)}.$$

The first-order conditions (6a)–(6b) thus imply

$$r^* = r_M(x) \text{ if } \int_x^M [G(x) - F(x)]U'(x)dx \geq 0,$$

$$= r_L(x) \text{ if } \int_x^M [G(x) - F(x)]U'(x)dx < 0,$$

where $U' = e^{-\int r^*}$ is evaluated at the optimal r^*.

IMPLICATIONS

Proposition 4: (stochastic dominance with respect to a function)

$f(x) \geq^* g(x)$ for all $U(x) \in U_f \equiv U[r_L(x), r_M(x)]$ if and only if

$$\int_L^M U'(x)[G(x) - F(x)] \geq 0$$

where $U'(x) = e^{-\int r^*}$ is evaluated at the optimal r^* of the above minimization problem.

Proposition 4 provides a framework to choose between $f(x)$ and $g(x)$ when we know that $U(x) \in U_f$, i.e. that risk preferences are nonsatiated ($U' > 0$) and satisfy the following bounds for the Arrow–Pratt risk aversion coefficient: $r_L(x) \leq - U''(x)/U'(x) \leq r_M(x)$ for all x.

THE DISCRETE CASE

To implement Proposition 4, consider the case of two discrete random variables involving n data points x_i, $i = 1, 2, \ldots, n$, where $x_{i+1} > x_i$ for all i. Let $U_i = U(x_i)$, $i = 1, 2, \ldots, n$. Note that

$$E_f U(x) - E_g U(x) = \sum_{i=1}^{n} U_i[(F_i - F_{i-1}) - (G_i - G_{i-1})],$$

$$= \sum_{i=1}^{n} U_i[(F_i - G_i) - \sum_{i=1}^{n} U_i[(F_{i-1} - G_{i-1})],$$

$$= \sum_{i=1}^{n-1} (U_i - U_{i+1})(F_i - G_i).$$

Let $H_i \equiv U_{i+1} - U_i > 0$, $\Delta x_i = x_{i+1} - x_i > 0$, and $[H_i/\Delta x_i - H_{i-1}/\Delta x_{i-1}]/\Delta x_{i-1} = -r_i H_i/\Delta x_i$ (corresponding to the definition of the Arrow–Pratt absolute risk aversion coefficient r_i in the context of discrete changes). Then, consider the minimization of the Lagrangean

$$\text{Min}_{H,r} \left[\sum_{i=1}^{n} [- H_i(F_i - G_i) + \lambda_i(- r_i H_i \Delta x_{i-1}/\Delta x_i - H_i/\Delta x_i + H_{i-1}/\Delta x_{i-1})] \right],$$

where the $\lambda_i's$ are Lagrange multipliers. Assuming $H_i > 0$, the first-order conditions take the form

$$\partial L/\partial H_i = -(F_i - G_i) - \lambda_i(1/\Delta x_i + r_i \Delta x_{i-1}/\Delta x_i) + \lambda_{i+1}/\Delta x_i$$

$$= 0, \text{ for } i = 1, \ldots, n - 1, \tag{8a}$$

$$= -\lambda_n(1/\Delta x_n + r_n \Delta x_{n-1}/\Delta x_n) = 0, \text{ for } i = n, \tag{8b}$$

$$\partial L/\partial r_i = -\lambda_i H_i \Delta x_{i-1}/\Delta x_i, \text{ for } i = 1, \ldots, n, \tag{9a}$$

$$= \text{sign}(-\lambda_i) \quad \leq 0 \text{ when } r_i^* = r_M(x_i),$$

$$> 0 \text{ when } r_i^* = r_L(x_i), \tag{9b}$$

since the Lagrangean is linear in r_i, and

$$\partial L/\partial \lambda_i = -r_i H_i \Delta x_{i-1}/\Delta x_i - H_i/\Delta x_i + H_{i-1}/\Delta x_{i-1} = 0, \ i = 1, \ldots, n. \quad (10)$$

For $i = 1, \ldots, n-1$, note that substituting equation (10) into (8a) yields

$$G_i - F_i + \lambda_{i+1}/\Delta x_i - \lambda_i(H_{i-1}/H_i)/\Delta x_{i-1} = 0,$$

or

$$\lambda_i = [G_i - F_i + \lambda_{i+1}/\Delta x_i]/[(H_{i-1}/H_i)/\Delta x_{i-1}] = \text{sign}\,(G_i - F_i + \lambda_{i+1}/\Delta x_i).$$

It follows from (9) that sign $(\partial L/\partial r_i) = \text{sign}\,(-\lambda_i) = \text{sign}[-(G_i - F_i + \lambda_{i+1}/\Delta x_i)]$. This suggests the following algorithm:

1. Choose $\lambda_n = 0$, $r_n^* = r_M(x_n)$, and $H_n^* = K > 0$. Let $i = n$.
2. Solve equation (10) $(\partial L/\partial \lambda_i = 0)$ for $H_{i-1}^* > 0$.
3. Let $i = i - 1$. Evaluate $[G_i - F_i + \lambda_{i+1}/\Delta x_i]$.
4. Choose $r_i^* = r_M(x_i)$ if $[G_i - F_i + \lambda_{i+1}/\Delta x_i] \geq 0$,
   $= r_L(x_i)$ if $[G_i - F_i + \lambda_{i+1}/\Delta x_i] < 0$.
5. Evaluate $\lambda_i = [G_i - F_i + \lambda_{i+1}/\Delta x_i]/[(H_{i-1}/H_i)/\Delta x_{i-1}]$. Then, go to step 2/ until $i = 1$.
6. Conclude that $f(x) \geq {}^*g(x)$ for all $U(x) \in U_f$ if $\{\Sigma_i[-H_i^*(F_i - G_i)]$: $i = 1, \ldots, n] \geq 0$.

This provides a practical way of assessing whether $f(x)$ is preferred to $g(x)$ for a class of utility function U_f where we have a priori information about the lower bound and upper bound of the Arrow–Pratt risk aversion coefficient at each data point.

PROBLEMS

Note: An asterisk (*) indicates that the problem has an accompanying Excel file on the Web page http://www.aae.wisc.edu/chavas/risk.htm.

*1. Consider the following pair of prospects of receiving an uncertain income x:

Prospect A		Prospect B	
x_i	$Pr(x_i)$	x_i	$Pr(x_i)$
2	0.2	3	0.6
3	0.3	6	0.4
5	0.5		

Analyze these two prospects in terms of:

- first-degree stochastic efficiency
- second-degree stochastic efficiency
- third-degree stochastic efficiency

Interpret your results.

*2. Three alternative rice production technologies have returns that are normally distributed with parameters given in the table:

Technology	Mean	Standard Deviation
A	1200	400
B	1000	300
C	500	100

a. Plot the distribution functions of returns for each technology.
b. Which technologies are efficient according to second-degree stochastic dominance? Interpret.

*3. Two possible technologies are available to maize growers in a region. The distributions of yield (t/ha) are described by two sets of fractiles.

Fractile	0	0.25	0.50	0.75	1.0
Technology A	0.75	1.25	1.50	2.00	3.50
Technology B	1.00	2.00	3.10	4.50	6.00

Suppose the net value of grain is $100/t and the variable costs associated with these technologies are $50/ha for technology A and $100/ha for technology B.

a. Plot the distribution functions of returns for each technology (assume that the functions are piece-wise linear).
b. Analyze the efficiency of each technology using stochastic dominance. Interpret your results.

Chapter 6

Mean-Variance Analysis

Under the expected utility model, consider a utility function $U(x)$ where $x \equiv (w + a)$ is terminal wealth. Analyzing behavior under risk in a mean-variance context implies that expected utility can be expressed as $EU(x) = W(M, V)$, where $M \equiv E(x)$ is the mean of x and $V \equiv \text{Var}(x)$ is the variance of x. This mean-variance approach is quite attractive in applied risk analysis given that the estimation of the first two moments of the distribution of x is often relatively easy to obtain empirically. But, besides its convenience, can we justify this mean-variance approach under fairly general conditions? This chapter evaluates the arguments underlying the mean-variance approach.

THE CASE OF CARA PREFERENCES UNDER NORMALITY

We showed in Chapter 4 that, under constant absolute risk aversion (CARA) and the normality of the distribution of x, maximizing $EU(x)$ is equivalent to maximizing $[M - r/2\ V]$, where $r = -U''/U'$ is the constant Arrow–Pratt absolute risk aversion coefficient. In this case, decision analysis under risk can be conducted in the context of an additive mean-variance objective function. While convenient, both the normality assumption and CARA preferences appear rather restrictive. For example, this does not allow risky prospects that have skewed probability distribution. Also, CARA implies the absence of wealth effects.

THE CASE OF A QUADRATIC UTILITY FUNCTION

Also, we have shown that, under a quadratic utility function, maximizing expected utility is equivalent to maximizing a mean-variance reference function $W(M, V)$. One advantage of this result is that it does not impose any restriction on the probability distribution of x. However, we have also shown that a quadratic utility function exhibits increasing absolute risk aversion (IARA). This appears restrictive in the sense that it excludes the more intuitive case of decreasing absolute risk aversion (DARA).

THE GENERAL CASE

So we know of two cases (CARA with normality and quadratic utility) where mean-variance preferences apply. But these cases appear rather restrictive. As a result, we are looking for more general results under which the mean-variance approach can be justified. Below, we present the arguments presented by Meyer (1987).

Consider the case where $x = M + \sigma e$, where $M = E(x)$ is the *mean* of x (= a *location* parameter), e is a random variable with mean zero ($E(e) = 0$) and $\sigma > 0$ is a *mean preserving spread* (or a *scale* parameter). In the special case where $\text{Var}(e) = 1$, the parameters M and σ can be interpreted as the mean and the standard deviation of x respectively. Note that, as long as the mean $E(x)$ exists, this representation does not impose any restriction on the form of the probability function of x (or e).

Consider the case where a decision-maker chooses among random variables of the form $x = M + \sigma e$, where all random variables differ from each other only by the location parameter M and/or the scale parameter σ. Then, under the expected utility model, the expected utility of the decision-maker takes the form

$$EU(x) = EU(M + \sigma e) = W(M, \sigma).$$

Note that *this does not impose any restriction on the form of the probability function of e, nor on the shape of the utility function U(x)*. Thus, the objective function $W(M, \sigma)$ provides a general way to motivate a mean standard deviation analysis (or mean variance analysis with $V = \sigma^2$). The properties of the mean-standard deviation utility frontier $W(M, \sigma)$ and the linkages with risk preferences are examined next.

NOTATION

$$\text{Let} \quad W_M = \partial W / \partial M = EU'$$
$$W_\sigma = \partial W / \partial \sigma = E(U'e)$$
$$W_{MM} = \partial^2 W / \partial M^2 = EU''$$
$$W_{\sigma\sigma} = \partial^2 W / \partial \sigma^2 = E(U''e^2)$$
$$W_{\sigma M} = \partial^2 W / \partial \sigma \partial M = E(U''e).$$

Let W_0 denote some constant level of expected utility. Differentiating $W_0 = W(M(\sigma), \sigma)$ with respect to σ gives

$$W_M \partial M / \partial \sigma + W_\sigma = 0,$$

or

$$\partial M / \partial \sigma = -W_\sigma / W_M = S(M, \sigma),$$

where $S(M, \sigma) = \partial M / \partial \sigma$ is the *slope of the indifference curve between M and σ*, holding expected utility at the constant level W_0. It also measures the *marginal rate of substitution between M and σ*. This notation provides the framework to analyze the risk preferences associated with the mean variance function $W(M, \sigma)$ and to link them with the properties of the underlying utility function $U(x)$.

IMPLICATIONS

The implications of risk preferences for the properties of the properties of the mean variance function $W(M, \sigma)$ are presented next.

Proposition 1: $W_M \geq 0$ if and only if $U' \geq 0$ for all (M, σ).

Proposition 1 simply means that, under nonsatiation ($U' > 0$), the function W is increasing in M. This is an intuitive result: higher expected return M makes the decision-maker better off.

Proposition 2: $W_\sigma \leq 0$ if and only if $U'' \leq 0$ for all (M, σ).

Proof:
$$W_\sigma = E(U'e) = \text{COV}(U', e) = \text{sign}(\partial U' / \partial e) = \text{sign}(U''\sigma) = \text{sign}(U'').$$

Proposition 2 implies that, under risk neutrality ($U'' = 0$), the function W is independent of σ. Alternatively, under risk aversion ($U'' < 0$), then the function W is decreasing in σ. This is intuitive: increasing risk (as measured by σ) makes any risk averse decision-maker worse off.

Proposition 3: $S(M, \sigma) \geq 0$ *if* $U'' > 0$, $U'' < 0$ for all (M, σ).

   Proof: $S(M, \sigma) = -W_\sigma/W_M = -E(U' e)/EU' = \text{sign}(U''/U')$.

Proposition 3 shows that, under risk neutrality (with $U' > 0$ and $U'' = 0$), the marginal rate of substitution between M and σ is zero: $S(M, \sigma) = 0$. Alternatively, under risk aversion (with $U' > 0$ and $U'' < 0$), the marginal rate of substitution between M and σ tends to be positive: $S(M, \sigma) \geq 0$. This means that, under risk aversion, any increase in risk (as measured by σ) must be compensated by an increase in expected return M to keep the decision on the same welfare level.

Proposition 4: $W(M, \sigma)$ is a concave function of (M, σ) if and only if $U'' < 0$ for all (M, σ).

   Proof: $\partial^2 W/\partial(M, \sigma)^2 = E\left[U''\begin{bmatrix}1\\e\end{bmatrix}[1\ e]\right]$, which is a negative semi-definite matrix if and only if $U'' < 0$.

Proposition 4 establishes the concavity of the mean-variance function $W(M, \sigma)$ under risk aversion ($U'' < 0$). Note that this implies that set $\{M, \sigma: W(M, \sigma) \geq W_0\}$ is a *convex set*. This is illustrated in Figure 6.1, which shows the general shape of the indifference curve between M and σ under risk aversion, holding expected utility constant at W_0. The slope of the curve in Figure 6.1 is $S(M, \sigma)$, the marginal rate of substitution between M and σ (which is positive under risk aversion).

Note that, under risk aversion, $W(M, \sigma)$ is a concave function of σ (the standard deviation of e). However, it is not necessarily a concave function of σ^2 (the variance of e). This indicates that a "mean-standard deviation" analysis appears more convenient than a "mean-variance" analysis.

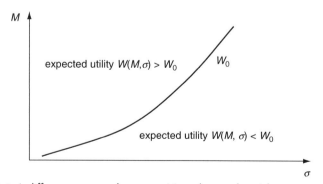

Figure 6.1 Indifference curve between M and σ under risk aversion, holding expected utility at W_0

Proposition 5: $\partial S(M, \sigma)/\partial M\{ <, =, > \} 0$ if and only if $U(x)$ exhibits {DARA, CARA, IARA} for all (M, σ), given $U' > 0$.

Proof:
$$\partial S(M,\sigma)/\partial M = -W_{\sigma M}/W_M + W_{MM}W_\sigma/(W_M)^2$$
$$= [-W_{\sigma M}W_M + W_{MM}W_\sigma]/(W_M)^2$$
$$= \text{sign}[-E(U''e)EU' + EU''E(U'e)]$$
$$= \text{sign}\{EU'[-E(U''e) + EU''z]\} \text{ where } z = E(U'e)/EU',$$
$$= \text{sign}\{E[U''(z-e)]\}$$
$$= \text{sign}\{E[rU'(e-z)]\} \text{ where } r = -U''/U',$$

Note that $E[U'(e - z)] = \int U'(e - z)f(e)de = 0$, where $f(e)$ is the probability function of e. Since $f(e) \geq 0$ *and* $U' > 0$, it follows that $[U'(e - z)f(e)]$ changes sign only once (from negative to positive) as e increases. Thus

- {r = constant} implies that $E[rU'(e - z)] = 0$ and $\partial S/\partial M = 0$,
- {r = increasing} implies that $E[rU'(e - z)] > 0$ and $\partial S/\partial M > 0$,
- {r = decreasing} implies that $E[rU'(e - z)] < 0$ and $\partial S/\partial M < 0$.

Proposition 5 shows the implications of the patterns of absolute risk aversion for the marginal rate of substitution $S(M, \sigma)$. For example, it implies that the marginal rate of substitution $S(M, \sigma)$ is independent of M under constant absolute risk aversion (CARA). This means a parallel upward shift in the indifference curve between M and σ as M increases. Proposition 5 also shows that, under decreasing absolute risk aversion (DARA), the slope of the indifference curve, $S(M, \sigma)$, decreases with M. This is illustrated in Figure 6.2. Intuitively, it shows that under DARA, the decision-maker becomes less concerned with risk (as measured by σ) as his/her expected wealth rises.

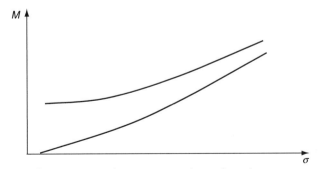

Figure 6.2 Indifference curves between M and σ under risk aversion and decreasing absolute risk aversion

Proposition 6: $\partial S(tM,\ t\sigma)/\partial t\{<,\ =,\ >\}$ 0 if and only if $U(x)$ exhibits {DRRA, CRRA, IRRA} for all $(M,\ \sigma)$, given $U' > 0$.

Proof: Evaluated at $t = 1$, $S(tM,\ t\sigma) = -W_\sigma/W_M = -E(U'\ e)/EU'$. It follows that

$$\partial S(tM,\ t\sigma)/\partial t = -E(U''x\ e)/EU' + E(U''\ x)E(U'\ e)/(EU')^2$$
$$= \text{sign}\{-E(U')E(U''x\ e) + E(U''x)E(U'e)\}$$
$$= \text{sign}\{E[\bar{r}U'(e-z)]\}$$

where $\bar{r} = -xU''/U'$ and $z = E(U'\ e)/EU'$.

We have shown that $E[U'(e-z)] = \int U'(e-z)f(e)\ de = 0$, and that $[U'(e-z)f(e)]$ changes sign only once (from negative to positive) as e increases. Thus

- $\{\bar{r} = \text{constant}\}$ implies that $E[\bar{r}U'(e-z)] = 0$ and $\partial S/\partial t = 0$,
- $\{\bar{r} = \text{increasing}\}$ implies that $E[\bar{r}U'(e-z)] > 0$ and $\partial S/\partial t > 0$,
- $\{\bar{r} = \text{decreasing}\}$ implies that $E[\bar{r}U'(e-z)] < 0$ and $\partial S/\partial t < 0$.

Proposition 6 shows the implications of the patterns of relative risk aversion for the marginal rate of substitution $S(M,\ \sigma)$. It implies that, under constant relative risk aversion (CRRA), the marginal rate of substitution $S(M,\ \sigma)$ remains unaffected by a proportional change in M and σ. This is illustrated in Figure 6.3. Figure 6.3 shows that, under CRRA, the slope of indifference curves between M and σ remain constant along a ray through the origin.

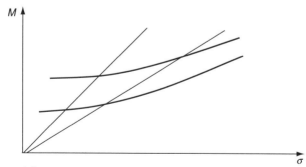

Figure 6.3 Indifference curves between M and σ under risk aversion and constant relative risk aversion (CRRA)

IMPLICATIONS

The previous analysis shows that a mean-variance specification (or mean-standard deviation specification) can be reasonably flexible in risk analysis. First, as long as one works with a flexible objective function $W(M, \sigma)$, this does not impose a priori restriction on risk preferences. Second, the shape of this function can provide insights on mean-variance trade-off, with useful linkages to the nature of risk aversion. Third, the arguments were presented for an arbitrary distribution function for the random variable representing uncertainty. This suggests its broad applicability to a variety of risky situations. Finally, the empirical estimation of mean and variances from sample information has a long tradition in statistics and econometrics. All these arguments indicate that a mean-variance analysis provides a powerful framework to conduct applied risk analysis. This gives strong support for the extensive use of mean-variance models in the empirical investigation of risk management issues. This will be further illustrated in the following chapters.

Yet, there are situations where the mean-variance model may be inappropriate. The main issue relates to the specification of the random variable $x = M + \sigma e$. It allows changes in the distribution of risk only through M (the mean) and σ (the standard deviation). This appears restrictive in at least two situations: when there is a focus on the management of "downside risk"; and when the analysis considers the case of "rare events."

One of the main issues with the mean-variance approach is that it fails to distinguish between "upside risk" (where the random variable is above its mean) and "downside risk" (where the random variable is below its mean). For example, the estimated variance from a random sample treats deviations from the mean symmetrically; it does not distinguish between being $X\%$ above the mean versus being $X\%$ below the mean. The problem is that most decision-makers treat upside risk and downside risk differently. As seen is Chapter 4, it is common for many individuals to exhibit *decreasing absolute risk aversion* (DARA), where "local" risk aversion decreases with wealth. It means that most decisions-makers are strongly averse to downside income risk exposure, while being only mildly risk averse (or even becoming risk lovers) with respect to upside income risk. As argued by Savage, this can explain why some individuals insure against downside risk while at the same time gambling to increase their exposure to upside risk. It suggests that the analysis of insurance schemes should distinguish between upside risk and downside risk. In general, under DARA, decision-makers are particularly concerned about reducing their exposure to downside income risk. It means that risk management and insurance contracts typically focus on reducing downside risk exposure. But this is not captured well by a mean-variance approach. As shown in Chapter 4, DARA implies aversion to negative skewness (representing downside risk exposure) and a relative preference for positive skewness (representing upside risk exposure). In situations where downside risk management is deemed important, this implies a need to go beyond the first two moments of the distribution (mean and variance) and to include the third moment (skewness) in risk analysis. This can be done by using a general moment-based approach (as discussed in Chapter 4). Alternatively, this can be handled by studying how the whole probability function representing uncertainty is shifted through risk management. Implications for decision-making can then be based on the expected utility model if risk preferences are known, or using stochastic dominance analysis if risk preferences are imprecisely known (see Chapter 5).

Another issue is related to the management of "rare" risky events. A *rare event* is any event that occurs with very low probability. The fact that they occur with low probability means that there can be a very large number of rare events that remain consistent with probability theory (where the sum of all probabilities equals 1). Note that, in the case where the probability function is unimodal (i.e., with a single peak), rare events are necessarily associated with values of random variables that are far from their mean. This raises questions about how information about rare events is used and processed by decision-makers. If there are many rare events, it may prove difficult for any individual to process the associated information. Bounded rationality arguments or the cost of obtaining information can imply that it is optimal to ignore much of this information in decision-making (this issue is addressed in Chapter 10). However, this does not imply that all rare events are ignored. As just discussed, under DARA, decision-makers are particularly concerned about reducing their exposure to rare events associated with "downside risk." It includes downside risk associated with rare catastrophic events such as risk of death, natural disasters, and catastrophic accidents or illness. The management of such risk is often seen as a significant concern for many individuals. In general, such management involves changes in small probabilities. Mean-variance models appear poorly equipped to handle the analysis of such effects. Again, a refined analysis would require addressing how risk management affects the lower tail of the distribution and assessing the perceived benefits associated with a lower exposure to rare downside risk.

PROBLEMS

1. Consider the mean-standard deviation representation of individual risk preferences: $W(M, \sigma) = a_1 M + a_1\sigma + a_2\sigma^2$.

    a. For what values of the a's is the decision-maker risk neutral? Risk averse?

    b. What is the marginal rate of substitution between M and σ?

    c. For what values of the a's does the decision-maker exhibit constant absolute risk aversion?

    d. Can the decision-maker exhibit decreasing absolute risk aversion? Why or why not?

2. You know that a decision-maker exhibits constant relative risk aversion (CRRA).

    a. Show that the marginal rate of substitution between M and σ must take the form $S = g(M/\sigma)$.

    b. Find a risk preference function $W(M, \sigma)$ that is consistent with CRRA.

3. Let $W(M, \sigma, s)$ represent individual risk preferences over terminal wealth x, where $M = E(x)$ is the mean of x, σ is the standard deviation of x, and s is the third central moment: $s = E[(x - M)^3]$. You know that the individual is risk averse and exhibit decreasing absolute risk aversion. Under the expected utility hypothesis, discuss the properties of the risk preference function $W(M, \sigma, s)$.

Chapter 7

Alternative Models of Risk Behavior

THE EXPECTED UTILITY MODEL REVISITED

The expected utility model provides the basis for most of the research on the economics of risk. It was the topic presented in Chapter 3. Under the expected utility model, individuals make decisions among alternative wealth levels x by maximizing $EU(x)$ where E is the expectation operator. The utility function $U(x)$ is defined up to a positive linear transformation. It is sometimes called a von Neumann–Morgenstern utility function. We saw in Chapter 4 that risk aversion, risk neutrality, or risk loving preferences correspond to the function $U(x)$ being respectively concave, linear, or convex.

One of the main advantages of the expected utility model is its empirical tractability. This is the reason why it is commonly used in risk analysis. But is the expected utility model a good predictor of human behavior? Sometimes, it is. And sometimes, it is not. This chapter evaluates some of the evidence against the expected utility model. It also reviews alternative models that have been proposed to explain behavior under risk.

The first challenge to the expected utility model is the following: Is it consistent with the fact that some individuals *both insure and gamble* at the same time? Friedman and Savage proposed to explain this by arguing that, for most individuals, the utility function $U(x)$ is probably concave (corresponding to risk aversion and a positive willingness to insure) for low or moderate monetary rewards, but convex (corresponding to risk loving and a positive willingness to gamble) for high monetary rewards. In this context, a particular individual can insure against "downside risk" while at the same time gambling on "upside risk" and still be consistent with the expected utility model.

In addition, the expected utility model hypothesis has been under attack on the ground that it is not always consistent with actual behavior under risk. We have shown that under some assumptions (Assumptions A_1–A_5), behavior under risk is necessarily consistent with the expected utility model (see Chapter 3). Thus, from a logical viewpoint, arguing that the expected utility model is not consistent with risk behavior is equivalent to arguing that some of these assumptions are not appropriate. Each of these assumptions has been challenged in the literature. For example, the ordering assumption (e.g., as in "fuzzy sets") and the transitivity assumption (e.g., as in "regret theory") have been questioned. Also, as discussed below, the continuity assumption (Assumption A3) and the independence assumption (Assumption A2) have been the subject of much scrutiny.

RELAXING THE CONTINUITY ASSUMPTION: SAFETY FIRST

In "safety first," a safety level is assumed to exist with preferences being quite different above the safety level compared to below this level. The safety level is sometimes called a "subsistence level" or a "disaster level." Intuitively, one expects decision-makers to behave in a way that would minimize the odds of being below the subsistence level. This is the motivation for using the term "safety first." It suggests that risk behavior may differ significantly for events located above versus below the subsistence level. There are some situations where such differences may imply inconsistencies with the continuity of the utility function $U(X)$ in the expected utility model.

To illustrate, consider the case where z is a subsistence level and x is random wealth with a subjective probability function $f(x)$. The formulation of safety-first modeling has taken different forms in the literature.

MINIMIZING THE PROBABILITY OF DISASTER

Assume that concerns about safety can be represented by decisions that minimize the probability of being below the subsistence level. This means that decisions are made in a way consistent with the minimization problem: Min $Pr(x \leq z)$. Since $Pr(x \leq z) = 1 - Pr(x > z)$, it follows that minimizing the probability of disaster is equivalent to maximizing

$$\text{Max } Pr(x > z) = \text{Max}\left[\int U(x)f(x)dx\right] = \text{Max } EU(x)$$

where the utility function $U(x)$ takes the form

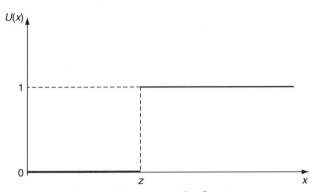

Figure 7.1 A step utility function

$$U(x) = 1 \text{ if } x > z$$
$$= 0 \text{ if } x \le z.$$

This is illustrated in Figure 7.1. It shows that there is a utility function $U(x)$ that is consistent with the minimization of the probability of disaster. However, the utility function has a very peculiar shape: it is a step function, which is discontinuous at the subsistence level z. This discontinuity means that the decision-maker views events above the subsistence level very differently from events below the subsistence level. This is inconsistent with the continuity assumption (assumption A3).

While concerns about meeting subsistence needs are quite intuitive, it remains unclear whether this necessarily implies a discontinuity in individual preferences.

MAXIMIZING EXPECTED RETURN SUBJECT TO A SMALL DISASTER PROBABILITY

Just minimizing the probability of disaster may be seen as a rather extreme objective for a decision-maker. A possible alternative to safety concerns is to combine this assessment with the evaluation of expected return. This suggests that the decision-maker may want to maximize expected return subject to a small probability of disaster

$$\text{Max}\{E(x): Pr(x \le z) \le \alpha\}.$$

This is a constrained maximization problem. It can be expressed in terms of the Lagrangean $L(x, \lambda) = \int_{-\infty}^{\infty} xf(x)dx + \lambda[\alpha - \int_{-\infty}^{z} f(x)dx]$, where $\lambda \ge 0$ is the Lagrange multiplier associated with the constraint $[Pr(x \le z) \le \alpha]$. Then, the constrained optimization problem implies the maximization of

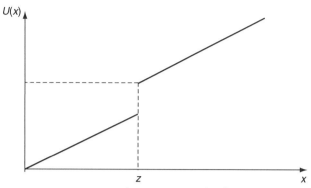

Figure 7.2 A discontinuous utility function

$\{\int_{-\infty}^{\infty} xf(x)dx - \lambda[\int_{-\infty}^{z} f(x)dx]\}$. This suggests that the decision-maker would behave as an expected utility maximizer with utility function

$$U(x) = x \text{ if } x > z$$
$$= x - \lambda \text{ if } x \leq z.$$

This utility function is piece-wise linear. When the constraint is not binding, then $\lambda = 0$, the utility function is linear, corresponding to a risk neutral decision-maker. However, when, the constraint is binding, then $\lambda > 0$ and the utility function is discontinuous at the subsistence point z. This is illustrated in Figure 7.2.

MAXIMIZING A FRACTILE OF THE DISTRIBUTION

Alternatively, safety concerns may lead individuals to make decisions so as to minimize their exposure to downside risk. This exposure can be measured by the probability of being in the lower tail of the distribution of income x, $Pr(x \leq z)$. This suggests that individuals may want to make choices under risk by maximizing

$$\text{Max}\{z: Pr(x \leq z) \leq \alpha\},$$

where z is a critical income level defined such that there is given probability $\alpha > 0$ that income will be less than z. While perhaps less intuitive, this formulation has an attractive approximation. Indeed, note that Chebychev inequality gives

$$Pr(x \leq z) \leq \text{Var}(x)/[E(x) - z]^2.$$

This suggests that the above maximization can be approximated by

$$\text{Max}\{z: \text{Var}(x)/[E(x) - z]^2 \le \alpha\},$$
$$= \text{Max}\{z: \sigma/[E(x) - z] \le \beta^{-1}\}, \text{ assuming that } [E(x) - z] > 0,$$
$$= \text{Max}\{E(x) - \beta\sigma\},$$

where $\sigma^2 = \text{Var}(x)$, σ is the standard deviation of x, and $\beta = \alpha^{-1/2}$. This approximation generates an additive mean-standard deviation model. In this context, $[\beta\sigma]$ is an approximate measure of the risk premium where the parameter β can be interpreted as a measure of "risk aversion."

RELAXING THE INDEPENDENCE ASSUMPTION

Much research has been done on the empirical validity of the independence assumption (Assumption A2). This is the assumption that underlies the fact that the expected utility model is "linear in the probabilities." In that sense, questioning the independence assumption A2 is equivalent to looking for evidence that risk preferences may be nonlinear in the probabilities. Is there any a priori basis to think that individual risk preferences should be linear in the probabilities? Not really. However, linearity is a property that is convenient in analytical research as well as empirical work. But how realistic is it? Below, we present an overview of the evidence presented both in favor and against the independence axiom.

THE ALLAIS PARADOX

Let the random variable x take three possible values: $x_1 < x_2 < x_3$, where $p_i = Pr(x = x_i)$, $i = 1,\ 2,\ 3$, $\sum_i p_i = 1$. Under the expected utility model, it follows that

$$EU(x) = p_1 U(x_1) + (1 - p_1 - p_3)U(x_2) + p_3 U(x_3).$$

Let U_0 be some reference utility level such that $EU(x) = U_0$. Then

$$U_0 = p_1 U(x_1) + (1 - p_1 - p_3)U(x_2) + p_3 U(x_3),$$

or

$$p_3 = \alpha + \beta p_1,$$

where the intercept is $\alpha = (U_0 - U(x_2))/(U(x_3) - U(x_2))$, and the slope is $\beta = -(U(x_1) - U(x_2))/(U(x_3) - U(x_2)) > 0$. The equation $\{p_3 = \alpha + \beta p_1\}$ above represents the *indifference curves* between p_1 and p_3, holding expected utility constant at U_0. Note that α and β are parameters that do not depend on p, and that β does not depend on U_0. It follows that, under the expected

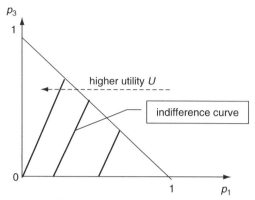

Figure 7.3a Indifference curves under the expected utility model

utility model, the indifference curves between p_1 and p_3 are *linear and parallel* to each other for different values of U_0. This is an implication of the independence assumption (which implies linearity in the probabilities). It is illustrated in Figure 7.3a.

However, there is empirical evidence that the indifference curves are not always parallel. This has been interpreted as evidence that the independence assumption (or the linearity in the probabilities) is not consistent with risk behavior. Allais proposed the following experiment to investigate this issue. It is known as the *Allais paradox* (although it does not really involve any paradox).

Choose between a_1 = receiving \$1,000 with probability 1,
  a_2 = receiving \$5,000 with probability 0.10,
    \$1,000 with probability 0.89,
    \$0 with probability 0.01.

Then choose between a_3 = receiving \$5,000 with probability 0.10,
    \$0 with probability 0.90,
  a_4 = receiving \$1,000 with probability 0.11,
    \$0 with probability 0.89.

Allais and others have found that, typically, a majority of individuals prefer a_1 over a_2, and a_3 over a_4. However, this ranking is *inconsistent* with the expected utility model. To see that, let $U(0) = 0$, $U(1000) = u$, *and* $U(5000) = 1$. Then, under the expected utility model, choosing a_1 over a_2 implies

$$u > .10 + (.89)u$$

or

$$u > 10/11.$$

Alternatively, under the expected utility model, choosing a_3 over a_4 implies

$$.1 > (.11)u$$

or

$$u < 10/11.$$

Obviously, the two inequalities cannot hold simultaneously, indicating that the expected utility model is not consistent with the choices of a majority of individuals. This is interpreted as evidence that *individual preferences are not linear in the probabilities* and thus violate the independence assumption in the expected utility model. This is illustrated in Figure 7.3b, where $p_1 = Pr(0)$ *and* $p_3 = Pr(5,000)$. In Figure 7.3b, if a_1 is preferred over a_2, *and* a_3 is preferred over a_4, then *the indifference curves cannot be parallel*, implying that such choices are necessarily inconsistent with the expected utility model. This can be interpreted to imply that preferences are nonlinear in the probabilities, the nonlinearity being such that the indifference curves "fan out" from the origin. Note that, in the Allais experiment, the probabilities involved in a_1 *and* a_2 are very different from the probabilities involved in a_3 and a_4.

PROSPECT THEORY

Psychologists have conducted much research on risk preferences. The research has provided some nice empirical evidence on the nature of individual risk preferences. In general, there is great complexity in human

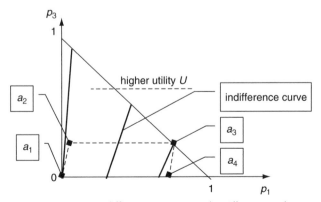

Figure 7.3b Indifference curves in the Allais paradox

decision-making under uncertainty, and the processing of information supporting it can be quite complex. As a result, no simple model can be found that would provide a general representation of risk preferences. To some extent, the expected utility model is one such simple model. As suggested by the Allais' paradox, there are situations where the expected utility model can fail to provide a precise representation of risk preferences. Following, we review an alternative model, termed "prospect theory," developed by Kahneman and Tversky. (See also Kahneman and Tversky 1979 for further refinements.)

Based on extensive experimental evidence, Kahneman and Tversky (KT) proposed some modifications to the expected utility model:

KT *reject asset integration* where preferences are expressed in terms of terminal wealth $x = w + a$, where w denotes initial wealth. Instead, they propose that risk preferences depend only on the net gain "a."

KT propose a preference function $W(\cdot)$ of the form

$$W(\cdot) = \Sigma_i q(p_i) U(a_i)$$

where a_i is the i-th realization of the random variable "a", $i = 1, \ldots, n$, $U(\cdot)$ is the utility function of the decision-maker, $p_i = Pr(a = a_i)$ is the probability of facing outcome a_i, and $q(\cdot)$ is a weight function.

KT propose that the weight function $q(p)$ is *nonlinear*: it tends to "underweight" high probabilities and "overweight" low probabilities. See Figure 7.4. Note that this nonlinearity contradicts the independence assumption in the expected utility model. Also, it suggests that rare events (i.e., events with low probabilities) are given relatively more weights compared to the expected utility model.

KT propose that the utility function $U(a)$ is concave for gains, convex for losses, and has a kink at "a" $= 0$ such that \$1 of gains is "worth less" than \$1

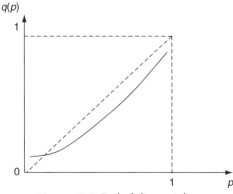

Figure 7.4 Probability weights

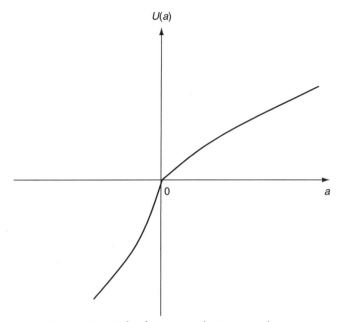

Figure 7.5 Utility function under Prospect theory

of losses. See Figure 7.5. This suggests significant aversion to losses (as opposed to gains).

SOME GENERALIZATIONS

The Allais paradox shows empirical evidence that the expected utility model does not provide an accurate representation of individual risk preferences. Prospect theory has been proposed as a generalization to the expected utility model. Other generalized expected utility models have also been put forward (Quiggin 1982, 1992; Yaari 1987). They all involve some form of nonlinearity in the probabilities. Such models are trying to improve the predictive power of economic modeling. But they are also more complex and more difficult to use empirically. This raises the question, how significant are the inaccuracies associated with the expected utility model? These issues have been discussed in the economic literature (e.g., see Harless and Camere 1994; Hey and Orme 1994). Following, we present some of the arguments presented by Machina (1982, 1987).

If the independence assumption does not hold, then preferences are not linear in the probabilities. This suggests that general risk preferences could be written in general as $W(F)$, where F is the distribution function $F(x)$ of a random variable x. The function $W(F)$ is thus a preference functional over the whole distribution of x. It allows for nonlinearity in the probabilities. What are the implications of this general formulation for economic analysis?

Let x_i = the i-th realization of the random variable x, $i = 1, \ldots, n$. Then, under differentiability, the preference function W(F) can be approximated locally by a first-order Taylor series expansion around some distribution function G:

$$W(F) - W(G) \approx \sum_i [\partial W/\partial G(x_i)] [F(x_i) - G(x_i)].$$

Define a function $U(x,G)$ such that $U(x_{n+1}, G) =$ some constant, and $U(x_{i+1}, G) - U(x_i, G) = -\partial W/\partial G(x_i)$, $i = n, \ldots, 1$. Substituting this into the above approximation yields

$$W(F) - W(G) \approx \Sigma_i \{U(x_i, G)[F(x_i) - G(x_i)] - U(x_{i+1}, G)[F(x_i) - G(x_i)]\}$$
$$\approx \Sigma_i \{U(x_i, G)[F(x_i) - G(x_i)] - U(x_i, G)[F(x_{i-1}) - G(x_{i-1})]\}$$
$$\approx \Sigma_i \{U(x_i, G)[F(x_i) - F(x_{i-1})] - U(x_i, G)[G(x_i) - G(x_{i-1})]\}$$
$$\approx E_F U(x, G) - E_G U(x, G).$$

This result is important. It shows that, under a general nonlinear preference function $W(F)$, a small movement in the distribution function from $F(\cdot)$ to $G(\cdot)$ changes the value of the preference function $W(F)$ by the difference in the expected value of $U(x, \cdot)$ with respect to the distributions $F(\cdot)$ and $G(\cdot)$. In other words, *the decision-maker would rank a small change in the distribution $F(\cdot)$ exactly as would an expected utility maximizer with a "local utility function" $U(x, \cdot)$.*
This has two important implications.

1. The independence assumption implies the restriction that the local utility function $U(x, \cdot)$ is the same for all distribution functions $G(\cdot)$. The Allais paradox suggests that $U(x, \cdot)$ is *not the same for all probability distributions $G(\cdot)$*. On one hand, the inaccuracies in the expected utility model would be easier to uncover when an individual faces large changes in probability distributions (e.g., as done in the Allais experiment). On the other hand, to the extent that the local utility function $U(x, \cdot)$ is approximately constant in the neighborhood of $G(\cdot)$, this means that the expected utility model would provide a good approximation to risk preferences for small changes in the probability distribution.

2. The Arrow–Pratt *local* characterizations of risk behavior are appropriate in the general case (where the preference function is $W(F)$) since

they are motivated "in the small," i.e., where $U(x, G)$ gives a valid *local* (not global) representation of risk preferences. In other words, the Arrow–Pratt absolute risk aversion coefficient $[-(\partial^2 U/\partial x^2)/(\partial U/\partial x)]$ provides a meaningful characterization of local risk behavior even if the independence assumption is violated. On that basis, Machina (1982) has suggested that most decisions-makers may exhibit risk preferences satisfying the following hypotheses:

a. $[-(\partial^2 U(x, G)/\partial x^2)/(\partial U(x, G)/\partial x)]$ is a nonincreasing function of x.

This is a *local* version of the decreasing absolute risk aversion (DARA) hypothesis. However, this is not a global characterization of DARA because the global effect of initial wealth on the willingness to insure will in general involve changes in G as well. Note that this first hypothesis implies $\partial^3 U(x, G)/\partial x^3 \geq 0$, i.e. *local* downside risk aversion.

b. $[-(\partial^2 U(x, G)/\partial x^2)/(\partial U(x, G)/\partial x)]$ is a nondecreasing function of G.

Machina (1982) argues that this second hypothesis can explain the Allais paradox as well as the "greater sensitivity" to small probabilities (e.g., as found in prospect theory).

THE CASE OF INDUCED PREFERENCES

So far, we have treated economic decisions generically. Yet, economic analysis often focuses on a subset of decisions. This is typically done for two reasons: (1) this simplifies the analysis, and (2) the investigator is interested only in a particular decision (e.g., a production decision, a consumption decision, or an investment decision). Does this affect our understanding of risk preferences? Machina (1984) has argued that it does.

To see that, consider the case of a decision-maker with utility function $U(y, a)$, where $y = (y_1, y_2)$ is a vector of decision variables and "a" is a random vector that can take n possible values a_i, $i = 1, \ldots, n$, with $p_i = Pr(a = a_i)$. Under the expected utility model, the decision-maker chooses y by maximizing $[PMax_y EU(y, a)]$. Assume that the economist is interested only in the decision variable y_1. This suggests the two-stage decomposition

$$\text{Max}_y\, EU(y, a) = \text{Max}_{y_1}[\text{Max}_{y_2}[EU(y_1, y_2, a)]] = \text{Max}_{y_1} W(P, y_1)$$

where

$$W(P, y_1) = \text{Max}_{y_2}[EU(y_1, y_2, a)]$$

is an "induced preference function" where $P = (p_1, \ p_2, \ \ldots, \ p_n)$ is the vector of probabilities. In general, $W(P, \ y_1)$ is a nonlinear convex function of the probabilities P. Thus, focusing on the decisions y_1, as represented by $[\text{Max}_{y_1} W(P, \ y_1)]$, corresponds to a problem where the objective function is nonlinear in the probabilities. In other words, even under the expected utility model, nonlinearity in the probabilities can be generated by the existence of auxiliary decisions (y_2) that are not modeled explicitly. It suggests that the assessment of risk preferences can be influenced by the context in which decisions are being made. Such complexities should be kept in mind in the analysis of economic behavior under risk.

THE STATE PREFERENCE APPROACH

So far, we have relied on probabilities as a means of measuring the riskiness of events. This requires that the decision-maker first assesses the probability distribution of its risky environment, say $F(x)$. Then, the individual evaluates the risky prospects. In general, this evaluation is made in a way consistent with the rankings provided by his/her preference function general $W(F)$. Consider the case where x has a discrete distribution, i.e., where it can take any of n possible values: $x_1, x_2, \ldots, x_n$, each with probability $Pr(x_i), i = 1, \ldots, n$. Then, the risk preference function is $W(Pr(x_1), \ Pr(x_2), \ \ldots, Pr(x_n))$. This allows for nonlinearity in the probabilities. It would include as a special case the expected utility model, where $W(\cdot)$ is linear in the probabilities and satisfies $W(\cdot) = \sum_i Pr(x_i)U(x_i)$.

A further generalization is possible. Consider the preference function $W(x_1, \ x_2, \ \ldots, x_n)$. It depends directly on the states $x_1, \ x_2, \ \ldots, x_n$. As such, while it still requires an assessment of ex-ante preferences over alternative states, it does not require an explicit evaluation of probabilities. This is the state-preference approach proposed by Debreu. It is very general in the sense that it does not rely on probability measurements. This is good if one analyzes situations where individual assessment of probabilities appears difficult or unreliable, or if one is interested in a general theory of behavior under risk. As such, the state-dependent approach provides a broad conceptual framework for theoretical analyses of economic behavior (Chambers and Quiggin 2000).

Note that the analysis of risk aversion or of the risk premium applies in this general context. To see that, consider the case where x is a random variable distributed with mean μ and variance σ^2. Let $x_i = \mu + e_i$, where e_i is random variable with mean 0 and variance σ^2. Then, the risk premium is defined as the value R that satisfies $W(\mu - R, \ \ldots, \mu - R) = W(x_1, \ \ldots, x_n)$. When x measures monetary returns, R is the largest amount of money the decision-maker is willing to pay ex ante to replace the risky prospect $(x_1, \ldots, x_n)$ by the sure prospect $(\mu, \ldots, \mu)$. As discussed in the context of the expected utility model, the risk premium R provides a measure of the implicit cost of private risk bearing. By definition, risk aversion corresponds to $R > 0$, while $R = 0$ under risk neutrality, and $R < 0$ under risk-loving behavior. And assuming that W is strictly increasing in $(\mu - R)$, then $(\mu - R)$ can be interpreted as the "certainty equivalent" in the sense that maximizing $W(x_1, \ldots, x_n)$ is equivalent to maximizing $(\mu - R)$.

While the state preference approach is very general, note that the number of uncertain states facing any particular individual can be large. Working with discrete random variables, each state would be characterized by a distinct realization of each of the relevant random variables facing an individual. For example, if each random variable can take 10 possible values, then the number of states is 10 if there is one random variable, 100 if there are two random variables, and 10^k is there are k random variables. Thus, even with a moderate number of random variables, the number of states can be quite large. Evaluating risk preferences over a large number of states is empirically difficult. This is the main reason why the state-preference approach has not been used much in empirical work. This identifies a significant trade-off between conceptual generality and empirical tractability. In this context, while empirical assessment of probabilities does impose a priori structure on the characterization of uncertainty, such structure has one significant advantage: It makes the empirical analysis of risk behavior easier.

ADDITIONAL EVIDENCE ON RISK PREFERENCES

In addition to the experimental evidence previously discussed, there has been empirical research evaluating the nature of individual risk preferences. Although uncertainty exists in any decision-making process, there are two situations where it appears particularly prevalent. The first one is uncertainty facing agricultural households. Weather uncertainty exposes farm households to significant production risks (as well as price risks) that are often difficult to manage. This stresses the need to understand the role of risk and risk preferences in farm household decisions around the world. The second is uncertainty involved in gambling games. Knowledge of risk preferences can provide useful insights into the behavior of bettors.

First, consider the risk behavior of agricultural households. Lin et al. (1974) investigated the behavior of a sample of California farmers. Three alternative models of behavior under risk were evaluated: (1) expected profit maximization, (2) expected utility maximization given a direct elicitation of the utility function $U(\cdot)$, and (3) a "safety first" model. Among the three models, Lin et al. found that the expected profit maximization model gave the worst predictions of farmers' behavior. In particular, this model failed to explain the observed diversification strategies implemented by California farmers. Lin et al. also found that the safety-first model was a poor predictor of farmers' behavior. Their empirical results showed that the expected utility model gave more accurate predictions of behavior. The elicited utility functions were typically concave. This suggests that most farmers are risk averse and that risk aversion can help explain observed diversification strategies.

Moscardi and de Janvry (1977) investigated the risk behavior of a sample of Mexican farmers. They used a mean-standard deviation model to study the impact of risk aversion on fertilizer demand. Risk aversion was estimated indirectly by comparing the model predictions with actual fertilizer demand. Moscardi and de Janvry found that risk aversion tends to be high and to discourage fertilizer use. They also found that risk aversion tends to decrease with off-farm income, land holding, and the presence of solidarity groups.

Dillon and Scandizzo (1978) examined the risk preferences of a sample of Brazilian farmers. They used the expected utility hypothesis along with a direct elicitation of $U(\cdot)$. They found that most farmers are risk averse, although the degree of risk aversion varied greatly across farmers.

Binswanger (1981) studied the risk preferences of a sample of Indian farmers. He conducted a direct elicitation of risk preferences (under the expected utility model) using *actual* lotteries. He found empirical evidence against safety-first models. In the context of the expected utility model, Indian farmers were found to exhibit:

- risk aversion (where $U'' < 0$),
- decreasing absolute risk aversion (DARA, where $-U''/U'$ decreases with w),
- increasing partial relative risk aversion (IPRA, where $-aU''/U'$ increases with a),
- decreasing relative risk aversion (DRRA, where $-xU''/U'$ decreases with x), with x being terminal wealth, w being initial wealth, "a" being income, and $x = w + a$.

Antle (1987) also analyzed the risk preferences of a sample of Indian farmers. He used a moment-based approach to the expected utility model. After estimating the production technology, he used observed behavior to estimate $(-U''/U')$ and (U'''/U'). He found empirical evidence in favor of risk aversion $(-U''/U' > 0)$, and of downside risk aversion $(U'''/U' > 0)$.

Chavas and Holt (1996) studied econometrically the risk preferences of United States farmers. Under the expected utility model, they used observed acreage decisions to estimate the underlying utility function. They found evidence of both risk aversion and decreasing absolute risk aversion (DARA).

Finally, Jullien and Salanie (2000) estimated the risk preferences of racetrack bettors in the United Kingdom. They found evidence of risk aversion similar to that proposed by Friedman and Savage (1948). They also examined the explanatory power of alternative nonexpected utility models.

Chapter 8

Production Decisions Under Risk

This chapter investigates the implications of risk for production decisions. It is motivated by the fact that production decisions are often subject to uncertainty. This includes price uncertainty as well as production uncertainty. Typically, firms face many sources of risk for which risk markets are absent. Under incomplete risk markets, risk-averse firms cannot easily transfer risk to other agents. This means that, in large part, firms must manage their risk exposure privately. This chapter focuses on risk management of an owner-operated firm facing incomplete risk markets. The analysis of risk markets and contracts will be discussed in Chapter 11.

In an owner-operated firm, the manager/decision-maker is also the residual claimant. Then, in the absence of risk, the manager has an incentive to maximize profit. Indeed, as long as the manager's preferences are non-satiated in income, increasing profit will necessarily make him/her better off. Thus, one can expect the manager to make production decisions in a way consistent with profit maximization. What happens when we introduce risk in the analysis? This chapter examines how risk affects the production decisions made in an owner-operated firm. We investigate the production behavior of a risk-averse decision-maker. This provides useful insights on the implicit cost of risk and its role in firm decisions. We start with the simple case of a single-output firm facing output price uncertainty. Then, we extend the analysis to include production uncertainty. We also examine the implications of risk and risk aversion for diversification strategies for a multi-output firm, as well as for hedging strategies for a firm participating in futures markets.

FIRM DECISIONS UNDER UNCERTAINTY

PRICE UNCERTAINTY

First, we consider the case of a competitive firm producing a single output under price uncertainty. The firm is competitive if it is relatively small and cannot affect prices on the markets where it trades. The price uncertainty is often associated with production lags, corresponding to situations where the production process is not instantaneous. Then, there is some delay between the time a production decision is made and the time the corresponding output reaches the market. During this delay, the market price can change in some unforeseen way. As a result, the output price is not known at the time the production decision is made. This creates price uncertainty for the firm. What are the implications of this uncertainty for production decisions?

We start with the case where the firm only sells its output on a commodity market. The situation where it also participates in a futures market is discussed in the following paragraphs. The firm chooses n inputs $x = (x_1, \ldots, x_n)'$ in the production of firm output y. The firm production technology is represented by the production function $y = f(x)$, where $f(x)$ measures the largest feasible output the firm can obtain when using inputs $x = (x_1, \ldots, x_n)'$. At this point, we assume that there is no uncertainty in the production process (the situation of production risk will be discussed in the following paragraphs). At the time production decisions are made, the firm manager tries to anticipate the uncertain market price it will receive for its output. As such it treats the output price p as a random variable, with a given subjective probability distribution. Being a competitive firm, the firm decisions do not affect this probability distribution.

Let $v = (v_1, \ldots, v_n)'$ denote the prices paid for inputs x. Then, the firm's cost of production is $v'x = \sum_{i=1}^{n} v_i x_i$. And its (uncertain) revenue is: py. It follows that the firm's profit is: $\pi = py - v'x$. In addition, let w denote initial wealth. (Alternatively, w could also represent exogenous income, or, if negative, fixed cost). Then, the firm terminal wealth is: $w + py - v'x$. For an owner-operated firm, this is the amount of money received by the owner/manager. Under output price uncertainty, terminal wealth is also uncertain. Assume that the manager behaves in a way consistent with the expected utility model. Then, the objective function of a competitive firm is

$$EU(w + py - v'x) = EU(w + \pi),$$

where E is the expectation operator based on the subjective probability distribution of the random variable p. We will assume that the entrepreneur/decision-maker has *risk-averse preferences* represented by the utility function $U(\cdot)$ which satisfies $U' \equiv \partial U/\partial w > 0$ *and* $U'' \equiv \partial^2 U/\partial w^2 < 0$. Focusing on *risk aversion* is motivated by the fact that most decision makers appear to be risk averse (see Chapters 3 and 7).

Let $\mu = E(p)$ be the expected output price, and $p = \mu + \sigma e$, where e is a random variable with mean zero. The random variable e can exhibit any distribution for which both the mean and variance exist. In this context, σ can be interpreted as the standard deviation of output price p. More generally, σ can be interpreted as a mean-preserving spread parameter for the distribution of p. Following the analysis presented by Sandmo, we will characterize the probability distribution of p by the mean μ and the mean preserving spread parameter σ.

Under the expected utility model, the production decisions can be represented by

$$Max_{x,y}\{EU(w + py - v'x: \; y = f(x)\}.$$

This simply states that production decisions are made in way consistent with expected utility maximization.

1. The Firm Minimizes Cost:

In the absence of production uncertainty, expected utility maximization implies cost minimization. To see that, note that the above maximization problem can be written as

$$Max_y\{Max_x\{EU(w + py - v'x: \; y = f(x)\} \}$$
$$= Max_y\{EU(w + py + Max_x\{ - v'x: \; y = f(x)\} \}$$
$$= Max_y\{EU(w + py - Min_x\{v'x: \; y = f(x)\} \}$$
$$= Max_y\{EU(w + py - C(v,y)\},$$

where $C(v, y) = [Min_x\{v'x: \; y = f(x)\}]$ is the *cost function* in a standard cost minimization problem under certainty. For given input prices v, $C(v, y)$ measures the smallest possible cost of producing output y. This shows that, in the absence of production risk, the risk-averse firm has incentives to behave in a cost-minimizing fashion (just like in the case of perfect certainty). However, as we will see, this should not be interpreted to mean that risk and risk aversion have no effect on production decisions.

This last maximization problem will prove particularly convenient for our analysis. It involves choosing only one variable: y, the firm output. Assuming that the firm decides to produce positive output, $y > 0$, using the chain rule, the first-order necessary condition associated with the optimal choice of y is:

$$F(y, \cdot) \equiv E[U' \cdot (p - C')] = 0, \tag{1}$$

or, using $E(U' \cdot p) = E(U') \cdot \mu + \text{Cov}(U', p)$ from Appendix A,

$$\mu - C' + \text{Cov}(U', p)/EU' = 0,$$

where $C' \equiv \partial C/\partial y$ denotes the *marginal cost of production*, and $\text{Cov}(U', p) = E(U'\sigma e)$. The associated second-order sufficient condition for a maximum is:

$$D \equiv \partial F/\partial y \equiv E[U' \cdot (- C'')] + E[U'' \cdot (p - C')^2] < 0.$$

We saw in Chapter 3 that maximizing expected utility is equivalent to maximizing the "certainty equivalent." Here, the certainty equivalent is: $\mu y - C(r, y) - R(w, y, \cdot)$, where $R(w, y, \cdot)$ is the Arrow–Pratt risk premium measuring the implicit cost of private risk bearing, with $R > 0$ under risk aversion. It follows that the output decision can be alternatively written as

$$\text{Max}_y\{\mu y - C(r, y) - R(w, y, \cdot)\},$$

The associated first-order condition is

$$\mu - C' - R' = 0,$$

where $R' \equiv \partial R/\partial y$ is the *marginal risk premium*. Comparing this result with the first-order condition derived above, it follows that $R' = -\text{Cov}(U', p)/EU'$. This gives an intuitive interpretation for the covariance term: $[-\text{Cov}(U', p)/EU']$ is the *marginal risk premium* measuring the marginal effect of output y on the implicit cost of private risk bearing.

2. The Supply Function

The supply function is the function $y^*(w, \mu, \sigma)$ that satisfies the first-order condition $F(y, \cdot) = 0$ in (1), or

$$\mu = C' + R',$$

where $R' = -\text{Cov}(U', p)/EU'$ is the *marginal risk premium*. This implies that, at the optimum supply y^*, *expected price μ is equal to the marginal cost C', plus the marginal risk premium R'*. This means that expressing $(C' + R')$ as a function of output y gives the *supply function*. It generates the schedule of output produced by a risk-averse decision-maker for each level of expected output μ.

Note that the covariance term $\text{Cov}(U', p)$ is always of the sign of $(\partial U'/\partial p)$. [This can be seen as follows. If $\partial U'/\partial p > 0$ (< 0), then, U' and p tend to move in the same direction (in opposite directions), implying a positive (negative) covariance.] But $\text{sign}(\partial U'/\partial p) = \text{sign}(U'' \cdot y)$. Thus, risk aversion (where $U'' < 0$) implies that $\text{Cov}(U', p) < 0$. It follows that the marginal risk premium is positive under risk aversion: $R' = -\text{Cov}(U', p)/EU' > 0$. This in turn implies that $\mu > C'$ at the optimum.

This is an important result. Under price uncertainty and risk aversion, the firm produces at a point where *expected output price exceeds marginal cost*. This is illustrated in Figure 8.1. It is the first hint that, under risk aversion, risk can have significant effects on resource allocation. Indeed, finding that $\mu > C'$ is inconsistent with the standard "marginal cost pricing" rule (output price equals marginal cost) obtained in a riskless world. Instead, our analysis shows that, while risk does not involve any explicit cost, its implicit cost (as measured by the marginal risk premium R') needs to be added to the marginal cost of production C' in the evaluation of optimal production decisions.

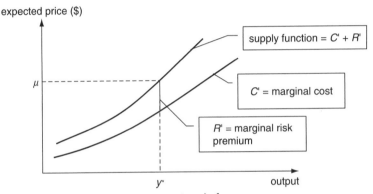

expected price ($)

supply function = C' + R'

μ

C' = marginal cost

R' = marginal risk premium

y^*

output

Figure 8.1 Supply function

3. Comparative Static Analysis

If risk affects production decisions under risk aversion, it will be useful to investigate its effects in more detail. This can be done by conducting a comparative static analysis of the output decision y in equation (1). Let $\alpha = (w, \mu, \sigma)$ be a vector of parameters of the supply function $y^*(\alpha)$. Differentiating the first-order condition $F(y, \alpha) = 0$ at the optimum $y = y^*(\alpha)$ yields

$$\partial F / \partial \alpha + (\partial F / \partial y)(\partial y^* / \partial \alpha = 0,$$

or, with $D = \partial F / \partial y < 0$,

$$\partial y^* / \partial \alpha = -D^{-1} \partial F / \partial \alpha$$
$$= -D^{-1} \partial \{E[U' \cdot (p - C')]\} / \partial \alpha$$
$$= \text{sign}(\partial \{E[U' \cdot (p - C')]\} / \partial \alpha.$$

This result will be used repeatedly in the analysis of the properties of the supply decision $y^*(\alpha)$ under risk and risk aversion.

a. The effect of initial wealth w

The effect of changing initial wealth w is given by

$$\partial y^*/\partial w = -D^{-1}\{\partial\{E[U' \cdot (p - C')]\}/\partial w\} = -D^{-1}\{E[U'' \cdot (p - C')]\}.$$

But $E[U'' \cdot (p - C')] >$, $=$, or < 0 under decreasing absolute risk aversion (DARA), constant absolute risk aversion (CARA), or increasing absolute risk aversion (IARA), respectively. To see that, consider the Arrow–Pratt absolute risk aversion coefficient $r = -U''/U'$ (see Chapter 4). Let π_0 denote the value profit π when evaluated at $p = C'$. Under DARA,

$$r(\pi) < (>)r(\pi_0) \text{ if } p > (<)C'.$$

It follows that

$$-U''/U' < (>) \, r(\pi_0) \text{ for } p > (<)C',$$

or

$$U'' > (<) - r(\pi_0) \, U' \text{ for } (p - C') > 0 \, (< 0),$$

or

$$U'' \cdot (p - C') > -r(\pi_0) \cdot U' \cdot (p - C'),$$

or, taking expectation,

$$E[U'' \cdot (p - C')] > -r(\pi_0) \cdot E[U' \cdot (p - C')] = 0,$$

from the first-order condition (1). Following similar steps, it can be shown that $E[U''' \cdot (p - C')] < 0 \, (= 0)$ under IARA (CARA). This implies that

$$\partial y^*/\partial w > 0 \text{ under DARA}$$
$$= 0 \text{ under CARA}$$
$$< 0 \text{ under IARA}.$$

Thus, under DARA, changing initial wealth, fixed cost or exogenous income (w) influences supply. This differs from the standard result obtained in the absence of risk. Without risk, a change in fixed cost or in initial wealth has no effect on profit-maximizing decisions. Under risk, such a result is obtained only under CARA preferences. Intuitively, this associates CARA risk preferences to the absence of income or wealth effects. However, many decision-makers appear to exhibit DARA preferences (see Chapters 4 and 7). Under DARA, wealth effects are positive. This means that the absence of income or wealth effects is not expected to apply to production decisions under risk. Intuitively, under DARA, private wealth accumulation tends to reduce the private cost of risk bearing (see Chapter 4). To the extent that the

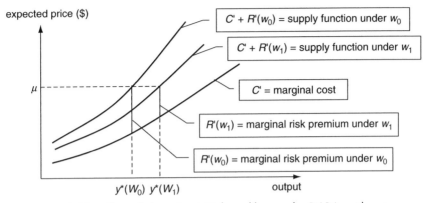

Figure 8.2 The effect of changing initial wealth w under DARA, with $w_1 > w_0$

implicit cost of risk provides a disincentive to produce (see following), this means that increasing initial wealth (or reducing fixed cost) tends to stimulate firm supply.

This is illustrated in Figure 8.2. Figure 8.2 shows that, under DARA, increasing initial wealth w from w_0 to w_1 tends to reduce the marginal risk premium $R'(w, \cdot)$. This is intuitive: under risk aversion and DARA, private wealth accumulation reduces the risk premium (as it is a substitute for insurance motives; see Chapter 4). This reduction in the risk premium R is accompanied by a reduction in the marginal risk premium R', which generates a rightward shift in the supply function $(C' + R')$. As a result, under DARA, increasing initial wealth w reduces the implicit cost of private risk bearing and stimulates supply.

To the extent that price risk exposure, risk aversion, and DARA preferences are rather common, we expect initial wealth to have a positive effect on supply. It means that, contrary to the prediction obtained without risk, the distribution of income or wealth within an industry can affect aggregate supply. For example, under DARA, *income transfers* to firms affect production decisions. Such transfers can be represented by a rise in w. This would tend to reduce the risk premium R, thus increasing the certainty equivalent and making the firm decision-maker better off. But it would also stimulate production by shifting the supply schedule to the right (since $\partial y^*/\partial w > 0$ under DARA). Given a downward sloping aggregate demand function, this would put downward pressure on the output price p. The associated decline in p would make consumers better off, but would also reduce the welfare of the firm. These effects will be further evaluated in Chapters 11, 12, and 13. At this point, it is sufficient to stress that such effects would not exist under certainty.

b. The effect of expected price μ

The effect of changing expected output price μ is given by

$$\partial y^*/\partial \mu = -D^{-1}\{\partial\{E[U' \cdot (p - C')]/\partial \mu\}\} = -D^{-1}\{E[U' + yEU'' \cdot (p - C')]\}.$$

Define $\partial y^c/\partial \mu \equiv -D^{-1}[EU']$ as the *compensated expected price effect*. Given $D < 0$ (from the second order condition for a maximization), it follows that $\partial y^c/\partial \mu > 0$. It follows that the *"compensated" supply function is always upward sloping* with respect to expected price μ.

We have just shown that $\partial y^*/\partial w = -D^{-1}E[U'' \cdot (p - C')]$. This generates the following Slutsky equation:

$$\partial y^*/\partial \mu = \partial y^c/\partial \mu + (\partial y^*/\partial w) \cdot y^*,$$

where the expected (uncompensated) price slope $\partial y^*/\partial \mu$, is equal to the compensated price slope, $\partial y^c/\partial \mu > 0$, plus a wealth (or income) effect, $(\partial y^*/\partial w) \cdot y^*$. The wealth effect, $(\partial y^*/\partial w) \cdot y^*$, can be positive or negative (depending on risk preferences). Given $\partial y^c/\partial \mu > 0$, the Slutsky equation means that the uncompensated price slope $\partial y^*/\partial \mu$ can also be either positive or negative. In particular, it shows that $\partial y^*/\partial \mu$ could be negative if the wealth effect, $(\partial y^*/\partial w) \cdot y^*$, is negative and sufficiently large. This seems counterintuitive. Why would optimal production decline when the expected output price increases? While theoretically possible, our analysis suggests that such a scenario is unlikely to be observed. Indeed, we have just shown that $\partial y^*/\partial w > , = , < 0$ under DARA, CARA or IARA. Given $\partial y^c/\partial \mu > 0$, it follows from the Slutsky equation that *CARA or DARA preferences are a sufficient condition for supply to exhibit a positive uncompensated price slope*: $\partial y^*/\partial \mu > 0$. Under CARA preferences, wealth effects are zero, meaning that compensated and uncompensated price slopes are the same. This generates the classical result also obtained in the absence of risk: profit incentives imply that supply functions are upward sloping. More generally, DARA preferences generate positive wealth effects and (from the Slutsky equation) a positive supply response to an expected output price increase. In other words, under risk, if DARA preferences characterize most decision-makers, one obtains the intuitive result that an *increase in expected output price would tend to stimulate supply*.

This is illustrated in Figure 8.3, where an increase in expected price from μ_0 to μ_1 increases supply $y^*(\mu_1) > y^*(\mu_0)$, as the supply function is upward sloping under DARA. Figure 8.3 also shows that *both* the marginal cost C' and the marginal risk premium R' are higher at μ_1 compared to μ_0.

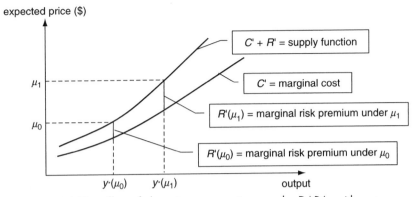

Figure 8.3 The effect of changing mean price μ under DARA, with $\mu_1 > \mu_0$

c. The effect of price risk σ

The effect of changing price risk σ (evaluated at $\sigma = 1$) is given by

$$\partial y^*/\partial\sigma = -D^{-1}\{\partial\{E[U' \cdot (p - C')]\}/\partial\sigma\} = -D^{-1}\{E(U' \cdot e) + yE[U'' \cdot (p - \mu)(p - C')]\}$$
$$= -D^{-1}\{E(U'' \cdot e) + yE[U'' \cdot (p - C' + C' - \mu)(p - C')]\}$$
$$= -D^{-1}\{E(U' \cdot e) + yE[U'' \cdot (p - C')^2] + y(C' - \mu)E[U'' \cdot (p - C')]\}.$$

But $E(U' \cdot e) = \mathrm{Cov}(U', p) = \mathrm{sign}(U''y) < 0$ under risk aversion. Also, $E[U'' \cdot (p - C')^2] < 0$ under risk aversion (where $U'' < 0$). Finally, we have shown that $(C' - \mu) < 0$ under risk aversion, and that $E[U'' \cdot (p - C')] > 0$ under DARA. It follows that

$$\partial y^*/\partial\sigma < 0 \quad \text{under DARA,}$$

i.e., that an increase in risk (as measured by σ) has a negative effect on supply under DARA. This is an important result. If risk aversion and DARA preferences characterize most decision-makers, it shows that *exposure to price risk provides a general disincentive to produce.* This implies that, in general, *risk can be expected to have adverse effects on production.*

This is illustrated in Figure 8.4, where an increase in price risk from σ_0 to σ_1 reduces supply. This is intuitive. Increasing risk exposure tends to increase the private cost of risk bearing (as measured by the risk premium R). Under DARA, this is accompanied by a rise in the marginal risk premium R', and a leftward shift in the supply function $(C' + R')$.

d. The effect of a profit tax t

Consider the case of profit tax. For simplicity, we assume that $w = 0$. Then, the objective function of the firm is $EU[(1 - t) \cdot \pi]$, where t is the

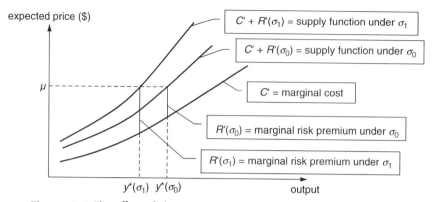

Figure 8.4 The effect of changing price risk σ under DARA, with $\sigma_1 > \sigma_0$

tax rate on profit π. Conducting comparative static analysis using (1) yields

$$\partial y^*/\partial t = -D^{-1}\{\partial\{E[U' \cdot (p - C')]\}/\partial t\} = -D^{-1}\{E[-U'' \cdot (p - C')\pi]\}$$

But $E[U'' \cdot (p - C')\pi] > , = ,$ or < 0 under decreasing relative risk aversion (DRRA), constant relative risk aversion (CRRA), or increasing relative risk aversion (IRRA). To see that, consider the relative risk aversion coefficient $\bar{r} - \pi U''/U'$ (see Chapter 4). Let π_0 denote the value profit π when evaluated at $p = C'$. Under DRRA,

$$\bar{r}(\pi) < (>)\quad \bar{r}(\pi_0) \text{ if } p > (<)C'.$$

It follows that

$$-\pi U''/U' < (>)\, \bar{r}(\pi_0) \text{ for } p > (<)C',$$

or

$$U'' \cdot \pi > (<)- \bar{r}(\pi_0)U' \text{ for } (p - C') > 0\, (< 0),$$

or, taking expectation,

$$U'' \cdot (p - C')\pi > -\, \bar{r}(\pi_0)U' \cdot (p - C'),$$
$$E[U'' \cdot (p - C')\pi] > -\bar{r}(\pi_0)\, E[U' \cdot (p - C')] = 0,$$

from the first-order condition (1). Following similar steps, it can be shown that $E[U'' \cdot (p - C')\pi] < 0\, (= 0)$ under IRRA (CRRA). This implies that

$$\partial y^*/\partial t < 0 \text{ under DRRA}$$
$$= 0 \text{ under CRRA}$$
$$> 0 \text{ under IRRA.}$$

Thus, a change in the profit tax t has no effect on production decisions under CRRA. This is the standard result also obtained in the absence of risk. However, this result no longer applies under nonconstant relative risk aversion. This shows how risk and risk preferences can affect the influence of fiscal policy on production decisions.

4. Long Run Analysis

So far, we have focused our analysis on a single firm in an industry. At this point, it will be useful to consider the implications of risk and risk aversion at the industry level. For that purpose, consider the simple case of an industry made of identical firms facing free entry and exit. We focus on a long-run situation, where firms have enough time to act on their entry or exit decisions in the industry. Then, we will argue that the industry equilibrium must satisfy

$$EU(w + py - C(v, y)] = U(w). \tag{2}$$

Indeed, if $EU(w + py - C(v, y)] > U(w)$, then there is an incentive for potential entrants to enter the industry. Under free entry, they would do so, implying a disequilibrium situation. And if $EU(w + py - C(v, y)] < U(w)$, then there is an incentive for current firms to exit the industry. Under free exit, they would do so, again implying a disequilibrium situation. Thus, equation (2) must be satisfied in long-run equilibrium.

Using the certainty equivalent formulation where $R(y, \cdot)$ is the Arrow–Pratt risk premium (see Chapter 4), note that (2) can be written as

$$w + \mu y - C(v, y) - R(y, \cdot) = w,$$

or

$$\mu y = C(v, y) + R(y, \cdot),$$

or

$$\mu = C(v, y)/y + R(y, \cdot)/y.$$

where $R > 0$ under risk aversion. It follows that, *in long-run equilibrium, the expected price μ must be equal to the average cost, C/y, plus the average risk premium, R/y.* Under risk aversion, the risk premium is positive, $R > 0$, implying that

$$\mu > C(v, y)/y,$$

or

$$E(\pi) = \mu y - C(v, y) > 0.$$

Thus, *in the long run, risk aversion implies that expected price must exceed the average cost of production, and that expected profit must be positive.* Intuitively, the positive expected profit can be interpreted as a means of compensating the risk-averse firm for its (implicit) cost of private risk bearing.

How does this long-run equilibrium relate to "short run" expected utility maximization discussed previously? To answer this question, consider the minimization of $[C(v, y)/y + R(y, \cdot)/y]$ with respect to output y. This involves the minimization of "average cost of production," $C(v, y)/y$, plus "average risk premium," $R(y, \cdot)/y$. Here, while the average cost per unit of output $C(v, y)/y$ is explicit, the average risk premium $R(y, \cdot)/y$ is an implicit measure of the shadow cost of private risk bearing per unit of output. The associated necessary first-order condition is

$$C'/y - C/y^2 + R'/y - R/y^2 = 0,$$

or

$$C' + R' = C/y + R/y.$$

Recall the short-run equilibrium condition: $\mu = C' + R'$; and the long-run equilibrium condition: $\mu = C/y + R/y$. It follows that both short-run and long-run equilibrium conditions are satisfied at the minimum of $[C/y + R/y]$. If the $[C/y + R/y]$ function has a U-shape with respect to output y, it follows that the short-run as well as long-run equilibrium conditions satisfy

$$\mu = \text{Min}_y[C(v, y)/y - R(y, \cdot)/y].$$

This shows that, under free entry and exit, the equilibrium expected output price must equal the smallest possible "average cost plus average risk premium." And this is consistent with both short-run expected utility maximization and long-run equilibrium. In addition, under risk aversion (where $R > 0$), this implies that $\mu > \text{Min}_y[C(v, y)/y]$. Thus, under free entry and exit, the standard "average cost pricing" rule obtained under certainty (where output price equals average cost of production) does not apply. It means that, compared to the riskless case, equilibrium expected price is higher under risk and risk aversion. This is illustrated in Figure 8.5. It suggests that reducing price uncertainty would lower expected price μ, which would tend to benefit consumers. (See Chavas et al. (1988) for a further analysis, and Chavas (1993) for an application to the Ricardian land rent). This issue is further explored in Chapter 13.

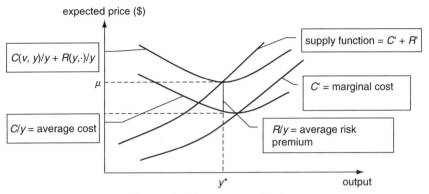

Figure 8.5 Long run equilibrium

PRODUCTION UNCERTAINTY

So far, we have focused our attention on a firm facing only price uncertainty. However, often firms also face significant production uncertainty. This can be due to many factors: technological change, equipment failure, unanticipated labor strike, unexpected resignation of workers, weather or disease effects influencing productivity, etc. This means that while managers choose some inputs, the outcome of the production process is typically not perfectly known and firm output is uncertain.

1. The General Case

Under general production uncertainty, firm output is a random variable at the time when inputs are chosen. The production technology can be represented by a stochastic production function denoted by $y(x, e)$, where y is output, x is a vector of inputs, and e is a random variable reflecting production uncertainty (e.g., weather in agricultural production). Here, $y(x, e)$ gives the largest possible output that can be obtained when inputs x are chosen and the random variable takes a particular value e. The manager has information about the production uncertainty, information represented by a subjective probability distribution of the random variable e. Building on the price uncertainty case, let p denote output price, v denote input prices, and w denote initial wealth. Then, $p\, y(x, e)$ is firm revenue, $v'x = \sum_{i=1}^{n} v_i x_i$ is production cost, $\pi = py(x, e) - v'x$ is firm profit, and $[w + \pi]$ is terminal wealth. If we also allow for price uncertainty (in the presence of production lags), the decision-maker does not know both e and p at the time of the input decisions. Then, the firm faces *price and production uncertainty*. In this context, the decision-maker treats both e and p as random variables with a subjective joint distribution. Under the expected utility model, assume that the objective function of the decision-maker is to choose inputs x so as to maximize the expected utility of terminal wealth

$$\text{Max}_x\{EU[w + py(x, e) - v'x]\},$$

where E is the expectation operator based on the subjective distribution of the random variables (p, e). Using the chain rule, the necessary first-order conditions for the optimal choice of inputs x are:

$$E[U' \cdot (p\partial y(x, e)/\partial x - v)] = 0,$$

or

$$E[p\partial y(x, e)/\partial x] = v - \text{Cov}[U', p\partial y(x, e)/\partial x]/EU',$$

or

$$E(p)E[\partial y(x, e)/\partial x] + \text{Cov}[p, \partial y(x, e)/\partial x] = v - \text{Cov}[U', p\partial y(x, e)/\partial x]/EU'.$$

We saw in Chapter 4 that maximizing expected utility is equivalent to maximizing the corresponding certainty equivalent. Here, the certainty equivalent of terminal wealth is $w + E[py(x, e)] - v'x - R(x, \cdot)$, where $R(x, \cdot)$ is the Arrow–Pratt risk premium. Thus the choice of input x can be alternatively written as

$$\text{Max}_x\{w + E[py(x, e)] - v'x - R(x, \cdot)\}$$

The associated necessary first-order conditions are

$$\partial E[py(x, e)]/\partial x - v - \partial R(x, \cdot)/\partial x = 0,$$

or

$$\partial E[py(x, e)]/\partial x = v + \partial R(x, \cdot)/\partial x,$$

where $\partial R(x, \cdot)/\partial x$ is the *marginal risk premium*. Comparing this result with the first-order condition derived above indicates that the marginal risk premium takes the form: $\partial R(x, \cdot)/\partial x = -\text{Cov}[U', p\partial y(x, e)/\partial x]/EU'$. This result provides an intuitive interpretation of the covariance term: $-\text{Cov}[U', p\partial y(x, e)/\partial x]/EU'$ is the *marginal risk premium* measuring the effect of inputs x on the implicit cost of private risk bearing. It also shows that, at the optimal input use, the expected marginal value product, $\partial E[py(x, e)]/\partial x$, is equal to the input cost v, plus the marginal risk premium, $\partial R(x, \cdot)/\partial x$.

In general, the marginal risk premium can be either positive, zero, or negative depending on the nature of the stochastic production function $y(x, e)$. For a risk-averse firm, when $\partial R(x, \cdot)/\partial x_i > 0$, the i-th input increases the implicit cost of risk, providing an incentive to reduce the use of this input. Alternatively, when $\partial R(x, \cdot)/\partial x_i < 0$, the i-th input reduces the implicit cost of risk, giving an incentive to increase the demand for this input. It is largely an empirical matter to evaluate whether a particular input increases or decreases the implicit cost of risk.

2. Some Special Cases

Alternative approaches have been used in the empirical assessment of the stochastic technology.

a. Multiplicative Production Uncertainty

This is the case where the stochastic production function is specified as:

$$y(x, e) = ef(x),$$

where $E(e) = 1$. Let $q = pe$ denote the revenue per unit of expected output. Then, the expected utility maximization problem becomes

$$\text{Max}_x\{EU[w + qf(x) - v'x]\}.$$

After replacing p by q, this becomes equivalent to the price uncertainty case discussed previously. Thus, all the results we obtained under price uncertainty apply. However, note that this specification implies the following results for the variance of output: $\text{Var}(y) = \text{Var}(e)f(x)^2$, and $\partial\text{Var}(y)/\partial x = 2\,\text{Var}(e)f(x)\partial f(x)/\partial x$. Given $f(x) > 0$ and $\partial f(x)/\partial x > 0$, it follows that $\partial\text{Var}(y)/\partial x > 0$. Thus, this stochastic production function specification restricts *inputs to be always variance increasing*. This seems rather restrictive.

b. Additive Production Uncertainty

This is the case where the stochastic production function takes the form

$$y(x, e) = f(x) + e,$$

where $E(e) = 0$. This simple specification implies that $\text{Var}(y) = \text{Var}(e)$, and $\partial\text{Var}(y)/\partial x = 0$. Thus, this stochastic production function specification restricts *input use to have no impact on the variance of output*. Again, this seems rather restrictive.

c. The Just–Pope Specification

In an attempt to develop more flexible specifications, Just and Pope (1978, 1979) proposed the following stochastic production function specification

$$y(x, e) = f(x) + e[h(x)]^{1/2},$$

where $E(e) = 0$ and $\text{Var}(e) > 0$. It implies:

$$. E(y) = f(x) \text{ and } \partial E(y)/\partial x = \partial f(x)/\partial x,$$

$$.\mathrm{Var}(y) = \mathrm{Var}(e)h(x) \text{ and } \partial\mathrm{Var}(y)/\partial x = \mathrm{Var}(e)\cdot \partial h(x(/\partial x >,$$
$$=, < 0 \text{ as } \partial h(x)/\partial x >, =, < 0$$

Note that this production function can be interpreted as a regression model exhibiting heteroscedasticity (i.e., nonconstant variance). Of particular interest are the effects of inputs on the variance of output, $\mathrm{Var}(y)$. Inputs can be classified as *risk increasing, risk neutral, or risk decreasing* depending upon whether $\partial\mathrm{Var}(y)/\partial x$ is positive, zero, or negative, respectively. Thus, in the Just–Pope specification, an input is risk increasing, risk neutral, or risk decreasing when $\partial h(x))/\partial x$ is positive, zero, or negative, respectively. When applied to agricultural production, Just and Pope (1979) found evidence that fertilizer use tends to increase expected yield ($\partial f(x)/\partial x >$) 0, as well as the variance of yield ($\partial h(x)/\partial x > 0$). This indicates that fertilizer is a *risk-increasing* input. However, other inputs can be *risk reducing*. Examples include irrigation (reduces the effects of uncertain rainfall on production) or pesticide use (reduces the effects of pest damage). In situations where inputs affect production risk, firms can then manage their risk exposure through input choice. Under risk aversion, managers have an extra incentive to use risk-reducing inputs (which reduce risk exposure and its implicit cost). And they have an extra disincentive to use risk-increasing inputs (which increase risk exposure and its implicit cost). In such situations, risk has a direct effect on input demand and production decisions.

d. The Moment-Based Approach

While mean-variance analysis is particularly convenient in applied analysis, there are situations where it may not capture all the relevant information about risk exposure. An example is related to downside risk exposure. If decision-makers are averse to downside risk, then it is relevant to assess their exposure to downside risk. Yet, as discussed in Chapter 6, the variance does not distinguish between upside risk versus downside risk. In this context, there is a need to go beyond a mean-variance approach. One way to proceed is to estimate the probability distribution of the relevant random variables. This would provide all the relevant information for risk assessment (see Chapter 2). An alternative approach is to rely on moments of the distribution (Antle 1983). Note that this includes mean-variance analysis as a special case (focusing on the first two moments). More interestingly, this provides a framework to explore empirically the role and properties of higher-order moments.

In the context of a general stochastic production function $y(x, e)$, let

$$\mu(x) = E[y(x, e)]$$

denote mean production given inputs x, and

$$M_i(x) = E\{[y(x,e) - \mu(x)]^i\}$$

be the i-th central moment of the distribution of output y given x, $i = 2, 3, \ldots$ Then, $M_2(x) = \text{Var}(x)$ is the variance of output, and $M_3(x)$ is the skewness of output, conditional on inputs. Here, the sign of $M_3(x)$ provides information on the asymmetry of the distribution, and thus on downside risk exposure. For example, comparing two distributions with the same mean and same variance, a higher (lower) skewness means a lower (greater) exposure to downside risk. As discussed in Chapter 4, this is particular relevant for decision-makers who are averse to downside risk.

To make the moment-based approach empirically tractable, consider the following specifications:

(1) $y = \mu(x) + u$,

(2) $[y - \mu(x)]^i \equiv u^i = M_i(x) + v_i$, $i = 2, 3, \ldots$

where $E(u) = 0, E(v_i) = 0, \text{Var}(u) = M_2(x)$, and

$$\text{Var}(v_i) \equiv E[u^i - M_i]^2 = E(u^{2i}) + M_i^2 - 2E(u^i)M_i = M_{2i} - M_i^2.$$

After choosing some parametric form for $\mu(x)$ and $M_i(x)$, specifications (1) and (2) become standard regression models that can be estimated by regression (using weighted least squares to correct for heteroscedasticity). Antle and Goodger (1984) have used this approach to investigate the effects of input choice on production risk. They found evidence that input use can influence mean production μ, the variance of production M_2, as well as the skewness of production, M_3.

THE MULTIPRODUCT FIRM UNDER UNCERTAINTY

So far, we have focused our attention on a single product firm. Next, we explore the implications of risk for a multiproduct firm.

PRICE UNCERTAINTY

Consider a firm producing m products where $y = (y_1, \ldots, y_m)'$ is an output vector with corresponding market prices $p = (p_1, \ldots, p_m)'$. Under price uncertainty, the output prices p are not known at the time production decisions are made due to production lags. Let $p_i = \mu_i + \sigma_i e_i$, where $E(e_i) = 0, i = 1, \ldots, m$. Under the expected utility model, the firm manager has risk preferences represented by the utility function $U(w + p'y - C(v, y))$, where w is initial wealth, $p'y = \sum_{i=1}^{m} p_i y_i$ denotes firm revenue, and $C(v, y)$ denotes the cost of production. Then, production decisions are made in a way consistent with the maximization problem

$$\text{Max}_y[EU(w + p'y - C(v, y))],$$

where E is the expectation operator over the subjective probability distribution of the random variables p. Let y^* be the optimal supply decisions associated with the above maximization problem. Some properties of y^* generalize from the single product firm model:

- $\partial y^*/\partial w = 0$ under constant absolute risk aversion (CARA),
- $\partial y^*/\partial t = 0$ under constant relative risk aversion (CRRA), where t is the tax rate,
- The Slutsky decomposition applies: $\partial^* y/\partial \mu = \partial^c y/\partial \mu + (\partial^* y/\partial w)y$, where $\partial^c y/\partial \mu$ is a symmetric, positive semi-definite matrix of compensated price effects, and $(\partial^* y/\partial w)y^*$ denotes the income effect.

However, other properties of the optimal supply function y^* are difficult to obtain in general. The reason is that they depend on both the joint probability distribution of $p = (p_1, \ldots, p_m)'$ and on the multiproduct firm technology. Of special interest are the effects of the correlation among output prices and their implications for production decisions under risk. Since such effects are difficult to predict in general, it will prove useful to focus our attention on a more restrictive specification: the mean-variance model (as discussed in Chapter 6).

MEAN-VARIANCE ANALYSIS

Consider a firm making m decisions under risk. Let $y = (y_1, \ldots, y_m)'$ be the vector of m decisions, and $p = (p_1, \ldots, p_m)'$ be the vector of net return per unit of products y. Then, firm profit is $\pi = p'y = \sum_{i=1}^{m} p_i y_i$. The net returns $p = (p_1, \ldots, p_m)$ are uncertain and are treated as random variables. Denote the mean of p by $\mu = (\mu_1, \ldots, \mu_m)' = E(p)$ and the variance of p by $A = \text{Var}(p)$

$$= \begin{bmatrix} \sigma_{11} & \sigma_{12} & \cdots & \sigma_{1m} \\ \sigma_{12} & \sigma_{22} & \cdots & \sigma_{2m} \\ \vdots & \vdots & \ddots & \vdots \\ \sigma_{1m} & \sigma_{2m} & \cdots & \sigma_{mm} \end{bmatrix},$$

a $(m \times m)$ symmetric positive semi-definite matrix, where $\sigma_{ii} = \text{Var}(p_i)$ is the variance of p_i, and $\sigma_{ij} = \text{Cov}(p_i, p_j)$ is the covariance between p_i and p_j, $i, j = 1, \ldots, m$. In a mean-variance framework, the objective function of the firm is represented by a utility function $U[E(\pi), \text{Var}(\pi)]$. The firm decisions are then consistent with the maximization problem

$$\text{Max}_y\{U[E(\pi), \text{Var}(\pi)]: \pi = p'y, y \in Y\}$$

where Y is the feasible set for y. We assume that $\partial U/\partial E > 0$ and $\partial U/\partial \text{Var} < 0$. This implies *risk aversion* since increasing risk (as measured by $\text{Var}(\pi)$) makes the decision-maker worse off. Note that expected return is given by $E(\pi) = \mu'y = \sum_{i=1}^{m} \mu_i y_i$, while the variance of return is $\text{Var}(\pi) = y'Ay = \sum_{i=1}^{m} \sum_{i=1}^{m} (y_i y_j \sigma_{ij})$. Then, the above optimization problem can be written as

$$\text{Max}_y\{U[\mu'y, y'Ay]: y \in Y\}$$

Denote by y^* the solution of this maximization problem. We want to investigate the properties of the optimal decisions y^*.

1. The E-V frontier

The previous mean-variance problem can be decomposed into two stages:

Stage 1: First, consider choosing y holding expected return $E(\pi) = \mu'y$ to be constant at some level M:

$$W(M) = \text{Min}_y[y'Ay: \mu'y = M, y \in Y].$$

where $W(M) = y^+(M)'Ay^+(M)$ is the indirect objective function, and $y^+(M)$ is the solution to this optimization problem for a given M. The function $W(M)$ gives the smallest possible variance attainable for given levels of expected return M. The function $W(M)$ is called the "E-V frontier" (which is short for "expected-value variance" frontier). The *E-V frontier* is the boundary of the feasible region in the mean-variance space.

Note that *a risk-averse decision-maker will always choose a point on the E-V frontier*. It means that, under risk aversion, utility maximization always implies the stage-one optimization. Indeed, with $\partial U/\partial \text{Var} < 0$, for any given expected return M, he/she would always prefer a reduction in variance up to a point on the E-V frontier. This is illustrated in Figure 8.6. Figure 8.6 shows that that point A is feasible but generates a high variance. From point A, holding expected return constant, a feasible reduction in variance is always possible and improves the welfare of a risk-averse decision-maker. The largest feasible reduction in variance leads to a move from point A to point B, which is located on the EV frontier. Another way to obtain the same result is to consider the choice of expected return for a given risk exposure. With $\partial U/\partial E > 0$, for a given variance, a risk-averse decision-maker would always choose a higher mean return up to a point on the E-V frontier. For example, in Figure 8.6, he/she would always choose to move from point C (exhibiting low expected return) to point B on the E-V frontier.

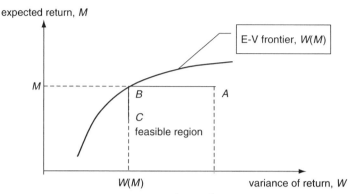

Figure 8.6 The E-V frontier

When the feasible set Y can be expressed as a set of linear inequalities, the above stage-one optimization is a standard quadratic programming problem. It can be easily solved numerically on a computer. This makes this approach simple and convenient for empirical analyses of economic behavior under risk. As discussed in the following paragraphs, it is commonly used in the investigation of risk management.

Stage 2: Next, consider choosing the optimal value for M (which was treated as fixed in stage 1):

$$\text{Max}_M U(M, W(M))$$

Denote the solution of this optimization problem by M^*. Under differentiability, this solution corresponds to the first-order necessary condition

$$\partial U/\partial M + (\partial U/\partial W)(\partial W/\partial M) = 0,$$

or

$$\partial W/\partial M = -(\partial U/\partial M)/(\partial U/\partial W).$$

This shows that, at the optimum, the slope of the E-V frontier, $\partial W/\partial \mu$, is equal to the marginal rate of substitution between mean and variance, $-(\partial U/\partial M)/(\partial U/\partial W)$. This marginal rate of substitution is also the slope of the indifference curve between mean and variance. This is illustrated in Figure 8.7.

Of course, putting the two stages together is always consistent with the original utility maximization problem. Recall that $y^+(M)$ corresponds to the point on the E-V frontier where expected return is equal to M. This generates the following important result: $y^* = y^+(M^*)$. It states that *the optimal choice y^* is always the point on the E-V frontier corresponding to M^*.*

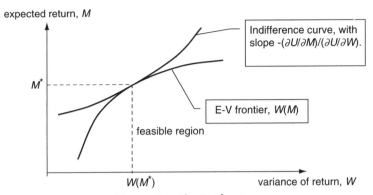

Figure 8.7 The E-V frontier

Note that *stage 1 does not depend on risk preferences*. Since risk preferences can be difficult to evaluate empirically (e.g., as they typically vary among decision-makers), this suggests the following popular approach:

1. Given estimates of μ and A, solve the stage 1 problem parametrically for different values of M. This traces out numerically the E-V frontier $W(M)$. This also generates the conditional choices $y^+(M)$.
2. Show the decision-maker the E-V frontier (and its associated choices $y^+(M)$), and let him/her choose his/her preferred point on the E-V frontier. Choosing this point determines M^*.
3. Obtain $y^* = y^+(M^*)$.

This provides a convenient framework to analyze risk behavior and/or to make recommendations to decision-makers about their risk management strategies.

2. Diversification

The above mean-variance model exhibits two attractive characteristics: (1) it is easy to implement empirically, and (2) it provides useful insights into diversification strategies. To illustrate the second point, consider the simple case where $m = 2, y = (y_1, y_2)$, and $\pi = p_1 y_1 + p_2 y_2, p_i$ being the net return per unit of activity y_i, $i = 1, 2$. Let $\mu_i = E(p_i), \sigma_i^2 = \text{Var}(p_i)$, and $\rho =$ the correlation coefficient between p_1 and p_2, $-1 \le \rho \le 1$. Then,

$$E(\pi) = \mu_1 y_1 + \mu_2 y_2$$

and

$$\text{Var}(\pi) = \sigma_1^2 y_1^2 + \sigma_2^2 y_2^2 + 2\rho \sigma_1 \sigma_2 y_1 y_2.$$

The stage-one optimization takes the form:

$$W(M) = \text{Min}_y[\sigma_1^2 y_1^2 + \sigma_2^2 y_2^2 + 2\rho\sigma_1\sigma_2 y_1 y_2 : \mu_1 y_1 + \mu_2 y_2 = M, y \in Y]$$

or

$$W(M) = \text{Min}_y[\sigma_1^2 y_1^2 + \sigma_2^2 (M - \mu_1 y_1)^2/(\mu_2^2) + 2\rho\sigma_1\sigma_2 y_1 (M - \mu_1 y_1)/\mu_2 : y \in Y].$$

First, consider the extreme situation where $\rho = -1$. This is the case where there is a *perfect negative correlation* in the unit returns to the two activities y_1 and y_2. Then, the previous problem becomes

$$W(M) = \text{Min}_y[(\sigma_1 y_1 - \sigma_2 (M - \mu_1 y_1)/\mu_2)^2 : y \in Y]$$

Note that choosing $y_1 = M\sigma_2/(\mu_2\sigma_1 + \mu_1\sigma_2)$ implies $\text{Var}(\pi) = 0$. Thus, there exists a strategy that can eliminate risk altogether. It shows that $\rho = -1$ generates the greatest possibilities for diversification strategies to reduce risk exposure.

Second, consider the other extreme situation where $\rho = +1$. This is the case where there is a *perfect positive correlation* in the unit returns to the two activities y_1 and y_2. Then, the above problem becomes

$$W(M) = \text{Min}_y[(\sigma_1 y_1 + \sigma_2 (M - \mu_1 y_1)/\mu_2)^2 : y \in Y]$$

which implies that $[\text{Var}(\pi)]^{1/2} = \sigma_1 y_1 + \sigma_2 (M - \mu_1 y_1)/\mu_2$, i.e. that the standard deviation of π is a linear function of y_1. This generates no possibility for diversification strategies to reduce the variance of return.

Third, consider the intermediate cases where $-1 < \rho < +1$. This corresponds to intermediate situations where the possibilities for diversification and risk reduction decrease with the correlation coefficient ρ between p_1 and p_2.

This is illustrated in Figure 8.8, which shows the tradeoff between expected return and the standard deviation of return under alternative correlation coefficients ρ. Figure 8.8 shows that risk diversification strategies cannot help reduce risk exposure when there is a strong positive correlation in their unit return. Then, the least risky strategy is simply to specialize in the least risky activity. Conversely, Figure 8.8 shows that risk exposure can be greatly reduced through diversification when the decision-maker can choose among activities with negative correlation in their unit returns. It indicates that risk-averse decision-makers have an extra incentive to diversify among these activities to reduce their risk exposure. In other words, *risk and risk aversion provide economic incentives to diversify into economic activities that do not involve positively correlated returns*. This is intuitive. It is just a formal way of stating the well-known diversification rule: Do not put all your eggs in the same basket (since doing so would expose all eggs to the same risk of dropping the basket).

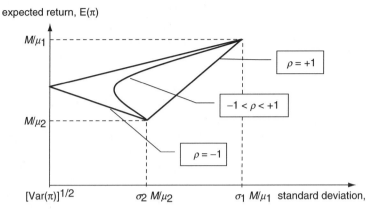

Figure 8.8 Risk diversification

THE USE OF FUTURES MARKETS

We have examined the behavior of a firm facing both price and production uncertainty. We have seen that risk-reducing inputs can help reduce exposure to production risk. Also, diversification strategies can help reduce the decision-maker risk exposure. But are there more direct ways of reducing price uncertainty? In this section, we investigate how futures markets can provide the firm a powerful way to reduce its exposure to price risk.

Over the last decades, futures markets have been one of the fastest growing industries in the world business economy. Futures markets involve the organized trading of futures contracts. A futures contract is a transferable, legally binding agreement to make or take delivery of a standardized amount of a given commodity at a specified future date. Futures markets perform several functions: (1) they facilitate risk management; (2) they aid firms in discovering forward prices; and (3) they provide a source of information for decision-making (Hull 2002). Our focus here is on the use of futures markets in managing price risk on the associated commodity market (also called *cash market*). This involves "hedging." A market participant is a *hedger* if he/she takes a position in the futures market opposite to a position held in the cash market. This contrasts with a *speculator*, defined as a market participant who does not hedge.

Following Feder et al. (1980), consider the case of a firm producing a commodity under price risk. Price uncertainty is associated with production lags, where input decisions are made before the output is marketed, i.e., before the cash market price for output is known. There are two relevant periods: the beginning of the production period (when input decisions are made), and the end of the production period (when output is marketed). If there is no futures market for the commodity produced (or if the firm decides not to participate in it), then the firm is a speculator in the cash market. This reduces to the Sandmo model discussed previously (where price uncertainty has adverse effects on production incentives under risk aversion). We now consider the case where a futures market exists for the commodity produced. We want to investigate the effects of hedging strategies for the firm. A hedger takes opposite positions in the cash market and the futures market. Thus, at the beginning of the production period, a hedging firm *sells* a futures contract at the same time as it *purchases* its inputs. And at the end of the production period (marketing time), a hedging firm *buys* a futures contract at the same time as it *sells* its output on the cash market. For simplicity, we assume that the firm faces no production uncertainty. Let

- . y = production output,
- . p = cash price of output at marketing time,
- . H = firm hedging on the futures market,
- . F = futures price at the beginning of the production period for delivery at marketing time.

At the beginning of the production period, the firm chooses the inputs used in the production of y units of output. At the same time, being a hedger, the firm *sells a futures contract* for H units of output to be delivered at marketing time. The unit price of this futures contract is F, generating a hedging revenue of $(F H)$. At the end of the production period (when output is marketed), the firm sells y units of output on the commodity market at cash price p. At the same time, to cancel its involvement in the futures market, the firm *buys a futures contract* for H units of output for immediate delivery.

Cash price and futures price typically differ. At any point of time, the *basis* is defined as the difference between a futures price (for a given futures contract) and a cash price. The basis evolves over time. To the extent that its evolution is not fully predictable, it exposes hedgers to a "basis risk." However, there is one situation where the basis is predictable. When the cash and futures markets are in the same location, one expects the basis to converge to zero as the futures contract approaches maturity. The two markets then become perfect substitutes at delivery time, meaning that a nonzero basis would be arbitraged away by market participants. In other words, a zero basis is an arbitrage condition at contract maturity. For simplicity, we focus on the case where the hedger chooses a futures contract maturity that matches its marketing time. Then, at the end of the production period (when output is marketed), the futures price for immediate delivery and the cash price (p) are assumed to coincide (corresponding to a zero basis). It follows that, for our hedging firm, the cost of buying back H units of futures contract is (pH).

The firm decisions involve choosing both production y and hedging H. For simplicity, we ignore time discounting. The firm's profit is $\pi = py - pH + FH - C(v, y)$, where ($py$) is the revenue from selling the output on the commodity market, $C(v, y)$ denotes the cost of production, (FH) is the revenue from hedging on the futures market, and (pH) is the cost of hedging activities (assuming that the futures price and the cash price coincide at marketing time). Under the expected utility model, this can be represented by the maximization problem

$$\text{Max}_{H, y} EU[w + py - pH + FH - C(v, y)],$$

where p is a random variable representing price uncertainty in the cash market. Again, we consider the case where the decision-maker is risk averse, where $U' > 0$ and $U'' < 0$. This provides a framework to investigate the implications of hedging for risk management and for production decisions.

1. Hedging Reduces Revenue Uncertainty

Note that, under price uncertainty,

$$\text{Var}[py - pH + FH - C(v, y)] = (y - H)^2 \, \text{Var}(p).$$

It follows that the variance of profit can be reduced to zero if $y = H$. It means that the firm has the possibility of eliminating revenue uncertainty if it decides to "fully hedge" its production. This shows that, in the absence of production uncertainty, hedging on the futures market is a very powerful tool for a firm to manage price uncertainty. In addition, note that $\text{Var}(\pi) = (y - H)^2 \, \text{Var}(p) < y^2 \, \text{Var}(p)$ whenever $0 < H < 2y$. This means that a "partial hedge" (where $0 < H < y$) always contributes to a reduction in the variance of profit. Thus, hedging can reduce the variance of firm revenue and thus risk exposure under price uncertainty. However, note that hedging cannot protect the firm against production uncertainty.

2. Under Optimal Hedging, Production Decisions are Unaffected by Price Risk or Risk Aversion:

While hedging helps manage price risk, does it also affect production decisions? To answer this question, consider the first-order necessary conditions associated with the expected utility maximization problem:

$$y: E[U' \cdot (p - C')] = 0$$

and

$$H: E[U' \cdot (-p + F)] = 0.$$

The optimal production y^* and optimal hedging H^* are the corresponding decisions that satisfy these two equations. In general, the hedging decision H^* depends on price expectations, risk, and risk aversion. However, note that substituting the second equation into the first gives

$$C' = F.$$

This shows that, at the optimum, production decisions are made such that the *marginal cost of production C' is equal to the futures price F*. This restores the "marginal cost pricing" rule for production decisions under price risk and risk aversion, except that the relevant price is now the futures price F (and not the expected cash price $E(p)$). Since this condition does not involve any random variable or risk preferences, it follows that under optimal hedging, neither price expectation, nor price uncertainty, nor risk aversion are to influence production decisions. This is in sharp contrast with our previous results obtained without hedging. It suggests that hedging strategies on futures markets can have profound effects on both private risk exposure and production decisions. More generally, it illustrates how the institutional context within which economic decisions are made can have significant effects on risk and resource allocation.

PROBLEMS

Note: An asterisk (*) indicates that the problem has an accompanying Excel file on the Web page http://www.aae.wisc.edu/chavas/risk.htm.

*1. Mr. Jones grows 100 ha of corn. His utility function for profit (π) is

$$U(\pi) = \pi - .00002\,\pi^2$$

Fixed costs are $100/ha. His subjective probability distribution for the price of corn (per kilogram) has a mean of $.04 and a variance of .0003. The decision variable of interest is nitrogen fertilizer priced at $.30 per kilogram. Mr. Jones judges that the mean and variance of corn yield (y measured in kg/ha) is

$$E(y) = 6000 + 30\,N - .1\,N^2$$
$$\text{Var}(y) = 800000 + 30000\,N$$

where N = kg of nitrogen fertilizer/ha.

    a. Assuming that yield and price are independently distributed, find the expected value and variance of profit for the farm.

    b. If the farmer maximizes his expected utility of profit, find the first-order conditions

- without risk,
- with price risk only,
- with yield risk only,
- with both price and yield risk.

c. Find the optimal nitrogen fertilizer use *for each case* in b. (use numerical methods). Interpret your results.

d. Under price and production uncertainty, how would an increase in fixed cost affect your answer in c? Interpret.

e. Discuss the management and policy implications of your results.

2. A firm faces two sources of risk: output price uncertainty and uncertainty in the value of its fixed cost.

a. Find the expected value of terminal wealth (allowing for possible correlation between the two sources of risk).

b. The firm decision-maker is risk averse. Under the expected utility model, obtain the first-order condition for optimal output. How does the presence of uncertain fixed cost affect your results?

c. Assume that marginal cost is constant and that the decision-maker has a quadratic utility function. Solve for the optimal output. Interpret your result.

3. A firm produces output y under a cost function $c(y) = k + y + 0.1y^2$, where k denotes fixed cost. The firm manager has risk preferences represented by the utility function $U(\pi) = -e^{-\pi}$, where $\pi = py - c(y)$, and p is output price.

a. How much would the firm produce if the output price is $p = 11$ for sure?

b. Now, the firm faces output price uncertainty where p has a normal distribution with mean 11 and standard deviation 2. What is the optimal firm supply? What is the marginal cost of risk?

c. How does your answer in b. change when fixed cost k increases? Interpret.

d. The standard deviation of output price p increases from 2 to 4. How does this affect firm supply and the marginal cost of risk? Interpret.

*4. Consider a decision-maker with $100 to invest among three risky prospects A, B, and C. The expected rate of return for each prospect is: $E(A) = .10, E(B) = .07$, and $E(C) = .03$. The standard deviation per unit return from each prospect is: $STD(A) = .06$, $STD(B) = .04$, and $STD(C) = .01$. The correlation among returns are: $R(A, B) = +0.4, R(B, C) = -1.0$, and $R(A, C) = -0.4$.

a. Find the E-V frontier and the associated investment strategies. Graph the E-V frontier. Interpret the results.

b. If the utility function of the decision-maker is $U(x) = x - .0045 x^2$, find the optimal investment strategy. Interpret the results.

c. Now assume that the correlation R(B,C) is equal to zero. How does that affect your results in a. and b.? Interpret.

Chapter 9

Portfolio Selection

This chapter focuses on optimal investment decision under uncertainty. A central issue is the role of risk and risk aversion in investment behavior. We start with the case of an investor choosing between two assets: a risky asset and a riskless asset. In this simple case, we obtain useful analytical insights on the effects of risk on portfolio selection. We then examine the general case of multiple risky assets. In a mean-variance context, we investigate the optimal portfolio selection among risky assets and its implications for empirical analysis. When taken to the market level, the optimal behavior of investors provides a framework to investigate the market price determination in the stock market. This is the standard capital asset pricing model (CAPM). Extensions to the capital asset pricing model are also discussed.

THE CASE OF TWO ASSETS

Consider an agent (it could be a firm or a household) choosing an investment strategy. We start with the simple case where there are only two investment options: a riskless asset and a risky asset. The investor has a one-period planning horizon. His/her investment decisions are made at the beginning of the period, yielding a monetary return at the end of the period. For each dollar invested, the riskless asset yields a sure return at the end of the period. The riskless asset can be taken to a government bond, which is considered to exhibit no risk of default. In contrast, the risky asset yields an uncertain return at the end of the period. The risky asset can be any activity yielding an uncertain delayed payoff (e.g., a stock investment). What should the investor decide?

At the beginning of the period, let I denote initial wealth of the investor. Let y denote the amount of money invested in the risky asset y, and let z denote the amount of money invested in the riskless asset. The investor faces the budget constraint:

$$I = y + z.$$

Denote by p the monetary return per unit of the risky asset y, and by r the monetary return per unit of the riskless asset z. While r is known ahead of time, p is uncertain at the time of the investment decision. Thus, the uncertain rate of return on y is $(p - 1)$, while the sure rate of return on z is $(r - 1)$. The uncertain variable p is treated as a random variable. In his/her risk assessment, the investor has a subjective probability distribution on p. At the end of the period, let C denote consumption (for a household), or terminal wealth (for a firm). It satisfies

$$C = py + rz,$$

Let $p = \mu + \sigma e$, where $\mu = E(p)$ and e is a random variable satisfying $E(e) = 0$. The parameters μ and σ can be interpreted respectively as the mean and standard deviation (or mean-preserving spread) of p. Under the expected utility model, let the preference function of the decision-maker be $U(C)$. We assume that $U' >$ and $U'' < 0$, corresponding to a risk-averse decision-maker. The investment decisions are then given by

$$\text{Max}_{y,z}\{EU(C): I = y + z, \ C = p\,y + r\,z\}$$

or

$$\text{Max}_y\{EU[p\,y + r \cdot (I - y)]\},$$

or

$$\text{Max}_y\{EU(r\,I + p\,y - r\,y)\}.$$

This is similar to Sandmo's model of the firm under price uncertainty discussed in Chapter 8. Indeed, the two models become equivalent if $w = r\,I$, and $C(v, y) = r\,y$. Let $y^*(I, \mu, \sigma, r)$ denote the optimal choice of y in the above maximization problem. It follows that the results obtained in Chapter 8 in the context of output price uncertainty apply to $y^*(I, \mu, \sigma, r)$. They are:

1. $\partial y^*/\partial I >$, $=$, < 0 under decreasing absolute risk aversion (DARA), constant absolute risk aversion (CARA), or increasing absolute risk aversion (IARA), respectively.

2. $\partial y^*/\partial \mu = \partial y^c/\partial \mu + (\partial y^*/\partial w)y^* > 0$ under DARA. This is the 'Slutsky equation' where $\partial y^c/\partial \mu$ is the compensated price effect and $[(\partial y^*/\partial w)y^*]$ is the income (or wealth) effect.
3. $\partial y^*/\partial \sigma < 0$ under DARA.
4. Denote by $Y = y/I$ the proportion of income invested in the risky asset. It implies that the maximization problem can be alternatively written as

$$\text{Max}_Y\{EU[I \cdot (r + pY - rY)]\}.$$

This is similar to Sandmo's model of the firm under price uncertainty discussed in Chapter 8 when $I = 1 - t$, t being the tax rate. Thus, the following result applies:

$\partial Y^*/\partial I = \partial(y^*/I)/\partial I >, =, < 0$ under decreasing relative risk aversion (DRRA), constant relative risk aversion (CRRA), or increasing relative risk aversion (IRRA), respectively.

Result 1 shows that, under DARA preferences, a higher income tends to increase investment in the risky asset (and thus to reduce investment in the riskless asset). Intuitively, under DARA, higher income reduces the implicit cost of risk, thus stimulating the demand for the risky asset. Result 2 has the intuitive implication that, under DARA, increasing the expected rate of return on the risky asset tends to increase its demand. Result 3 shows that, under DARA and risk aversion, increasing the riskiness of y (as measured by the standard deviation parameter σ) tends to reduce its demand. This is intuitive, as the implicit cost of risk rises, the risk-averse investor has an incentive to decrease his/her investment in the risky asset (thus stimulating his/her investment in the riskless asset). Finally, Result 4 indicates how risk preferences affect the proportion of the investor's wealth held in the risky asset, y^*/I. It implies that this proportion does not depend on income I under CRRA preferences. However, this proportion rises with income under DRRA, while it declines with income under IRRA. These results provide useful linkages between risk, risk aversion, and investment behavior.

MULTIPLE RISKY ASSETS

THE GENERAL CASE

We obtained a number of useful and intuitive results on investment behavior in the presence of a single risky asset. However, investors typically face many risky investment options. This implies a need to generalize our analysis. Here, we consider the general case of investments in m risky assets.

Let z be the risk free asset with rate of return $(r - 1)$, and y_i be the i-th risky asset with rate of return $(p_i - 1)$, where $p_i = \mu_i + \sigma_i e_i$, e_i being a random variable with mean zero, $i = 1, 2, \ldots, m$. This means that μ_i is the mean of p_i, and σ_i is its standard deviation (or mean-preserving spread), $i = 1, \ldots, m$.

Let $y = (y_1, y_2, \ldots, y_m)'$ denote the vector of risky investments, with corresponding returns $p = (p_1, p_2, \ldots, p_m)'$. Extending the two-asset case presented above, an expected utility maximizing investor would make investment decisions as follows

$$\text{Max}_y \{EU[r\, I + \sum_{i=1}^{m} (p_i - r)y_i]\},$$

where E is the expectation operator based on the joint subjective probability distribution of p. Let y^* denote the optimal portfolio choice of y in the above problem. Then, y^* satisfies the Slutsky equation:

$$\partial y^*/\partial \mu = \partial y^c/\partial \mu + (\partial y^*/\partial w)y^{*\prime}$$

where $\mu = (\mu_1, \mu_2, \ldots, \mu_m)'$ denotes the mean of $p = (p_1, p_2, \ldots, p_m)'$, $\partial y^c/\partial \mu$ is a $(m \times m)$ symmetric positive semidefinite matrix of compensated price effects, and $[(\partial y^*/\partial w)y^{*\prime}]$ is the income (or wealth) effect. Unfortunately, besides the Slutsky equation, other results do not generalize easily from the two-asset case. The reason is that the investments in risky assets y^* depend in a complex way on the joint probability distribution *of p*.

THE MEAN-VARIANCE APPROACH

The complexity of portfolio selection in the presence of multiple risky assets suggests the need to focus on a more restrictive model. Here we explore the portfolio choice problem in the context of a mean-variance model (as discussed in Chapter 6).

$$\text{Let } \pi = r\, I + \sum_{i=1}^{m} (p_i - r)y_i, \text{ and } A = \text{Var}(p) = \begin{bmatrix} \sigma_{11} & \sigma_{12} & \cdots & \sigma_{1m} \\ \sigma_{12} & \sigma_{22} & \cdots & \sigma_{2m} \\ \vdots & \vdots & \ddots & \vdots \\ \sigma_{1m} & \sigma_{2m} & \cdots & \sigma_{mm} \end{bmatrix}$$

$$= \text{a } (m \times m) \text{ positive}$$

definite matrix representing the variance of $p = (p_1, p_2, \ldots, p_m)'$, where σ_{ii} is the variance of p_i and σ_{ij} is the covariance between p_i and p_j, $i, j = 1, \ldots, m$. Assume that the investor has a mean-variance preference function $U(E(\pi),\ \text{Var}(\pi))$, where $\partial U/\partial E > 0$, $\partial U/\partial \text{Var} < 0$ (implying risk aversion). Note that

$$E(\pi) = r\,I + \sum_{i=1}^{m} (\mu_i - r)\,y_i,$$

and

$$\text{Var}(\pi) = y'Ay = \sum_{i=1}^{m}\sum_{j=1}^{m} y_i y_j \sigma_{ij}.$$

The decision problem thus becomes

$$\text{Max}_y\ \{U(E,\ \text{Var}): E = rI + \sum_{i=1}^{m} (\mu_i - r)y_i,\ \text{Var} = y'Ay\},$$

or

$$\text{Max}_y\{U(r\,I + \sum_{i=1}^{m} (\mu_i - r)\,y_i,\ y'Ay\}.$$

Let y^* denote the optimal solution to the previous problem. Next, we explore the implications of the model for optimal portfolio selection.

1. The Mutual Fund Theorem

The first-order necessary conditions to the above maximization problem are

$$(\partial U/\partial E)[\mu - r] + 2(\partial U/\partial \text{Var})\,A\,y = 0,$$

or

$$y^* = -(U_E/2U_V)A^{-1}[\mu - r],$$

where $U_E \equiv \partial U/\partial E > 0$, and $U_V \equiv \partial U/\partial \text{Var} < 0$. This gives a closed form solution to the optimal investment decisions. It implies that $y^* = (y_1^*, \ldots, y_m^*)$ is proportional to vector $(A^{-1}[\mu - r])$, with $-(U_E/2U_V) > 0$ as the coefficient of proportionality. Note that the vector $(A^{-1}[\mu - r])$ is independent of risk preferences. This generates the following "mutual fund theorem" (Markowitz 1952):

If all investors face the same risks, then the relative proportions of the risky assets in any optimal portfolio are independent of risk preferences.

Indeed, if all investors face the same risks, then each investor (possibly with different risk preferences) chooses a multiple $[-(U_E/2U_V) > 0]$ of a standard vector of portfolio proportions $(A^{-1}[\mu - r])$. Note that the mutual fund principle does not say anything about the proportion of the riskless asset in an optimal portfolio (this proportion will depend on individual risk preferences).

This is illustrated in Figures 9.1 and 9.2. These figures represent the relationships between expected return and the standard deviation of return. They are closely related to the evaluation of the E-V frontier discussed in Chapter 8. Here the standard deviation is used (instead of the variance) for reasons that will become clear shortly.

Figure 9.1 shows the feasible region under two scenarios. First, the area below the curve *ABC* gives the feasible region in the absence of a riskless asset (as discussed in Chapter 8). The curve *ABC* is thus the mean-standard

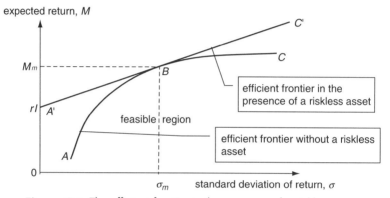

Figure 9.1 The efficient frontier in the presence of a riskless asset

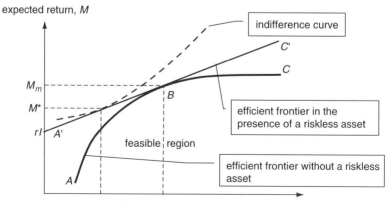

Figure 9.2 Portfolio choice in the presence of a riskless asset

deviation frontier when $z = 0$. Second, Figure 9.1 shows that the introduction of a riskless asset z expands the feasible region to the area below the line $A'BC'$. The line $A'BC'$ happens to be a straight line in the mean-standard deviation space (which is why the standard deviation is used in Figures 9.1 and 9.2). Points A' and B are of particular interest. Point A' corresponds to a situation where the decision-maker invests all his/her initial wealth in the *riskless asset*; it generates no risk (with zero variance) and an expected return equal to (r I). Point B corresponds to a situation where the decision-maker invests all his/her initial wealth in the *risky assets*. It identifies a unique market portfolio (M_m, σ_m) that is at the point of tangency between the curve ABC and the line going through A'. Knowing points A' and B is sufficient to generate all points along the straight line $A'BC'$. Note that moving along this line can be done in a simple way. Simply take a linear combination of the points A' and B. Practically, this simply means investing initial wealth I in different proportions between the riskless asset (point A') and the risky market portfolio given by point B. Thus, in the presence of a riskless asset, the feasible region is bounded by the straight line $A'BC'$ in Figure 9.1. As discussed in Chapter 8, a risk-averse decision-maker would always choose a point on the boundary of this region, i.e., on the line $A'BC'$. For that reason, the line $A'BC'$ is termed the *efficiency frontier*. Indeed, any point below this line would be seen as an inferior choice (which can always be improved upon by an alternative portfolio choice that increases expected return and/or reduces risk exposure). Note that the efficiency frontier $A'BC'$ does not depend on risk preferences.

Figure 9.2 introduces the role of risk preferences. As seen in Chapter 8, the optimal portfolio is obtained at a point where the indifference curve between mean and standard deviation is tangent to the efficiency frontier. In Figure 9.2, this identifies the point (M^*, σ^*) as the optimal choice along the efficiency frontier $A'BC'$. Of course, this optimal point would vary with risk preferences. Yet, as long as different decision-makers face the same risk, they would all agree about the risky market portfolio (M_m, σ_m) given at at point B. If this risky market portfolio represents a mutual fund, the only decision left would be what proportion of each individual's wealth to invest in the mutual fund versus the riskless asset. This is the essence of the mutual fund theorem: *the mutual fund (corresponding to the risky market portfolio B) is the same for all investors, irrespective of risk preferences.*

The mutual fund theorem does generate a rather strong prediction. When facing identical risks, all investors choose a portfolio with the same proportion of risky assets. In reality, the relative composition of risky investments in a portfolio is often observed to vary across investors. This means either that investors face different risks, or that the mean-variance model does not provide an accurate representation of their investment decisions. Before we explore some more general models of portfolio selection, we will investigate in more details the implications of the simple mean-variance model.

2. Two-Stage Decomposition

As seen in Chapter 8, in a mean-variance model, it is useful to consider a two-stage decomposition of the portfolio choice.

Stage 1: First, choose the risky investments y conditional on some given level of expected return M. Under risk aversion (where $U_V = \partial U / \partial \mathrm{Var} < 0$), this implies:

$$W(M) = \mathrm{Min}_y[y' \; Ay : rI + \sum_{i=1}^{m} (\mu_i - r)y_i = M],$$

where $W(M)$ is the mean-variance E-V frontier (as discussed in chapter 8). Let $y^+(M, \cdot)$ denote the solution to this stage-one problem.

Note that, in the presence of a riskless asset, it is always possible to drive the variance of the portfolio to zero by investing only in the riskless asset. This corresponds to choosing $y = 0$, which generates a return $m = r \, I$. This means that the E-V frontier necessarily goes through the point of zero variance when $M = r \, I$ (corresponding to $y^+(r \, I, \cdot) = 0$). In general, the E-V frontier $W(M)$ expresses the variance W as a nonlinear function of the mean return M. It is in fact a quadratic function as the frontier in the mean-standard deviation space, $W^{1/2}(M)$, is a linear function (as illustrated in Figures 9.1 and 9.2).

Stage 2: In the second stage, choose the optimal expected return M:

$$\mathrm{Max}_M[U(M, \; W(M)],$$

which has for first-order condition

$$U_E + U_V(\partial W / \partial M) = 0,$$

or

$$\partial W / \partial M = -U_E / U_V.$$

This states that, at the optimum, the slope of the E-V frontier $\partial W / \partial M$ is equal to the marginal rate of substitution between E and Var, $-U_E / U_V$ (which is the slope of the indifference curve between E and Var). (See Chapter 8.)

Let M^* denote the solution to the stage-two problem. Then the optimal solution to the portfolio selection problem is $y^* = y^+(M^*)$.

As noted in Chapter 8, solving the stage-one problem is relatively easy since it does not depend on risk preferences (which can vary greatly across investors). Thus, given estimates of $\mu = E(p)$ and $A = V(p)$, deriving the efficiency frontier $W(M)$ can be easily done by solving stage-one problem parametrically for different values of M. Then, choosing the point M^* on the efficiency frontier generates the optimal portfolio choice $y^* = y^+(M^*)$. In a mean-variance framework, this provides a practical way to assess optimal investment choice and to make recommendations to investors about optimal portfolio selection.

THE CAPITAL ASSET PRICING MODEL (CAPM)

The previous mean-variance model has one attractive characteristic: It gives a closed form solution to the optimal investment decisions. Given the simplicity of the investment decision rule, it will prove useful to explore its implications for market equilibrium. All it requires is to aggregate the decision rules among all market participants and to analyze the associated market equilibrium. This provides useful insights on the functioning of the stock market.

To see that, consider an economy composed of

. n firms

. h investors, each with an initial wealth w_i and a mean-variance utility function $U_i(E_i, \text{Var}_i)$, where $\partial U_i/\partial E_i > 0$ and $\partial U_i/\partial \text{Var}_i < 0$ (implying risk aversion), $i = 1, 2, \ldots, h$. We allow for different investors to have different utility function, i.e., different risk preferences.

Each firm has a market value P_j determined on the stock market, $j = 1, 2, \ldots, n$, and is owned by the h investors. We consider a one-period model where investors make their investment decisions at the beginning of the period and receive some uncertain returns at the end of the period. At the beginning of the period, each investor i decides:

. the proportion Z_{ij} of the j-th firm he wants to own,
. the amount to invest in a riskless asset z_i, with a rate of return of $(r - 1)$.

The *budget constraint* for the i-th investor is

$$w_i = z_i + \sum_{j=1}^{n} Z_{ij}P_j,$$

or

$$w_i = z_i + Z_i'P,$$

where $Z_i = (Z_{i1}, \ldots, Z_{in})'$ and $P = (P_1, \ldots, P_n)'$.

The value of each firm, P_j, may change in unforeseen fashion by the end of the period to X_j. Since X_j is not known ahead of time, it is treated as a random variable. Let $X = (X_1, \ldots, X_n)'$ be a vector of random variables with mean $\mu = E(X)$ and variance $A = V(X) =$

$$\begin{bmatrix} \sigma_{11} & \sigma_{12} & \cdots & \sigma_{1n} \\ \sigma_{12} & \sigma_{22} & \cdots & \sigma_{2n} \\ \vdots & \vdots & \ddots & \vdots \\ \sigma_{1n} & \sigma_{2n} & \cdots & \sigma_{nn} \end{bmatrix}.$$

The *end-of-period wealth* for the i-th investor is: $r\,z_i + Z_i'X = r\,z_i + \sum_{j=1}^{n} Z_{ij}X_j$. It follows that the mean end-of-period wealth is: $E_i = r\,z_i + Z_i'\mu$; and the variance of end-of-period wealth is: $\text{Var}_i = Z_i'AZ_i$. The maximization of utility $U(E_i, \text{Var}_i)$ for the i-th investor becomes

$$\text{Max}_{m,Z}\{U_i(rz_i + Z_i'\mu, Z_i'A\,Z_i): w_i = z_i + Z_i'P\}$$

or

$$\text{Max}_z\{U_i[r(w_i - Z_i'P) + Z_i'\mu, Z_i'AZ_i]\}.$$

The optimal investment proportions for the i-th investor, Z_i^*, satisfy the first-order conditions

$$(\partial U_i \partial E_i)\,(\mu - rP) + 2(\partial U_i/\partial V_i)AZ_i = 0,$$

which gives

$$Z_i^* = -[\partial U_i/\partial E_i)/2\partial U_i/\partial V_i]A^{-1}(\mu - rP), \; i = 1, \ldots, h. \quad (1)$$

Note that we are assuming that all investors face the same risk. This means that Z_i^* satisfies the *mutual fund theorem*: Z_i^* is proportional to $[A^{-1}(\mu - rP)]$, which does not depend on individual risk preferences. It follows that each investor holds the same relative proportion of the shares of each firm in the stock market.

MARKET EQUILIBRIUM

Given the optimal decision rule of the i-th investor given in equation (1), we now investigate its implications for market equilibrium. Assuming that each firm is completely owned by the h investors, then the market prices of the n firms, $P = (P_1, \ldots, P_n)'$, are determined on the stock market. The stock market provides the institutional framework for investors to exchange their ownership rights of the n firms. Market equilibrium in the stock market must satisfy

$$\sum_{i=1}^{h} Z_{ij} = 1, \; j = 1, \; \ldots, \; n,$$

or

$$\sum_{i=1}^{h} Z_i = \underline{1},$$

where $\underline{1} = (1, \ldots, 1)'$ is the $(n \times 1)$ unit vector. Substituting equation (1) into the market equilibrium condition yields

$$\sum_{i=1}^{h} \{ - [(\partial U_i / \partial E_i)/(2\partial U_i / \partial V_i)] \} A^{-1}(\mu - rP) = \underline{1}.$$

Let $\lambda = - \{ \sum_{i=1}^{h} [(\partial U_i / \partial E_i)/(2\partial U_i / \partial U_i / \partial V_i)] \}^{-1} > 0$. The parameter λ can be interpreted as the "market risk aversion parameter" (since it depends on the risk preferences of the h investors). Substituting λ into the above expression gives

$$\lambda^{-1} A^{-1}(\mu - rP) = \underline{1},$$

or

$$P = (\mu - \lambda A \underline{1})/r. \tag{2a}$$

Expression (2a) gives the market equilibrium value of the n firms on the stock market. It can be written alternatively as

$$P_j = \left[\mu_j - \lambda \left(\sum_{k=1}^{n} \sigma_{jk} \right) \right] \bigg/ r, \ j = 1, \ \ldots, \ n, \tag{2b}$$

where σ_{jj} is the variance of X_j, and σ_{jk} is the covariance between X_j and X_k. Expression (2b) states that, in equilibrium, the price of the j-th asset, P_j, equals the expected present value of future dividends μ_j / r, minus a risk premium, $\lambda(\sum_{k=1}^{n} \sigma_{jk})]/r$.

THE RATE OF RETURNS ON STOCKS

Given the determination of stock prices given in (2a) or (2b), we now examine the implications for the rate of return on stocks. Again, we assume that each firm is completely owned by the h investors who exchange their ownership rights of the n firms on the stock market.

Let $r_j = (1 +$ rate of return on stock $j)$
$= X_j / P_j =$ (end-of-period value)/(beginning-of-period value) for the j-th firm, $j = 1, \ldots, n.$

Let $X_m = \sum_{j=1}^{n} X_j = $ end-of-period value of all *n firms,*

with mean $\mu_m = E(X_m)$.

Let $P_m = \sum_{j=1}^{n} P_j = $ beginning-of-period value of all *n firms.*

Let $r_m = X_m/P_m = 1 + $ "market average rate of return."

Using equation (2b), we obtain:

$$E(r_j) = \mu_j/P_j = r + \lambda \left(\sum_{k=1}^{n} \sigma_{jk} \right) / P_j, \; j = 1, \dots, n,$$

$$E(r_m) = \mu_m/P_m,$$

$$\text{Cov}(X_j, \; X_m) \equiv \sigma_{jm} = \sum_{k=1}^{n} \sigma_{jk},$$

and

$$\text{Cov}(r_j, \; r_m) = \text{Cov}(X_j/P_j, \; X_m/P_m) = \sigma_{jm}/(P_j \, P_m).$$

Combining these results gives

$$\begin{aligned} E(r_j) &= r + \lambda \sigma_{jm}/P_j, \; j = 1, \dots, n, \\ &= r + \lambda P_m \, \text{Cov}(r_j, \; r_m), \\ &= r + \lambda P_m \, \text{Var}(r_m) \beta_j, \end{aligned}$$

where $\beta_j = \text{Cov}(r_j, \; r_m)/V(r_m)$ is the regression coefficient of r_m on r_j. This states that, in equilibrium, *the expected rate of return of a risky asset equals the risk-free return plus a risk premium.* Here the risk premium is: $\lambda P_m \text{Cov}(r_j, \; r_m)$. It depends on the market risk-aversion parameter λ and on the covariance between the asset return r_j and the market return r_m. Note that the above expression holds as well for r_m, implying that: $E(r_m) = r + \lambda P_m \text{Var}(r_m)$, or $[\lambda P_m \text{Var}(r_m)] = [E(r_m) - r]$. Substituting this result in the above expression gives

$$E(r_j) = r + [E(r_m) - r] \cdot \beta_j, \; j = 1, \; \dots, \; n.$$

This expression is the fundamental equation of the capital asset pricing model (CAPM) (Sharpe 1963). It states that the equilibrium expected rate of return on the *j*-th stock is *linear in its beta* (β_j), where β_j is the regression coefficient of r_j on r_m. This relationship is empirically tractable and provides a simple framework to investigate the functioning of capital markets. It expresses the expected rate of return on the *j*-th risky asset as the sum of two terms: the intercept measured by the risk free rate of return, and the term $\{[E(r_m) - r] \cdot \beta_j\}$ representing the market equilibrium risk premium, expressed as the difference between the expected market rate of return and the risk-free rate of return, multiplied by the corresponding beta. It means that, in equilibrium, the price of each risky asset must adjust until its mean rate of return, over and above the riskless rate of return, reflects its additional riskiness compared to the market. For example, if the j-th asset return is perfectly correlated with market risk, it would have a beta of one ($\beta_j = 1$), implying that $E(r_j) = E(r_m)$. Alternatively, if the j-th asset exhibits zero correlation with the market, then its beta is zero and $E(r_j) = r$. Intuitively, if an asset is weakly (strongly) correlated with the market, then the asset risk can (cannot) be easily diversified in the portfolio, implying a smaller (larger) equilibrium risk premium. Since both r and $[E(r_m) - r]$ are the same for all firms, it follows that differences in the rate of expected return across firms depend only on their β's: a higher (lower) β_j is associated with a higher (lower) rate of expected return $E(r_j)$.

THE CASE OF DEBT LEVERAGE

So far, we have assumed that the firms are entirely owned by investors-stockholders. This means that the firms are entirely equity financed. We now extend the analysis to allow for debt financing. Consider the case where firms can be financed by debts (i.e., bonds) as well as equity (i.e., stocks). The debt (bonds) is always paid first, and the equity holders (stockholders) are the residual claimants.

Let the value of debt of firm j at the beginning of the period be D_j. The debt is repaid with interest at the end of the period, the amount repaid being: $R_j = D_j r$. Then the equity return from firm j is: $X_j - R_j$, with mean $E(X_j - R_j) = \mu_j - R_j$, and variance $V(X_j - R_j) = V(X_j)$.

From equation (2b), we have

$$
\begin{aligned}
P_j &= \left[\mu_j - R_j - \lambda \left(\sum_{k=1}^{n} \sigma_{jk} \right) \right] / r, \; j = 1, \; \ldots, \; n, \\
&= \left[\mu_j - \lambda \left(\sum_{k=1}^{n} \sigma_{jk} \right) \right] / r - R_j / r, \\
&= \left[\mu_j - \lambda \left(\sum_{k=1}^{n} \sigma_{jk} \right) \right] / r - D_j,
\end{aligned}
$$

which implies

$$P_j + D_j = \left[\mu_j - \lambda \left(\sum_{k=1}^{n} \sigma_{jk} \right) \right] / r.$$

Define the value of the j-th firm to be: $P_j + D_j$. Also, define the *leverage ratio* for the *j*-th firm to be: $D_j/(P_j + D_j)$. For each firm, the leverage ratio is the proportion of debt to the value of the firm. Then, the above result gives the Miller–Modigliani theorem:

The value of the firm is independent of its leverage ratio.

This is a strong result. Under the CAPM, the relative amount of debt is not expected to affect the value of firms. But is it realistic? Intuitively, we may think that the extent of debt financing could possibly affect asset values. From the above analysis, this can only be the case if some basic assumptions made in the CAPM model are violated. This has stimulated the development of more general models that may also be more realistic. They are discussed below.

Finally, while the Miller–Modigliani theorem states that leverage does not affect the value of the firm, note that it does allow leverage to affect the rate of return on equity (since bonds are paid first and stockholders are the residual claimants).

SOME EXTENSIONS

The mutual fund theorem, the CAPM pricing formula, and the Miller–Modigliani theorem were all obtained in the context of a mean-variance model. They illustrate how deductive reasoning can be used to derive behavioral relationships among economic variables under risk. This facilitates the empirical analysis of investment behavior and stock prices. But does the CAPM provide accurate representations of investment behavior, or of asset price? There is a fair amount of empirical evidence suggesting that it does not.

The evidence against the CAPM model takes several forms. An overview of some of the "anomalies" generated by the CAPM is presented in Campbell et al. (1997). One piece of evidence is the "equity premium" puzzle. The puzzle is that the historical average return on the United States stock market seems "too high" (compared to the riskless rate of return on government bond) to be easily explained by risk and risk aversion alone under the CAPM. Other anomalies involve the CAPM difficulties in explaining differences in mean return and risk across some firms (or some industries). Such anomalies suggest the presence of "excess returns" in some capital markets.

Many factors may contribute to the existence of these "anomalies." First, data problems can affect the empirical testing of the CAPM model. Second, the standard CAPM model is developed under some rather restrictive conditions. It is a static one-period model, with homogeneous expectations, no taxes, unlimited liability, zero transaction costs, and well-functioning capital markets. Relaxing these assumptions has been the subject of active research. (See Campbell et al. for a survey of the empirical literature.) First, alternative models of asset pricing have been developed. For example, one approach that does not rely on the mutual fund theorem is the arbitrage pricing model proposed by Ross. In contrast with the CAPM, it allows for multiple risk factors. Second, in general, the presence of asymmetric information invalidates all CAPM results. This includes heterogeneous expectation among investors, which is sufficient to invalidate the mutual fund theorem. And asymmetric information between firm managers and investors can create adverse incentives for firm decisions. Over the last twenty years, this has stimulated much research on the economics of corporate governance. The role of asymmetric information will be discussed in Chapters 11 and 12. Third, the presence of transaction cost in the capital markets modifies the CAPM pricing rule. This can help explain discrepancies between expected returns and CAPM predictions (e.g., see Shiha and Chavas for an application to the United States farm real estate market, 1995). By reducing the possibilities of arbitrage, transaction costs create frictions that reduce the mobility of capital, contribute to market segmentations, and affect asset prices. This segmentation can be national within the international capital markets, or sectorial within a particular economy (e.g., the case of farm real estate market within the broader equity markets). The role of transaction costs will be evaluated in Chapter 11. Finally, introducing dynamics has provided useful insights into the interactions between risk, intertemporal allocation, and asset pricing (e.g., see Epstein and Zin 1991; Chavas and Thomas 1999). The analysis of dynamic decisions under risk is the topic of the next chapter.

PROBLEMS

Note: An asterisk (*) indicates that the problem has an accompanying Excel file on the Web page http://www.aae.wisc.edu/chavas/risk.htm.

*1. Consider a decision-maker with $100 to invest among one riskless prospect and three risky prospects A, B, and C. The expected rate of return for the riskless prospect is .02, and for each risky prospect: $E(A) = .10$, $E(B) = .07$, and $E(C) = .03$. The standard deviation per unit return from each prospect is: $STD(A) = .06$, $STD(B) = .04$, and $STD(C) = .01$. The correlation of the returns are: $R(A, B) = 0.4$, $R(B, C) = -0.5$, and $R(A, C) = -0.4$.

    a. Find the E-V frontier and the associated investment strategies. Graph the E-V frontier. Interpret the results.

    b. If the utility function of the decision-maker is $U(x) = x - .045\,x^2$, find the optimal investment strategy. Interpret the results.

    c. Now assume that the correlation $R(B, C)$ is equal to $+0.5$. How does that affect your results in a. and b.? Interpret.

  *2. Consider again Problem 1. Answer questions 1.b and 1.c knowing that the risky returns are normally distributed and the decision-maker has a utility function $U(\pi) = -e^{-4\pi}$.

Chapter 10

Dynamic Decisions Under Risk

So far, we have focused our attention on static, one-period analyses of economic behavior under risk. This has two important limitations. First, it does not capture the dynamic aspects of most decision-making processes. Second, it basically treats uncertainty as a given. In fact, uncertainty is only what decision-makers have not had a chance to learn before they make a decision. This suggests that an important aspect of risk management is information acquisition: The more an agent can learn about his/her economic environment, the less uncertainty he/she faces. We have delayed the analysis of learning for a simple reason. It is a very complex process (e.g., different individuals often process and retain information differently). In this chapter, we develop a multiperiod analysis to investigate the implications of learning for risk management and dynamic decision-making. We focus on individual decisions, leaving the analysis of risk transfers among individuals for the following chapters.

THE GENERAL CASE

We start with a general model of dynamic decisions for an individual. The individual could be a firm or a household. He/she has a T-period planning horizon. At each period, he/she makes decisions based on the information available at that time. However, under learning, the information can change over time. This requires addressing explicitly the learning process. At the beginning of the planning horizon, the decision-maker has initial wealth w. At period t, he/she makes some decision denoted by x_t, $t = 1, \ldots, T$. The individual also faces uncertainty due to unknown factors affecting his/her welfare during the T-period planning horizon. Let this uncertainty be represented by the random variables e. The information available about the random variables e is represented by a subjective probability distribution (as discussed in Chapter 2). However, under learning this probability distribution changes over time. Denote the subjective probability distribution of e based on the information available at time t by $f_t(e)$, $t = 1, \ldots, T$.

For simplicity, we assume that the decision-maker is an expected utility maximizer. Although this is not really required for the following analysis (as most results would still apply under nonexpected utility models), it will help simplify some of the arguments. The individual has preferences represented by the von Neumann–Morgenstern utility function $U(w, x_1, x_2, \ldots, x_T, e)$ satisfying $\partial U/\partial w > 0$. The decisions are made in a way consistent with the expected utility maximization problem

$$\text{Max}_{x_1, \ldots, x_n}\{EU(w, x_1, x_2, \ldots, x_T, e): x \text{ is feasible}\}$$
$$= \text{Max}_{x_1}\{E_1\{\text{Max}_{x_2}E_2\{\ldots \text{Max}_{x_T}E_T\{U(w, x_1, x_2, \ldots, x_T, e):$$
$$x \text{ is feasible}\}\ldots\}\}\},$$

where E_t is the expectation operator based on the subjective probability distribution of e at time t, $f_t(e)$, and where $x = (x_1, \ldots, x_n)$. This makes it explicit that, at each time period t, the decision x_t is made based on the information available at that time (as represented by E_t), $t = 1, \ldots, T$. This is a T-period version of the expected utility hypothesis. This is also a dynamic programming formulation, using backward induction (i.e. solving for x_T, then $x_{T-1}, \ldots, x_2$, and finally x_1). It includes as a special case the standard case where the utility function is time additive: $U(w, x_1, x_2, \ldots, x_n, e) = \sum_{t=1}^{T} \delta^{t-1} U_t(w, x_t, e)$, δ being the discount factor representing time preferences, $0 < \delta < 1$. This generates $\text{Max}_{x_1}\{E_1\{U_1(w, x_1, e)+\delta \text{Max}_{x_2}E_2\{\ldots + \delta \text{Max}_{x_T}E_T\{U_T(w, x_T, e): x \text{ is feasible}\}\ldots\}\}\}$, which can be solved using backward induction (see below).

LEARNING

The probability distribution of e, $f_t(e)$, changes from one time period to the next. We have seen in Chapter 2 that probability theory shows how probability assessments get updated under learning. This is formalized by Bayes' theorem, showing how new information transforms prior probabilities into posterior probabilities. As a result, it will be convenient to rely on the Bayesian approach as a representation of the learning process. Under Bayesian learning, a "signal" or "message" u_t is observed at time t,

$t = 1, 2, \ldots, T$. Thus, u_t is a random vector that is not known before time t but becomes known at time t and beyond. If u_t and e are independently distributed, then observing u_t provides no information about e. If u_t and e are perfectly correlated, then observing u_t provides perfect information about e. And if u_t and e are (imperfectly) correlated, then observing u_t provides some information about e.

Let $k(u_t|e; x_1, u_1; \ldots; x_{t-1}, u_{t-1}; x_t)$ denote the likelihood function of u_t. Then, Bayes' theorem gives

$$f_{t+1}(e, \cdot) = f(e|x_1, u_1; \ldots; x_t, u_t)$$
$$= k(u_t|e, \cdot)f_t(e) / \left[\int k(u_t|e, \cdot)f_t(e) \, de \right], \quad t = 1, \ldots, T.$$

where $f_{t+1}(e, \cdot)$ is the posterior probability function at time t as well as the prior probability function at time $t + 1$.

1. *The Case of Passive Learning*: Passive learning corresponds to the situation where $k(u_t|e, \cdot) = k(u_t|e; u_1; \ldots; u_{t-1})$ is *not a function of the decision variables* x for all t. This implies that $f_t(e, \cdot)$ is also not a function of x. In this case, learning takes place because u_t is observed at each time period $t = 1, \ldots, T$, but the decisions $x = (x_1, \ldots, x_T)$ do not affect the probability $f_t(e, \cdot)$, $t = 1, \ldots, T$.
2. *The Case of Active Learning*: In contrast, active learning corresponds to the situation where $k(u_t|e, \cdot) = k(u_t|e; u_1; \ldots; u_{t-1})$ *depends on the decision variables* x. This implies that $f_t(e, \cdot)$ is a function of x. In this case, the decisions $x = (x_1, \ldots, x_T)$ can influence the probability $f_t(e)$, $t = 1, \ldots, T$. For example, x_t can increase the correlation between u_t and e, and thus make the observations of u_t "more informative." Finally, note that when choosing x_t is called "an experiment," this corresponds to choosing an "optimal experimental design" that would provide information generating the greatest benefit to the decision-maker.

DYNAMIC PROGRAMMING RECURSION

Let

$$F_t(w, x_1, \ldots, x_{t-1}, e) = \text{Max}_{x_t} \{ E_t \{ \text{Max}_{x_{t+1}} E_{t+1} \{ \ldots \text{Max}_{x_T} E_T$$
$$\{ U(w, x_1, x_2, \ldots, x_T, e) : x \text{ is feasible} \} \ldots \} \} \},$$

where $F_t(w, x_1, \ldots, x_{t-1}, e)$ is an indirect utility function or "value function" at time t, $t = 1, \ldots, T$. Then, the general problem can be reformulated as

$$F_t(w,\ x_1,\ \ldots,\ x_{t-1},\ e) = \text{Max}_{x_t}\{E_t\{F_{t+1}(w,\ x_1,\ \ldots,\ x_t,\ e)\}:$$
$$x \text{ is feasible}\},\ t = T,\ T-1,\ \ldots,\ 2,\ 1.$$

where $W_{T+1}(w,\ x_1,\ \ldots,\ x_n,\ e) = U(w,\ x_1,\ \ldots,\ x_n,\ e)$. This is the *general recursion formula of dynamic programming*. It corresponds to a stage-wise decomposition of the original problem where each stage is a time period. Because it involves solving recursively for the function $F_t(w,\ x_1,\ \ldots,\ x_{t-1},\ e)$, it is a functional equation. Its optimal solution is the decision rule $x_t^*(x_1,\ \ldots,\ x_n,\ \cdot)$ expressing the choice of x_t as a function of past history $(x_1,\ \ldots,\ x_n)$ and of the information available at time t.

In the special case of a time additive utility function where $U(w,\ x_1,\ \ldots,\ x_n,\ e) = \sum_{t=1}^{T} \delta^{t-1} U_t(w,\ x_t,\ e),\ 0 < \delta < 1$, this generates the standard dynamic programming problem (Bertsekas)

$$F_t(w, x_1, \ldots, x_{t-1}, e) = \text{Max}_{x_t}\{E_1\{U_t(w, x_t, e) + \delta F_{t+1}(w, x_1, \ldots, x_t, e)\}$$
$$: x \text{ is feasible}\},\ t = T,\ T-1, \ldots, 1,$$

which can be solved using backward induction. The term δ is the "discount factor" measuring the rate of time preferences. With $0 < \delta < 1$, it means that the future always matters to the decision-maker ($\delta > 0$), but that it matters less than the present ($\delta < 1$). In this additive model, the discount factor is treated as given. It means that the rate of time preferences is treated as constant in standard dynamic programming problems. This is a convenient assumption that helps simplify the solutions to dynamic programming problems. This convenience is the main motivation for the common use of time additive preferences in the analysis of economic dynamics. Yet, time additivity imposes restrictions on intertemporal preferences and thus on dynamic behavior. For example, individuals facing poor prospects for survival (e.g., due to a terminal disease, or due to famine) may discount the future more heavily (compared to healthy individuals). This suggests that discounting the future may be endogenous. In other words, nonadditive preferences with nonconstant discounting may be needed to gain a better understanding of dynamic behavior. But nonadditive preferences are more difficult to specify and evaluate (see Chapter 3). This identifies significant trade-off between the convenience of simple models and their ability to represent dynamic behavior. For the sake of generality, we present the arguments below using a general (non time-additive) model. However, the reader should keep in mind that the time-additive model remains a popular framework for the analysis of dynamic behavior.

Note that, while $U(\cdot)$ is the "basic" preference function, $F_t(\cdot)$ is an "induced" preference function at time t, obtained from a stage-wise decomposition of the original optimization problem. It indicates that any dynamic problem can be analyzed such that the decisions x_t made at time t can be treated as a "one stage" optimization problem provided that one works with the "induced" preference function. However, this requires a good understanding of the properties of the induced preference function.

The above T-period model is very general. It can represent dynamic investment behavior under uncertainty. And when applied to a risk-averse household, it can provide insights into "consumption smoothing" behavior. However, solving the value function $F_t(\cdot)$ can be difficult when the decision-maker faces a lot of uncertainty. Indeed, $F_t(\cdot)$ depends on the information available at time t. Evaluating $F_t(\cdot)$ can be a difficult task when the information involves many random variables (e.g., weather effects, health effects, price and income uncertainty, etc.). In addition, $F_t(\cdot)$ depends on past history $(x_1, \ldots, x_{t-1})$. This can also be complex to evaluate. A standard simplification is to work with "Markovian structures." Under *Markovian structures*, at each time period, the influence of past history is summarized by a relatively small number of *state variables*. The state variables measure the position of the dynamic system at each time period. Solving the dynamic programming problem becomes simpler when the number of state variables is small (e.g., less than 3): the optimal decision rule for x then depends on just a few state variables. A further simplification is to work with "stationary" Markovian models. A Markovian model is *stationary* if the value function is stationary, i.e., if $F_t(\cdot)$ is the same function for each time period. Clearly, this requires that the decision-maker faces a situation where his/her payoff function and the law of dynamics do not change over time. Note that this does not imply that the same decision is made every period (e.g., each decision can still react to the latest information). But, it generates a key simplification: under stationarity, the decision rule expressing x_t as a function of the state variables at time t is the same for all periods.

SOME APPLICATIONS

THE STOCHASTIC DISCOUNT FACTOR UNDER TIME ADDITIVE PREFERENCES

Consider the case of a decision-maker with a *time additive* utility function $U(c_1, \ldots, c_T) = \sum_{t=1}^{T} \delta^{t-1} U(c_t)$, where c_t denotes consumption at time t, and δ is the discount factor, $0 < \delta < 1$. We assume risk aversion, with $U_t' = \partial U / \partial c_t > 0$ and $U_t'' = \partial^2 U / \partial c_t^2 < 0$. The decision-maker holds m assets at time t, $y_t = (y_{1t}, \ldots, y_{mt})'$, $t = 1, \ldots, T$. From time $(t-1)$ to t, the m assets generate a return $\pi(y_{t-1}, e_t)$ at time t, where e_t is a random variable representing uncertainty. This return can be either consumed or invested. At time t, the investment made in the i-th asset is $(y_{it} - y_{i,t-1})$. Thus, the net cost of investment at time t is: $p_t' \cdot (y_t - y_{t-1}) = \sum_{i=1}^{m} [p_{it} \cdot (y_{it} - y_{i,t-1})]$, where $p_t = (p_{1t}, \ldots, p_{mt})'$, p_{it} being the price of the i-th asset at time t. Note that the net cost of investment is positive under investment, but can become negative under disinvestment. Assuming that the price of the consumption good c_t is 1, it follows that the individual *budget constraint* at time t is:

$$\pi(y_{t-1}, e_t) = c_t + p_t' \cdot (y_t - y_{t-1}).$$

This simply states that, at time t, the return $\pi(y_{t-1}, e_t)$ is allocated between consumption c_t and investment, $[p_t' \cdot (y_t - y_{t-1})]$. Then, under the expected utility model, the optimal decisions for $[(c_t, y_t): t = 1, \ldots, T]$ are

$$\text{Max}_{c, y} \left\{ \sum_{t=1}^{T} \delta^{t-1} E_1 U(c_t) : \pi(y_{t-1}, e_t) = c_t + p_t' \cdot (y_t - y_{t-1}), \ t = 1, \ldots, T \right\}$$

$$= \text{Max}_y \left\{ \sum_{t=1}^{T} \delta^{t-1} E_1 U[\pi(y_{t-1}, e_t) - p_t' \cdot (y_t - y_{t-1})] \right\},$$

or using the dynamic programming formulation,

$$F_t(y_{t-1}) = \text{Max}_y \{ U[\pi(y_{t-1}, e_t) - p_t' \cdot (y_t - y_{t-1})] + \delta E_t[F_{t+1}(y_t)] \},$$
$$t = T, \ T-1, \ldots, 1.$$

The first-order condition (also called a *Euler equation*) with respect to y_{it} is

$$U_t' \cdot p_{it} = \delta E_t[U_{t+1}' \cdot (p_{i,t+1} + \pi_{i,t+1})],$$

where $U_t' = \partial U(c_t)/\partial c_t$ is the marginal utility of consumption at time t, and $\pi_{i,t+1} = \partial \pi(y_t, e_{t+1})/\partial y_{it}$ is the marginal return from the i-th asset from time t to time $(t+1)$, $i = 1, \ldots, m$. This first-order condition can alternatively be written as

$$1 = E_t[M_{t+1} \cdot g_{i,t+1}],$$

where $M_{t+1} \equiv \delta U_{t+1}'/U_t' > 0$ is the discounted ratio of marginal utilities, and $g_{i,t+1} \equiv (p_{i,t+1} + \pi_{i,t+1})/p_{it}$, $(g_{it} - 1)$ being the marginal rate of return on the i-th asset from time t to time $(t+1)$, $i = 1, \ldots, m$. The term M_{t+1} is the intertemporal marginal rate of substitution and represents time preferences. Because it is not known at time t, it is often called the *stochastic discount factor*.

The previous expression shows that optimal investment in the i-th asset takes place when the expected value of the stochastic discount factor M_{t+1} multiplied by $g_{i,t+1}$ equals 1, $i = 1, \ldots, m$. This formula is known as the *consumption-based capital asset pricing model* (CCAPM). Note that it can be alternatively written as

$$E_t(g_{i,t+1}) = 1/E(M_{t+1}) - \text{Cov}_t(M_{t+1}, g_{i,t+1})/E(M_{t+1}),$$

$i = 1, \ldots, m$. This expression shows that the expected return $E_t(g_{i,t+1})$ is the sum of two terms. The first term, $1/E(M_{t+1})$, is the inverse of the expected discount factor and represents time preferences. The second term is $[-\text{Cov}_t(M_{t+1}, g_{i,t+1})/E(M_{t+1})]$ and reflects risk aversion. Indeed, under risk neutrality (with $U_t'' = 0$), M_{t+1} would be a constant and the covariance term would vanish. This shows that, under risk aversion, the expected return $E_t(g_{i,t+1})$ is inversely related to $\text{Cov}_t(M_{t+1}, g_{i,t+1})$, the covariance between the stochastic discount factor M_{t+1} and $g_{i,t+1}$. Intuitively, as the covariance declines, the i-th asset tends to generate returns that are small when the marginal utility of consumption is high, i.e., when consumption is low. Since such an asset fails to generate wealth when wealth is most valuable, the investor demands a higher return to hold it.

As a special case, consider the utility function $U(c_t) = [c_t^{1-\gamma} - 1]/(1 - \gamma)$. With $U' = c_t^{-\gamma}$, it corresponds to *constant relative risk aversion*, where $\gamma = -c_t U''/U'$ is the relative risk aversion coefficient (see Chapter 4). Then, the stochastic discount factor is $M_t = \delta(c_{t+1}/c_t)^{-\gamma}$, and the CCAPM formula becomes

$$1 = E_t[\delta(c_{t+1}/c_t)^{-\gamma}, g_{i,t+1}],$$

$i = 1, \ldots, m$. Given empirical measurements on prices, consumption path, and rates of return, this expression is empirically tractable. It provides a basis for estimating the risk-aversion parameter γ. It has been at the heart of the "equity premium puzzle." The empirical evidence indicates that returns on equity seem to be too high to be consistent with observed consumption behavior unless investors are extremely risk averse (see Deaton 1992 or Campbell et al. 1997 for an overview). This has raised some doubts on the empirical validity of the CCAPM model.

SEPARATING RISK AVERSION AND INTERTEMPORAL SUBSTITUTION

One attempt to solve the equity premium puzzle involves relaxing the assumption of time additive preferences. Epstein and Zin proposed the following nonadditive specification:

$$U_t = U(c_1, \ldots, c_T) = \{(1 - \delta)c_t^\rho + \delta(E_t[U_{t+1}^\alpha])^{\rho/\alpha}\}^{1/\rho}.$$

This recursive specification involves three parameters: δ reflecting time preferences $(0 < \delta < 1)$; $\rho \leq 1$ capturing intertemporal substitution; and

$\alpha \leq 1$ reflecting risk aversion. Note that, when $\alpha = \rho \neq 0$, the Epstein–Zin specification reduces to $U_t = \{(1 - \delta)c_t^\alpha + \delta E_t[U_{t+1}^\alpha]\}^{1/\alpha} = (1 - \delta) E_t[\sum_{j \geq 0} \delta^j c_{t+j}^\alpha]^{1/\alpha}$, which is time additive. Thus, the Epstein–Zin specification nests the time-additive model as a special case (where $\alpha = 1$ corresponds to risk neutrality). It shows that the time additive model arises when $\alpha = \rho$, i.e. when the risk-aversion parameter and the intertemporal substitution parameter coincide. This highlights how restrictive time additive preferences can be; they cannot distinguish between risk aversion and intertemporal substitution. Epstein and Zin argue that this is unduly restrictive.

Consider the consumption/investment problem just discussed under the Epstein–Zin specification. The associated dynamic programming problem is

$$F_t(y_{t-1}) = \text{Max}_{y_t}\{[(1 - \delta)c_t^\rho + \delta(E_t[(F_{t+1}(y_t))^\alpha])^{\rho/\alpha}]^{1/\rho} : \pi(y_{t-1}, e_t)$$
$$= c_t + p_t' \cdot (y_t - y_{t-1})\},$$

or

$$F_t(y_{t-1}) = \text{Max}_{y_t}\{[(1 - \delta)[\pi(y_{t-1}, e_t) - p_t' \cdot (y_t - y_{t-1})]^\rho$$
$$+ \delta(E_t[(F_{t+1}(y_t))^\alpha])^{\rho/\alpha}]^{1/\rho}\},$$

$t = T, T - 1, \ldots, 1$. The first-order conditions (or Euler equation) with respect to y_t are derived in Epstein and Zin. Using observable data on prices, consumption flows and returns, Epstein and Zin estimate the parameters of these first-order conditions. They provide empirical evidence suggesting that the equity premium puzzle arises in part due to the failure of time-additive models to distinguish between risk aversion and intertemporal substitution (see Campbell et al. 1997 for an overview of the evidence). This suggests that nonadditive preferences can help provide improved insights into the dynamics of risk management.

DISCOUNTING IN THE PRESENCE OF A RISKLESS ASSET

We now investigate the role of a riskless asset in dynamic allocations. For that purpose, we introduce a riskless asset (e.g., a government security) in the above investment analysis. In addition to the m risky assets $y_t = (y_{1t}, \ldots, y_{mt})'$, we consider that the individual can hold a riskless asset z_t that generates a sure rate of return. Throughout, we assume that the unit purchase price of z_t is 1. We consider the case where the riskless asset produces a *constant rate of return* r from one period to the next. It means that buying one unit of z_t at any time t generates a return of $(1 + r)$ at time $(t + 1)$. In this context, z_t is a pure interest-bearing instrument, where r *is the interest rate on the riskless asset per unit of time*. Also, we now allow the price of the consumer good c_t to vary over time. Letting q_t denote the unit price of c_t, the individual budget constraint at time t is

$$\pi(y_{t-1}, e_t) + r\, z_{t-1} = q_t\, c_t + p_t' \cdot (y_t - y_{t-1}) + (z_t - z_{t-1}).$$

The left-hand side is the total return at time t. It includes the return from the risky assets, $\pi(y_{t-1}, e_t)$, plus the return from the riskless asset, $r\, z_{t-1}$. The right-hand side includes consumption expenditure, $q_t c_t$, plus the net cost of investment in the risky assets, $p_t' \cdot (y_t - y_{t-1})$, plus the net cost of investment in the riskless asset, $(z_t - z_{t-1})$. Note that, $(z_t - z_{t-1})$ can represent either saving/lending or borrowing at the riskless rate r: saving/lending corresponds to $(z_t - z_{t-1}) > 0$, while borrowing corresponds to $(z_t - z_{t-1}) < 0$. The budget constraint simply states that, at time t, total return is allocated between consumption and investment.

This budget constraint can be solved for z_{t-1}, yielding

$$z_{t-1} = \beta[q_t c_t + p_t' \cdot (y_t - y_{t-1}) - \pi(y_{t-1}, e_t) + z_t],$$

where $\beta = 1/(1 + r)$ is a *discount factor*. Note that the discount factor satisfies $0 < \beta < 1$ *when* $r > 0$. By successive substitution, this gives

$$z_{t-1} = \beta[q_t c_t + p_t' \cdot (y_t - y_{t-1}) - \pi(y_{t-1}, e_t)] + \beta^2[q_{t+1}c_{t+1} + p_{t+1}'$$
$$\cdot (y_{t+1} - y_t) - \pi(y_t, e_{t+1}) + z_{t+1}],$$

$$= \cdots$$

$$= \sum_{\tau=t}^{T} \beta^{\tau-t+1}[q_\tau c_\tau + p_\tau' \cdot (y_\tau - y_{\tau-1}) - \pi(y_{\tau-1}, e_\tau)] \text{ (assuming } z_T = 0),$$

or, after multiplying by $(1 + r)$,

$$(1 + r)z_{t-1} = \sum_{\tau=t}^{T} \beta^{\tau-t}[q_\tau c_\tau + p_\tau' \cdot (y_\tau - y_{\tau-1}) - \pi(y_{\tau-1}, e_\tau)].$$

This means that, at time t, the *intertemporal budget constraint* can be written as

$$(1 + r)z_{t-1} + \sum_{\tau=t}^{T}[\beta^{\tau-t}\pi(y_{\tau-1}, e_\tau)] = \sum_{\tau=t}^{T}[\beta^{\tau-t}q_\tau c_\tau] + \sum_{\tau=t}^{T}[\beta^{\tau-t}p_\tau' \cdot (y_\tau - y_{\tau-1})].$$

Given a monetary flow $(x_t, \ldots, x_T)$ and a discount factor β, define the *present value of this flow at time* t by

$$PV_t(x_t, \ldots, x_T) = \sum_{\tau=t}^{T}[\beta^{\tau-t}x_\tau],$$

$$= x_t + \beta x_{t+1} + \beta^2 x_{t+2} + \ldots + \beta^T x_T.$$

(Note that, in the case where x_t is constant over time, this reduces to $PV_t(x, \ldots, x) = \sum_{\tau=t}^{T} [\beta^{\tau-t}x] = x[1 - \beta^{T+1}]/[1 - \beta]$). It follows that the intertemporal budget constraint at time t becomes:

$$(1 + r)z_{t-1} + PV_t[\pi(y_{t-1}, e_t), \ldots, \pi(y_{T-1}, e_T)] - PV_t[p_t' \cdot (y_t - y_{t-1}), \ldots,$$
$$p_T' \cdot (y_T - y_{T-1})] = PV_t(q_t c_t, \ldots, q_T c_T).$$

This states that the present value of consumption expenditures, $PV_t(q_t c_t, \ldots, q_T c_T)$, must be equal to $[(1 + r)z_{t-1}]$, plus the present value of risky returns $PV_t[\pi(y_{t-1}, e_t), \ldots, \pi(y_{T-1}, e_T)]$, minus the present value of the net cost of investment, $PV_t[p_t' \cdot (y_t - y_{t-1}), \ldots, p_T' \cdot (y_T - y_{T-1})]$, with $\beta = 1/(1 + r)$ as discount factor. This generates the following important result:

In the presence of a riskless asset yielding a constant rate of return r, all future costs and returns should be valued according to their *present value*, with $\beta = 1/(1 + r)$ as discount factor.

Note the generality of this result. It applies irrespective of the uncertainty facing the decision-maker. And it applies independently of individual preferences with respect to risk or intertemporal substitution (e.g., it applies under risk aversion, as well as under preferences that are not time-additive). This makes sense when one realizes that the derivation relied solely on the individual budget constraint. Intuitively, it means that, given a constant riskless rate r, \$1 today is potentially worth $(1 + r)$ after one period. Alternatively, \$1 next period is worth $1/(1 + r)$ today. This implies that *any future benefit or cost should be discounted using the discount factor $\beta = 1/(1 + r)$, where the riskless interest rate r measures the temporal opportunity cost of money.*

It should be kept in mind that this result was obtained assuming a constant interest rate. This is a restrictive assumption. Note that if the riskless rate is not constant over time, then the analysis still applies but the discount factor needs to be modified and becomes more complex (e.g., see Luenberger 1998).

THE TWO-PERIOD CASE

Often, realistic models involve situations where the underlying dynamics require many state variables (e.g., reflecting physical capital, human capital, ecological capital, etc.). In this case, solving for the optimal decision rules can become extremely complex. This is called the *"curse of dimensionality"* in dynamic programming. It means that when dynamics involve many state variables, there is no practical way of finding a general solution to the dynamic optimization problem (even using the latest and fastest computers). Yet, individuals still make decisions. They develop decision rules that map current information into current decisions. This involves two significant difficulties: (1) assessing current information (which can be hard when it involves many random variables and/or many states); and (2) deciding how this information can be used in the design of individual decision rules. These difficulties suggest that the cost of obtaining and processing information can play a significant role in choosing decision rules. In some cases, this can lead the decision-maker to choose simple "rules of thumb" as a means of simplifying the decision-making process. The choice of simple decision rules can be associated with "bounded rationality" when the complexity of a decision means that the decision-maker is unable to process all the relevant information. More generally, simple decision rules can arise when the cost of obtaining and processing information is high. This can help justify why some costly information is often disregarded in decision-making. Yet invariably, at least some information is used and processed by the decision-maker (e.g., weather conditions, technology, market conditions). How much information is obtained is often subject to management. For example, weather forecasts can help anticipate future weather conditions. Experience can help generate information about technological possibilities. And market conditions can be anticipated through market and price analyses. In these cases, active learning (i.e., acquiring and processing information) is likely to be an important part of the decision-making process. Then, the choice of information must involve weighing the benefit of additional information against its cost. These issues are investigated below.

These arguments indicate how difficult it can be to conduct empirical analyses of dynamic economic behavior. This suggests the need for some simplifying assumptions. Below, we focus our attention on a two-period model ($T = 2$). A two-period model is the simplest possible dynamic model. While such a model may appear too simple to be realistic, it will provide a basis to generate insights on the role of risk in dynamic decisions. As a special case of the general model previously discussed, we consider the decisions $x = (x_1, x_2)$ made in a way consistent with the maximization problem

$$\text{Max}_{x_1} \; E_1\{\text{Max}_{x_2} \; E_2\{U(w, \; x_1, \; x_2, \; e)\}\},$$

where the choice of x is implicitly assumed subject to feasibility constraints. Note that this captures the essence of general dynamic optimization problems. Indeed, in the spirit of a stage-wise decomposition of dynamic programming, this can represent a general situation when the function $U(w, \; x_1, \; x_2, \; e)$ is interpreted as the "value function" at time $t = 2$, reflecting the effects of dynamic decisions made beyond the second period.

Assume that information is obtained between time $t = 1$ and $t = 2$ by observing random variables u_1. This informs the decision-maker about the uncertainty e, and helps him/her make the period-two decisions. Let x_1^* and x_2^* denote the optimal decisions in the above problem. Then x_1^* is the ex-ante decision made before the message u_1 is observed. In contrast $x_2^*(u_1, \cdot)$ is a decision rule that provides "feedback," reflecting how the message u_1 influences the x_2 decisions.

THE VALUE OF INFORMATION

The first relevant question is, is new information valuable in individual decision-making process? Answering this question requires defining the value of information. First, note that the second-period decision involves the maximization problem $\text{Max}_{x_2} E_2\{U(w, x_1, x_2, e)\}$. It means that, conditional on x_1, the ex-ante evaluation (based on the information available at time $t = 1$) of choosing x_2 at time $t = 2$ is given by the expected utility $E_1\{\text{Max}_{x_2} E_2\{U(w, x_1, x_2, e)\}\}$. We would like to know how the decision-maker is valuing the information that becomes available between the two periods.

1. The Selling Price of Information

Consider the case where the decision-maker is forced to make the second period decision without learning, i.e., without observing u_1. For a given x_1, this corresponds to the maximization problem $\text{Max}_{x_2} E_1\{U(w, x_1, x_2, e)\}$. Define S as the value implicitly satisfying:

$$\text{Max}_{x_2} E_1\{U(w + S, x_1, x_2, e)\} = E_1\text{Max}_{x_2} E_2\{U(w, x_1, x_2, e)\}.$$

S is the *selling price* of the information provided by u_1. Indeed, S is the smallest amount of money the decision-maker would be willing to accept to choose x_2 without knowing u_1, using the informed situation as a reference.

2. The Bid Price of Information

Alternatively, define B as the value implicitly satisfying:

$$\text{Max}_{x_2} E_1\{U(w, x_1, x_2, e)\} = E_1\text{Max}_{x_2} E_2\{U(w - B, x_1, x_2, e)\}.$$

B is the *bid price* of the information associated with u_1. Indeed, B is the largest amount of money the decision-maker would be willing to pay for the opportunity to choose x_2 knowing u_1, using the uninformed situation as a reference.

In general, note that B and S can differ (see Lavalle 1978). However, the bid price B and the selling price S of information can be shown to be identical under risk neutrality or under CARA preferences. These are situations where wealth effects vanish (see Problem 1 on page 159). In other words, differences between the bid price B and the selling price of information S can be attributed to income or wealth effects.

Both S and B can depend on initial wealth w (when risk preferences depart from risk neutrality or CARA) and on the period one decisions x_1. Thus, they take the general form: $S(w, x_1)$ *and* $B(w, x_1)$. This shows that both values of information are *conditional* on the x_1 decisions. This means that period-one decisions can have a direct effect on how valuable the forthcoming information is. As we will see below, this effect is particularly relevant in individual decision-making under situations of irreversibility.

3. Costless Information is Valuable

Both the selling price and the bid price of information have been evaluated by comparing decision-making with and without information. However, the change in information was implicitly assumed to be *costless*. This means that $S(w, x_1)$ *and* $B(w, x_1)$ measure the value of *costless information*. If information is actually costless, then they are the net value of information. Otherwise, they should be interpreted as measuring the *gross value of information*, i.e., the value of information before its cost is taken into consideration.

What can we say in general about the value of costless information (or equivalently about the gross value of information) in individual decision-making? The key result is the following:

The gross value of information is always nonnegative: $S(w, x_1) \geq 0$ and $B(w, x_1) \geq 0$ for any (w, x_1).

To see that, note that, by definition of a maximum,

$$\text{Max}_{x_2} \, E_2\{U(w, x_1, x_2, e)\} \geq E_2\{U(w, x_1, x_2, e)\},$$

or

$$\text{Max}_{x_2}\left\{\int f_2(e|u_1, \cdot)U(w, x_1, x_2, e)de\right\} \geq \int f_2(e|u_1, \cdot)U(w, x_1, x_2, e)de,$$

for any feasible (x_1, x_2). Let $f_1(e, u_1, \cdot)$ denote the joint probability function of (e, u_1) based on the subjective information available at time $t = 1$. Since $f_1(e, u_1, \cdot) \geq 0$, it follows that

$$\iint f_1(\varepsilon, u_1, \cdot)\text{Max}_{x_2}\left\{\int f_2(e|u_1, \cdot)U(w, x_1, x_2, e)de\right\}du_1 d\varepsilon$$

$$\geq \iint f_1(\varepsilon, u_1, \cdot)\int f_2(e|u_1, \cdot)U(w, x_1, x_2, e)dedu_1 d\varepsilon,$$

which can be written equivalently as

$$E_1 \text{Max}_{x_2} E_2\{U(w,\ x_1,\ x_2,\ e)\} \geq E_1\{U(w,\ x_1,\ x_2,\ e)\},$$

for any $(x_1,\ x_2)$. But this implies

$$E_1 \text{Max}_{x_2} E_2\{U(w,\ x_1,\ x_2,\ e)\} \geq \text{Max}_{x_2} E_1\{U(w,\ x_1,\ x_2,\ e)\}, \tag{1}$$

for any x_1. Given a positive marginal utility of wealth, $U' \equiv (\partial U/\partial w > 0$, this yields the key results: $S(w,\ x_1) \geq 0$ and $B(w,\ x_1) \geq 0$.

Thus, the value of costless information has zero as a lower bound. This shows that costless information is in general valuable. The reason is that new information helps refine the period-two decision rule $x_2^*(u_1,\ \cdot)$, thus improving the decisions made at time $t = 2$. At worst, the new information may be worthless (e.g., when the signals u_1 are distributed independently of e), in which case it would not be used ($x_2^*(u_1,\ \cdot)$ being the same for all u_1), yielding $S(w,\ x_1) = 0$ and $B(w,\ x_1) = 0$. But in all cases where the signals u_1 provide some information about e, then the period-two decisions $x_2^*(u_1,\ \cdot)$ will typically depend on u_1, yielding $S(w,\ x_1) > 0$ and $B(w,\ x_1) > 0$. In such situations, the gross value of new information is positive.

While the value of costless information has a lower bound (zero), does it also have an upper bound? Consider the case where u_1 is perfectly correlated with e. This is the situation where the message u_1 provides perfect information about e. In this case, S and B measure the *value of perfect information*. Denote them by S^+ *and* B^+. They measure the gross benefit of making the period-two decisions under perfect information, with $x_2^*(u_1,\ \cdot)$ being an ex post decision rule. Since it is not possible to learn beyond perfect information, it follows that S^+ *and* B^+ provide a general upper bound on the value of information. Thus, in general, the gross value of information is bounded as follows:

$$0 \leq S(w,\ x_1) \leq S^+(w,\ x_1),$$

and

$$0 \leq B(w,\ x_1) \leq B^+(w,\ x_1).$$

In any specific learning situation, the gross value of information (S or B) will always be between these bounds. It will be close to 0 when the quality of the information provided by u_1 is poor. And it will get close to its upper bound (S^+ or B^+) when the signals u_1 are particularly informative about e.

These results show that, if information were costless, the decision-maker would always choose to obtain perfect information. This means that imperfect information must be associated with costly information. Since imperfect information is pervasive in economic decision-making, this implies that costly information must also be pervasive. The issue of choosing information when it is costly will be further examined.

The Risk Neutral Case

Consider a *risk neutral* decision-maker facing an uncertain profit $\pi(x_1, x_2, e)$ where e is a random variable with a prior subjective probability function $f_1(e)$. A signal u_1 is observed after the first-period decision x_1 but before the second-period decision x_2. Let $k(u_1|e)$ denote the likelihood function of u_1 given e. (That this corresponds to passive learning if $k(\cdot)$ does not depend on x_1.) From Bayes' theorem, the posterior probability function of e given u_1 is: $f_2(e|u_1) = f_1(e)k(u_1|e)/[\sum_u \{f_1(e)k(u_1|e)\}]$ (assuming discrete random variables). And the marginal probability function of u_1 is $[\sum_e f_1(e)k(u_1|e)]$. Under risk neutrality, $S = B$. The value of information generated by the signal u_1 is

$$S = B = E_1 \max_{x_2} E_2\pi(x_1, x_2, e) - \max_{x_2} E_1\pi(x_1, x_2, e)$$

$$= \sum_u \left\{ \left[\sum_e f_1(e)k(u_1|e)\right] \max_{x_2} \sum_e f_2(e|u_1)\pi(x_1, x_2, e) \right\}$$

$$- \max_{x_2}\left\{ \sum_e f_1(e)\pi(x_1, x_2, e)\right\}$$

And the value of perfect information is

$$S^+ = B^+ = E_1 \max_{x_2}\pi(x_1, x_2, e) - \max_{x_2} E_1\pi(x_1, x_2, e)$$

$$= \sum_e \{f_1(e)\max_{x_2}\pi(x_1, x_2, e)\} - \max_{x_2}\left\{\sum_e f_1(e)\pi(x_1, x_2, e)\right\}.$$

Under risk neutrality, these expressions provide the basis for the empirical investigation of the value of information (see Problem 2 on page 159).

4. Relationship Between the Value of Information and the Risk Premium:

We have just shown that costless information is in general valuable in individual decision-making. This result has one striking characteristic. It was obtained under general risk preferences. In particular, such a result applies whether the decision-maker is risk neutral, risk averse, or even risk lover. This is in sharp contrast with the Arrow–Pratt risk premium, which was presented in Chapter 4 as a measure of the implicit cost of risk. Indeed, the risk premium does depend on risk preferences (e.g., the risk premium is positive if and only if the decision-maker is risk averse). Thus, it appears that both learning (the acquisition of information) and risk preferences (e.g., risk aversion) can influence individual behavior toward risk. This raises the question, is there any relationship between the risk premium (as discussed in Chapter 4) and the gross value of information?

To answer this question, consider the case discussed in Chapter 4 where $U(\cdot) = U(w + \pi(x_1,\ x_2,\ e))$ is the basic preference function, and $\pi(x_1 x_2,\ e)$ denotes the profit function. From the definition of the *selling price of information S*, we have

$$E_1 \text{Max}_{x_2} E_2 U(w + \pi(x_1,\ x_2,\ e)) = \text{Max}_{x_2} E_1 U(w + S(w,\ x_1,\ \cdot) \\ + \pi(x_1,\ x_2,\ e)), \tag{2}$$

Let $x_2^*(w,\ x_1,\ u_1)$ be the optimal choice of x_2 in the left-hand side optimization problem above. Also, denote by $F(w,\ x_1,\ u_1) = E_2 U[w + \pi(x_1,\ x_2^*(w, x_1,\ u_1),\ e)]$ the *induced preference* function. In general, the curvature of $F(\cdot)$ is different from the curvature of $U(\cdot)$. Thus, $F(\cdot)$ *and* $U(\cdot)$ have different implications for economic behavior toward risk.

To identify the role of risk aversion in the presence of learning, consider the *Arrow–Pratt risk premium R* based on the basic preference function $U(\cdot)$. Define it as the monetary value $R(w,\ x_1)$ that implicitly satisfies:

$$\text{Max}_{x_2} E_1 U(w + S(w,\ x_1) + \pi(x_1,\ x_2,\ e)) \\ = \text{Max}_{x_2} E_1 U(w + S(w,\ x_1) + E_1 \pi(x_1,\ x_2,\ e) - R(w,\ x_1)). \tag{3}$$

From equation (2), the left-hand side of (3) is the objective function for the period-one decisions x_1. It follows that the right-hand side in (3) is an alternative formulation for this objective function. This indicates how both the Arrow–Pratt risk premium R and the gross value of information S can affect period-one decisions x_1. In particular, it shows that the net welfare effect of risk is measured by the monetary value $[S(w,\ x_1) - R(w,\ x_1)]$, where S is the implicit benefit of reducing risk through learning, and R is the implicit cost of private risk bearing evaluated at time $t = 1$. In this context, dynamic risk management involves attempts to increase the net benefit $[S(w,\ x_1) - R(w,\ x_1)]$. This points to two directions: (1) the individual can try to learn about his/her uncertain environment so as to increase $S(w,\ x_1)$; and (2) the risk averse individual can try to reduce his/her exposure to ex-ante risk, thus lowering $R(w,\ x_1)$. This shows that both the value of information S and the risk premium R are relevant concepts in the evaluation of the welfare effects of risk, although they each measure something quite different. To the extent that decisions are typically made in a dynamic context, this stresses the need to distinguish between them in empirical risk evaluation.

THE VALUE OF ADAPTIVE STRATEGIES

In individual decision-making, the value of information has a useful corollary: the value of adaptive strategies. In a multiperiod planning horizon, a strategy is said to be adaptive if dynamic decisions are influenced by new information as it becomes available. In the two-period model, an adaptive strategy means that the decision rule for x_2 is expressed in "feedback form" $x_2^*(u_1, \cdot)$, which depends on the observed signal u_1.

The key result is stated next:

At the optimum, an adaptive strategy is always at least as good as a nonadaptive strategy.

To see that, from equation (1) derived previously, we have:

$$E_1 \text{ Max}_{x_2} E_2 U(w, x_1, x_2, e) \geq \text{Max}_{x_2} E_1 U(w, x_1, x_2, e) \geq E_1 U(w, x_1, x_2, e),$$

for any feasible $x = (x_1, x_2)$. It follows that

$$\text{Max}_{x_1} E_1 \text{ Max}_{x_2} E_2 U(w, x_1, x_2, e) \geq E_1 U(w, x_1, x_2, e), \qquad (4)$$

for any feasible $x = (x_1, x_2)$. The left-hand side of the above equation measures the ex-ante utility received by the decision-maker under an optimal adaptive strategy (where information feedback is used in the x_2 decisions). The right-hand side measures the ex-ante utility obtained by the decision-maker under arbitrary feasible strategies, including all possible nonadaptive strategies. The inequality in equation (4) establishes the general superiority of adaptive strategies. It simply means that individuals who acquire information about their economic environment and use this information in their decision-making tend to benefit from it. This is just a formal statement about the characteristics and rewards of good management.

IMPLICATIONS FOR PERIOD ONE DECISIONS

It is now clear that information management is important. But what does it imply for the period-one decisions? To investigate this issue, consider the adaptive dynamic programming problem:

$$\text{Max}_{x_1} E_1 \text{ Max}_{x_2} E_2 U(w, x_1, x_2, e)$$

By definition of the selling price of information S, we have

$$\text{Max}_{x_2} E_2 U(w, x_1, x_2, e) = \text{Max}_{x_2} E_1 U(w + S(w, x_1), x_1, x_2, e).$$

It follows that

$$\text{Max}_{x_1} E_1 \text{ Max}_{x_2} E_2 U(w, x_1, x_2, e) = \text{Max}_{x_1, x_2} E_1 U(w + S(w, x_1), x_1, x_2, e). \quad (5)$$

Note that these two expressions give equivalent optimal solutions for the period-one decision x_1. While the left-hand side in (5) is the standard dynamic programming solution, the right-hand side in (5) corresponds to an ex-ante decision where the decision-maker is compensated (through S) for not being able to learn over time. Under differentiability and assuming an interior solution, the first-order condition with respect to x_1 for the right-hand side problem is:

$$E_1 \partial U / \partial x_1 + E_1 (\partial U / \partial w) \partial S(w, \ x_1) / \partial x_1 = 0$$

or

$$\partial S(w, \ x_1) / \partial x_1 + (E_1 \partial U / \partial x_1) / (E_1 \partial U / \partial w) = 0.$$

This states that, at the optimum, the marginal net benefit of x_1 must be zero. Here, the marginal net benefit involves two additive parts: the marginal value of information, $\partial S(w, \ x_1) / \partial x_1$; and the more standard marginal benefit $(E_1 \partial U / \partial x_1) / (E_1 \partial U / \partial w)$. Note that this result is quite general (e.g., it applies under risk neutrality, risk aversion, or even risk-loving behavior). As such, it appears relevant in a wide variety of situations.

Note that there are scenarios under which the marginal value of information vanishes, with $\partial S(w, \ x_1) / \partial x_1 = 0$. This happens when the gross value of information $S(w, \ x_1) \geq 0$ is independent of x_1. Then, the first-period decision x_1 is not affected by learning; it is the same as the one that would be chosen without information acquisition. This happens to hold when the "certainty equivalent principle" applies. The *certainty equivalent principle* means that the optimal first-period decision can be obtained simply by replacing the random variable e by its mean $E(e)$. It is extremely convenient in empirical analyses; it basically separates the issues of uncertainty estimation from optimal control of a dynamic system. This has proved very useful in engineering applications. This is exemplified by the great success of NASA's space program. Under the certainty equivalent principle, large computers can calculate ahead of time optimal decision rules, rules that are then used to map quickly the latest information about the position of the spacecraft into an optimal response of its rocket to maintain the intended course. Under which conditions does the certainty equivalent principle holds? It applies when the objective function can be written in quadratic form (see Problems 3 and 4 on page 160). To the extent that quadratic functions can provide good second-order local approximations to any differentiable function, this may be seen as being approximately valid under rather general conditions. Unfortunately, quadratic approximations may not always be realistic. When applied to dynamic behavior under the expected utility hypothesis, the certainty equivalent principle would apply when the utility function $U(w, \ x_1, \ x_2, \ e)$ is quadratic. But we saw in Chapter 3 that quadratic utility functions are indeed restrictive (e.g., they cannot exhibit decreasing absolute risk aversion). In other words, quadratic approximations can be rather poor in the analysis of risk behavior.

This suggests that the certainty equivalent principle does not apply to many situations of human decision-making under uncertainty. Again, this points to the existence of empirical tradeoffs between the convenience of simple models and realism. If the certainty equivalent principle does not hold, we need to evaluate how new information affects decisions. In the context of our two-period model, this means understanding how the gross value of information $S(w, x_1)$ varies with the first-period decision x_1. It appears that such effects are *pervasive* in the economics of risk. The value of information S can vary with x_1 in two ways. It can be increasing in x_1, corresponding to situations where learning tends to increase the use of x_1. Or it can be decreasing in x_1, corresponding to scenarios where new information tends to reduce the choice of x_1. The exact nature of these effects depends on the particular situation considered. This is illustrated in the following example:

The Case of Irreversible Decisions

Following Arrow and Fisher, consider the following decision problem. At time t, a manager must choose between implementing a given project (denoted by $x_t = 1$), or not (denoted by $x_t = 0$), $t = 1, 2$. The project development is *irreversible*. The irreversibility is represented by: $x_1 + x_2 \leq 1$. This implies that

. if $x_1 = 0$, then $x_2 =$ either 0 or 1, yielding $S(w, 0) \geq 0$,
. if $x_1 = 1$, then $x_2 = 0$, yielding $S(w, 1) = 0$ (since there is no flexibility in making the x_2 decision).

Using equation (5), the x_1 decision can be represented by the maximization problem

$$\text{Max}_{x_1, x_2} \ EU(w + S(w, x_1), x_1, x_2, e)$$

This implies

choose $x_1 = 1$, if $E_1 U(w, 1, 0, e) > \text{Max}_{x_2} E_1 U(w + S(w, 0), 0, x_2, e)$
   $= 0$, otherwise.

The term $S(w, 0)$ has been called the "*quasi-option value*" by Arrow and Fisher. The above result shows that the value of information $S(w, x_1)$ (the quasi-option value) reflects the valuation of keeping a flexible position in future decisions. It provides an *incentive to delay an irreversible decision*. This has two important implications. First, it means that neglecting the role of information would generate recommendations that would be incorrectly biased in favor of the irreversible development. Second, it illustrates that in the presence of irreversibility, information valuation provides incentives to avoid the irreversible state. Note that this result is quite general and does not depend on risk preferences. It gives important insights into management decisions under risk and irreversibility (see Dixit and Pindyck 1994). Classical examples of irreversibility include soil erosion (at least when topsoil is thin) or species extinction; if lost, neither soil nor endangered species can be replaced within any human planning horizon. This shows that the valuation of information provides extra economic incentives for conservation strategies trying to prevent the irreversible state.

ACTIVE LEARNING UNDER COSTLY INFORMATION

We have argued that active learning is a pervasive characteristic of individual decision-making. In general, acquiring information involves search, experimentation, etc. To illustrate the optimality of active learning, consider the simple case where x_1 is a vector of information gathering activities *only*, $C(x_1)$ denoting the cost of gathering and processing the information produced by x_1. This corresponds to the following problem:

$$\text{Max}_{x_1} \, E_1 \, \text{Max}_{x_2} \, E_2 U(w - C(x_1), \, x_2, \, e).$$

Define the gross value of information to be the selling price $S(w, \, x_1)$ satisfying:

$$\text{Max}_{x_2} \, E_1 U(w - C(x_1) + S(w, \, x_1), \, x_2, \, e) = E_1 \, \text{Max}_{x_2} \, E_2 U(w - C(x_1), \, x_2, \, e).$$

From equation (5), the x_1 decision can be written as

$$\text{Max}_{x_1, x_2} E_1 U(w - C(x_1) + S(w, x_1), x_2, e) = \text{Max}_{x_1} E_1 \, \text{Max}_{x_2} E_2 U(w - C(x_1), x_2, e)$$

Using the left-hand side of the above expression, and assuming a positive marginal utility of wealth ($U' = \partial U / \partial w > 0$), it follows that optimal learning corresponds to

$$\text{Max}_{x_1} \{ S(w, \, x_1) - C(x_1) \}.$$

This defines the *net value of information* (S – C) as being equal to the *gross value of information* $S(w, \, x_1)$ minus the *cost of information* $C(x_1)$. It indicates that optimal learning takes place when the net value of information is maximized with respect to x_1. Note that this intuitive result is general in the sense that it applies under risk aversion, risk neutrality, as well as under risk-loving behavior. Under differentiability, the first-order condition for an interior solution is

$$\partial S / \partial x_1 = \partial C / \partial x_1.$$

This gives the classical result that optimal learning takes place at the point where the marginal value $\partial S/\partial x_1$ equals marginal cost $\partial C/\partial x_1$.

However, there may be situations where the solution for x_1 is a corner solution: $x_1 = 0$. This may occur when the cost of information C is high and the value of information S is relatively low (e.g., because the information is complex, difficult to process, and/or difficult to use). In such situations, there would be little incentive to learn. This may be prevalent when individuals face a complex economic environment involving many sources of uncertainty. Then, individuals may obtain and use only a small fraction of the available information. This would generate an incentive for individuals to *specialize* to process only the subset of information that is closely associated with some specific task. Having different individuals specializing in different tasks and processing different information may then appear efficient. But that requires exchanges among differentially informed individuals. Evaluating the decision rules supporting such exchanges is the topic of the following chapters.

PROBLEMS

Note: An asterisk (*) indicates that the problem has an accompanying Excel file on the web page http://www.aae.wisc.edu/chavas/risk.htm.

1. Consider a risk-averse decision-maker facing an uncertain profit $\pi(x_1, x_2, e)$. His/her risk preferences are represented by the utility function $U(w + \pi(x_1, x_2, e))$.

   a. Assume that the decision-maker exhibits *constant absolute risk aversion*.

   - How does the selling price of information S differ from its bid price B?
   - How does the gross value of information vary with initial wealth w?

   b. Assume that the decision-maker exhibits *decreasing absolute risk aversion*.

   - How does the selling price of information S differ from its bid price B?
   - How does the gross value of information vary with initial wealth w?

*2. Mr. Smith has to choose between contracts to purchase either 1,000, 1,200, or 1,600 cattle for fattening on summer pasture. His profit depends on whether the pasture growing season is good, fair, or poor—for which events his subjective likelihood is .3, .4, and .3 respectively. The budgeted consequences, in terms of dollar profits per animal, are as follows:

Type of season	Buy 1,000	Buy 1,200	Buy 1,600
good	18	20	25
fair	10	8	6
poor	8	2	−8

If desired, Mr. Smith can purchase a forecast of the type of season for $300. His subjective likelihoods for this forecast are as follows:

		forecast (u)		
likelihood of forecast, k(u|e)		good	fair	poor
Type of season (e)	good	.6	.3	.1
	fair	.2	.5	.3
	poor	.1	.3	.6

Mr. Smith is risk neutral.
   a. What is the prior optimal act?
   b. What is the value of a perfect weather predictor?
   c. What is the maximum price that Mr. Smith would pay for the actual weather prediction?
   d. Should Mr. Smith purchase the weather forecast?
   e. What is Mr. Smith's optimal strategy?
Interpret your results.
   3. Consider a risk-neutral decision-maker facing an uncertain profit $\pi(x_1, x_2, e)$. Assume that the profit function is *quadratic*: $\pi(x_1, x_2, e) = a_0 + a_1x_1 + 0.5a_2\,x_1^2 + a_3x_2 + 0.5a_4x_2^2 + a_5x_1x_2 + b_1e + b_2e^2 + b_3ex_1 + b_4ex_2$, where $a_4 < 0$ and e is a random variable with mean $E(e) = 0$ and variance $V(e) = \sigma^2$.
   a. Find the optimal ex post decision for x_2.
   b. What is the value of perfect information?
   c. The decision-maker obtains information before choosing x_2 by observing a random variable u that is correlated with e. What is the value of information associated with observing u?
   d. Does the value of information varies with x_1? Interpret.
   4. Consider a risk-neutral decision-maker facing an uncertain profit $\pi(x_1, x_2, e)$. Assume that the profit function is: $\pi(x_1, x_2, e) = a_0 + a_1x_1 + 0.5a_2x_1^2 + a_3x_2 + 0.5a_4x_2^2 + a_5x_1x_2 + b_1e + b_2e^2 + b_3ex_1 + b_4ex_2 + b_5ex_1x_2$, where $a_4 < 0$ and e is a random variable with mean $E(e) = 0$ and variance $V(e) = \sigma^2$. (Note the presence of the third-order term "$b_5\,e\,x_1\,x_2$.")
   a. Find the optimal ex post decision for x_2.
   b. What is the value of perfect information?
   c. The decision-maker obtains information before choosing x_2 by observing a random variable u that is correlated with e. What is the value of information associated with observing u?
   d. Does the value of information vary with x_1? Interpret.

Chapter 11

Contract and Policy Design Under Risk

Previous chapters have analyzed the implications of risk for the welfare and behavior of a decision-maker. We have investigated how an individual can manage risk and information. However, individual decision-making must always be situated within its broader economic context. The institutions and economic environment surrounding an individual can themselves be sources of uncertainty (e.g., the case of theft). Alternatively, the economic institutions affecting individual behavior are themselves subject to management. This includes the establishment of property rights, the development and enforcement of contracts among individuals, and the design and implementation of policy rules. Such schemes play an important role in risk management for two reasons. First, they condition the type and magnitude of risk exposure facing a particular individual. Second, they allow for risk transfers among individuals. These risk transfers can take many forms: risk sharing schemes as specified in contracts (e.g., the case of sharecropping under uncertainty); insurance protection (e.g., fire or medical insurance); limited liability rules (e.g., bankruptcy protection); or social safety nets (e.g., disaster relief managed by government or NGO). The design and implementation of risk transfer schemes among individuals are an important aspect of risk management. This chapter focuses on the economics and efficiency of such schemes.

We will first develop a general model of resource allocation among individuals. This will include individual risk management as well as risk transfers across individuals. This provides a basis for analyzing the efficiency of resource allocation, as well as the efficiency of risk transfers. The generality of the analysis means that it can be applied to a variety of empirical situations. It will provide the general guidelines for evaluating the efficiency of risk allocation. The problem is that such evaluations can become quite complex. This means that making the analysis empirically tractable is a significant challenge. This chapter focuses on the general principles of efficient risk allocation. Specific applications are discussed in Chapter 12.

A GENERAL MODEL

Consider n individuals making allocation decisions under risk. Each individual is involved in the production, exchange, and/or consumption of m private goods. The production activities of the i-th individual involve choosing the m inputs-outputs $x_i = (x_{1i}, \ldots, x_{mi})$, $i = 1, \ldots, n$. It will be convenient to the use netput notation where outputs in x_i are positive and inputs are negative. Let $y_i = (y_{1i}, \ldots, y_{mi})$ denote the quantities of the m commodities consumed by the i-th individual. In addition to production and consumption decisions, the n individuals can exchange the m commodities with each other. Let $t_{ij} = (t_{1ij}, \ldots, t_{mij})$ denote the quantities of the m goods traded from individual i to individual j (including exchange with oneself when $i = j$). Exchange may involve the use of resources (e.g., information, transportation). Denote by $h_i = (h_{1i}, \ldots, h_{mi})$ the amount of the m goods used by the i-th individual in the exchange process. In general, the $h_i's$ reflect the presence of transaction costs; it measures the amount of resources used in exchange among the n individuals. Finally, the n individuals face a vector of public goods q (e.g., infrastructure). We want to investigate the efficiency of the allocation $z = (q, h, x, y, t)$, where $h = (h_1, \ldots, h_n)$, $x = (x_1, \ldots, x_n)$, $y = (y_1, \ldots, y_n)$, and $t = (t_{ij} : i, j = 1, \ldots, n)$.

The n individuals make decisions under uncertainty. The uncertainty is represented by discrete random variables. The realized values of these random variables define mutually exclusive states. Assume there are S mutually exclusive states, represented by $e = (e_1, \ldots, e_s)$. In principle, when made by informed decision-makers, the decision z can depend on the states e. Thus, we consider *state-dependent decision rules* $z^e = z(e) = (z_1(e), z_2(e), \ldots)$, where $z_k(e) = (z_k(e_1), \ldots, z_k(e_s))$, and $z_k(e_s)$ is the k-th decision made under the s-th state of nature, $s = 1, \ldots, S$. This includes $t(e)$, the state-dependent exchange of goods among the n individuals. When this exchange is state-dependent, it allows the transfer of risk across individuals. Now we must evaluate the efficiency of such risk transfers.

The i-th individual has preferences represented by an ex-ante utility function $u_i(q^e, y_i^e)$, where $q^e = q(e) = (q(e_1), \ldots, q(e_s))$, and $y_i^e = y_i(e) = (y_i(e_1), \ldots, y_i(e_s))$, $q(e_s)$ denoting the public goods under state s, and $y_i(e_s)$ denoting the i-th individual consumption of the m private goods under state s,

$i = 1, \ldots, n$. Following Debreu (1959), this is a *state-dependent preference function* (see Chapter 4). It represents the i-th individual ex-ante subjective evaluation of the allocation y_i^e for all states. Note that this is quite general since the subjective evaluation can be made without relying on a probability distribution. However, it is often convenient to make explicit use of probability assessments. For example, if the i-th individual assigns a probability $Pr(e_s, i)$ to the s-th state, then the ex-ante utility function may take the form $u_i(q^e, y^e, Pr(e_1, i), \ldots, Pr(e_s, i))$, which can be nonlinear in the probabilities. This includes as a special case the expected utility model: $u_i(\cdot) = \sum_{s=1}^{s} Pr(e_s, i) v_i(q(e_s), y(e_s))$, where $v_i(\cdot)$ is the von Neumann–Morgenstern utility function representing the risk preferences of the i-th individual, $i = 1, \ldots, n$. This shows that while the following analysis applies under the expected utility model, it actually holds under much more general conditions (including situations where risk preferences are nonlinear in probabilities).

First, we need to characterize feasible allocations. One aspect of feasibility relates to the information available to decision-makers. This information can impose restrictions on the state-dependent decision rules $z^e = z(e) = (z_1(e), z_2(e), \ldots)$. Assume that each decision is made based on possibly different information. This allows for asymmetric information across individuals as well as learning (if different decisions are made at different times based on different information). Assume that the k-th decision is made based on information characterized by an information partition $P_k = (P_{k1}, P_{k2}, \ldots)$ of the set of states $\{e_1, e_2, \ldots, e_s\}$. For each k, the P_{kj}'s are mutually exclusive subsets of $\{e_1, e_2, \ldots, e_s\}$ and their union is the set $\{e_1, e_2, \ldots, e_s\}$. Intuitively, each P_{kj} contains the states that are not distinguishable for the purpose of making the k-th decision. It means that the k-th decision must satisfy the information constraint

$$z_k(e_s) = z_k(e_{s'}) \text{ for any two } e_s \text{ and } e_{s'} \text{ both in } P_{kj} \text{ for each } j, k = 1, 2, \ldots \quad (1)$$

Equation (1) reflects how information affects the decision rule $z_k(e)$. It includes as a special case two extreme situations. At one extreme, perfect information corresponds to $P_{ks} = e_s, s = 1, \ldots, S$. Then, $z_k(e)$ is chosen ex-post and can vary across states as (1) imposes no restriction. At the other extreme, no information corresponds to $P_{k1} = \{e_1, e_2, \ldots, e_s\}$. Then, (1) implies that the decision $z_k(e)$ is chosen ex-ante and is constrained to be the same across all states. In intermediate situations, equation (1) restricts the k-th decision to be the same across states that are not distinguishable, but allows it to differ across states otherwise. Given that $P_k = (P_{k1}, P_{k2}, \ldots)$ is the information supporting the k-th decision, we denote by $P = \{P_1, P_2, \ldots\}$ the information structure supporting all decisions across all individuals.

In addition to the information constraint (1), an allocation must be feasible. Besides satisfying budget constraints, consumption feasibility reduces to nonnegativity restrictions on the consumption goods: $y_i^e = y_i(e) \geq 0$, $i = 1, \ldots, n$. Denote production feasibility by $(q^e, x^e) = (q(e), x(e)) \in X(P)$, where the feasible set $X(P)$ represents the production technology under information structure P. This simply means that the goods (q^e, x^e) are feasibly produced in the economy from the activities of the n individuals. Finally, the quantities traded t can also involve both private goods h (e.g., transportation activities) and public goods q (e.g., infrastructure) used to support exchange. Exchange feasibility is denoted by $(q^e, h^e, t^e) \in T(P)$, where the feasible set $T(P)$ represents the exchange technology under information structure P. When transactions are costly, this simply means that feasible trade t requires the use of resources (as reflected by q^e and h^e).

Note that, besides the public goods q^e that are available to all individuals, the model allows for *external effects* across individuals. External effects arise when an individual makes a decision that also affects directly the feasible set or the welfare of some other individual. In this model, the externalities can take place in production as well as in trade. Indeed, the feasible set X allows for external effects in production activities across individuals. These external effects can be positive (e.g., the case of the fruit producer who benefits from his/her beekeeper neighbor) or negative (e.g., the case of pollution). Similarly, the feasible set T allows for externalities in trade activities. This will provide useful insights on the effects of externalities on efficient resource allocation.

Finally, the feasibility of exchanging the m private goods among the n individuals must satisfy

$$\sum_{j=1}^{n} t_{ij}(e_s) \leq x_i(e_s) - h_i(e_s), \tag{2a}$$

and

$$y_i(e_s) \leq \sum_{j=1}^{n} t_{ji}(e_s), \tag{2b}$$

for $i = 1, \ldots, n$, $s = 1, \ldots, S$. Equation (2a) states that the i-th individual cannot export more than his/her production, net of private resources used in exchange. And equation (2b) states that the i-th individual cannot consume more than he/she can produce (t_{ii}) or import from others (t_{ji}, $j \neq i$). These two restrictions guarantee that aggregate consumption of the private goods cannot exceed aggregate production, net of aggregate resource used in exchange.

Thus, in addition to $y^e \geq 0$ and the technological constraints: $(q^e, x^e) \in X$ and $(q^e, h^e, t^e) \in T$, a feasible allocation $z^e = z(e)$ must satisfy the information constraint (1) and the exchange constraints (2a)–(2b).

PARETO EFFICIENCY

The question of interest is, how do we choose an allocation among all the feasible ones? The key concept to evaluate this choice is the concept of *efficiency*.

A feasible allocation is Pareto efficient if there does not exist another feasible allocation that could make one individual better off without making anyone else worse off.

As a corollary, this identifies inefficiency as situations where there exist other feasible allocations that can make some individual better off without making anyone worse off. Intuitively, it means that inefficient allocations are undesirable. This motivates the focus of economic analysis on efficient allocations. But how do we know that a particular allocation is efficient (or inefficient)? Making such an evaluation can be difficult empirically.

The Pareto efficiency criterion involves a welfare evaluation of the n individuals affected by the decision-making process for z^e. This requires measuring the benefits received by the n individuals. Measuring individual benefits can be using a reference bundle of private goods. It will be convenient to choose "money" as the reference bundle. For our purpose, we identify the m-th private commodity as "money". We denote one unit of money by $g = (0, \ldots 0, 1)$. And we denote one unit of *sure money* by $g^e = (g(e_1), \ldots g(e_s)) = (g, \ldots, g)$. Although we allow for transaction costs for the first $(m-1)$ private goods, we assume throughout that money can be exchanged costlessly among the n individuals.

Given the ex-ante utility function $u_i(q^e, y_i^e)$ of the i-th individual and using sure money g^e as the reference bundle, define the i-th *individual benefit function* as

$$b_i(q^e, y_i^e, U_i) = \max_\beta \{\beta : u_i(q^e, y_i^e - \beta g^e) \geq U_i; y_i^e - \beta\, g^e \geq 0\}, \qquad (3a)$$

$i = -1, \ldots, n$. Then, the *aggregate benefit function* is

$$B(q^e, y^e, U) = \sum_{i=1}^{n} b_i(q^e, y_i^e, U_i), \qquad (3b)$$

where $y^e = (y_1^e, \ldots, y_n^e)$, *and* $U = (U_1, \ldots, U_n)$. The benefit function $b_i(q^e, y_i^e, u_i)$ measures the amount of sure money the i-th individual is willing to give up facing the allocation (q^e, y_i^e) to reach the utility level U_i. As such, it can be interpreted intuitively as an individual willingness-to-pay measure. And the benefit function $B(q^e, y^e, U)$ is the corresponding aggregate measure across all n individuals. They provide convenient welfare measurements. Throughout, we assume that transferring a positive quantity of the bundle g^e to any individual will make him/her better off (i.e., we assume that $u_i(\cdot)$ is increasing in income).

Intuitively, one would expect that more efficient allocations would generate greater welfare benefits to the n individuals. This suggests considering the allocations z^e that solve the following maximization problem (conditional on the utility levels $U = (U_1, \ldots, U_n)$):

$$V(U) = \text{Max}\{B(q^e, y^e, U): z^e \text{ is feasible}\}. \tag{4}$$

Let $z^{e^*}(U)$ denote the optimal allocation in (4). Such allocation is said to be *maximal* (Luenberger 1995). Equation (4) also identifies $V(U)$ as the largest feasible aggregate benefit that can be obtained when individuals receive utility levels $U = (U_1, \ldots, U_n)$. Allais (1953) interpreted $V(U)$ as measuring the *aggregate distributable surplus*; at the aggregate, it is the largest amount of money that can be generated for given individual utilities U. There are three possibilities: $V(U) < 0$, $V(U) > 0$, *and* $V(U) = 0$. First, the case where $V(U) < 0$ must be *infeasible*. Indeed, a negative aggregate willingness-to-pay indicates that the utility levels $U = (U_1, \ldots, U_n)$ are "too high" to be attained feasibly in the economy. Since $V(U) < 0$ implies infeasibility, it follows that $V(U) \geq 0$ characterizes feasible allocations. Second, the case where $V(U) > 0$ must correspond to an *inefficient* allocation. Indeed, if positive, the distributable surplus can always be redistributed to some individual. This would make that individual better off without making anyone else worse off. Third, consider the case where $V(U) = 0$. Since $V(U) \geq 0$ under feasibility and $V(U) > 0$ implies inefficiency, this gives the following key result:

If an allocation is Pareto efficient, then it is a maximal allocation associated with zero distributable surplus, $V(U) = 0$.

In combination with (4), this has the following intuitive interpretation: efficient allocations can be obtained among feasible allocations by first maximizing aggregate benefit (as given in (4)), and then redistributing entirely the resulting surplus $V(U)$ among the n individuals, yielding $V(U) = 0$ (see Luenberger 1995; Chavas and Bouamra-Mechemache 2002).

The distributable surplus function $V(U)$ is useful in another way. Solving $V(U) = 0$ for $U = (U_1, \ldots, U_n)$ involves solving one equation for n unknowns. This typically has an infinite number of solutions. The solutions trace out the *Pareto utility frontier*. This is illustrated in Figure 11.1 in the

Contract and Policy Design Under Risk 167

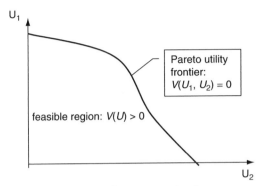

Figure 11.1 The Pareto utility frontier

context of two individuals ($n = 2$). The Pareto utility frontier gives the distribution of welfare generated by Pareto efficient allocations. Thus, any point on the Pareto utility frontier corresponds to a Pareto efficient allocation. And moves along the Pareto utility frontier (e.g., as generated by lump-sum income transfers) involve different welfare distributions among individuals. Finally, as illustrated in Figure 11.1, any point below the Pareto utility frontier corresponds to feasible but inefficient allocations (where $V(U) > 0$). This shows that the Pareto utility frontier gives the upper bound of utilities that are feasibly reached under efficiency.

Finally, what happens as one moves along the Pareto utility frontier? Clearly, the allocation $z^{e^*}(U)$ must change to affect the distribution of welfare among the n individuals. This can be broadly interpreted as changes in income distribution (e.g., associated with lump-sum income transfers). As the income distribution changes, all decisions $z^{e^*}(U)$ can possibly change. This would be the case in the presence of "income effects" where changes in individual income (or wealth) affect production or consumption decisions. We discussed such income effects in Chapter 4 and found them to be prevalent. This suggests that, in the presence of income effects, the efficient allocations $z^{e^*}(U)$ depend on income distribution. This appears intuitive and realistic. However, it makes economic analysis much more difficult. Indeed, it implies that efficiency and income distribution issues are closely linked. It means that it is not possible to make a specific recommendation about an efficient allocation without knowing the associated income distribution. As income distribution changes, so do the corresponding efficient allocations. Such complexities significantly reduce the empirical tractability of efficiency analysis. This has motivated the search for simplifying assumptions.

One such simplifying assumption involves "zero income effects." A particular decision z_k exhibits zero income effects if it is not affected by changes in individual income or wealth (e.g., the case of constant absolute risk aversion (CARA) discussed in Chapter 4). In such cases, changes in income distribution as one moves along the Pareto utility frontier have no impact on the efficient decision for z_k. In other words, $z_k^*(U)$ is independent of U. This means that it becomes possible to make a specific recommendation about an efficient allocation z_k^* without knowing the associated income distribution. Although probably less realistic, this greatly simplifies economic analysis and helps improve empirical tractability. As a result, "zero income effects" are often assumed in empirical investigation of economic efficiency. As long as income effects remain "sufficiently small," such simplifying assumptions may still provide an "approximate" characterization of efficient allocations. This illustrates some important tradeoffs between realism and empirical tractability.

Note: The previous results become empirically more tractable when the number of individuals is small. The simplest case is when there are only two individuals, $n = 2$. Then, the above characterization of the Pareto efficiency reduces to the following optimization problem:

$$\text{Max}\{u_1(q^e, y_1^e): u_2(q^e, y_2^e) \geq U_2, z^e \text{ is feasible}\}.$$

In Figure 11.1, this amounts to choosing some reservation utility level U_2 for individual 2, and choosing an allocation that maximizes the utility of individual 1 up to a point on the Pareto utility frontier. This is the basic structure of the principal-agent model, a model that has been commonly used in the analysis of contracts (see Chapter 12).

Note that, assuming that the Lagrangean approach applies (see Appendix B), this can be alternatively written as:

$$\text{Max}\{u_1(q^e, y_1^e) + \gamma u_2(q^e, y_2^e): \gamma \geq 0, z^e \text{ is feasible}\},$$

where γ is a Lagrange multiplier corresponding to the constraint $u_2(q^e, y_2^e) \geq U_2$. Then, the set of Pareto efficient allocations can be conveniently obtained by solving this optimization problem for different values of $\gamma > 0$ (where γ plays the role of "relative welfare weight" for individual 2).

INTERPRETATION

The characterization of efficiency presented above is very general. It applies in the presence of uncertainty, asymmetric information, transaction costs, public goods, as well as externalities. At this point, it is silent about the role of markets. This indicates that efficiency can be obtained without markets. This is the domain of *contracts* and *policy*. Indeed, the state-dependent decision rules $z^e = (q(e), h(e), x(e), y(e), t(e))$ can be the ones specified in a contract or in a policy rule. They can involve production decisions $x(e)$, trade and transfers $t(e)$ with associated transaction resources $h(e)$, as well as the provision of public goods $q(e)$.

What are the distinguishing features of a contract compared to a policy rule? A contract typically involves a relatively small number of individuals who bargain with each other to set up decentralized decision rules. In contrast, policy rules typically involve decisions made by centralized institutions (e.g., government) and affecting a large number of individuals. Thus, both the identity of the decision-makers and the level of centralization differ.

Contracts can play an important role in establishing efficient resource allocation. For example, Coase (1960) has shown that externality problems can be managed through bargaining among the individuals affected. The outcome of bargaining generates individual rights and obligations set out in a contract. Coase argued that, in the presence of externalities, a contract can be designed such that the outcome is Pareto efficient. However, Coase focused on a simple situation with no uncertainty, no transaction cost, and "zero income effects." As seen above, the latter means that the terms of the contract can be designed independently of income distribution. This generated much discussion on whether Coase's analysis applies under uncertainty, transaction cost, and in the presence of income effects. Our analysis provides the needed generalization. It shows that, if contracts can help implement efficient decision rules for $z(e)$, then they support a Pareto efficient allocation. This result applies in the presence of uncertainty, asymmetric information and learning, under transaction costs, nonzero income effects, and the presence of externalities and public goods.

Similar results apply to policy rules. If policy rules can help implement efficient decision rules for $z(e)$, then they support a Pareto efficient allocation. Again, this result applies in the presence of uncertainty, asymmetric information and learning, under transaction costs, nonzero income effects, and the presence of externalities and public goods.

Our analysis sheds some light on the design and evaluation of efficient contracts and of efficient policy-making. However, such design and evaluation can be quite complex. To see that, consider the maximal allocation given in (4). Solving this optimization problem can be quite difficult. When the number of individuals is large and/or the uncertainty complex, there may be no practical way of solving for the maximal allocation $z^{e^*}(U)$, even using the fastest computers. It is not that such attempts have not been made. For example, computable general equilibrium (CGE) models have been developed to evaluate the efficiency of general resource allocation. However, to be empirically tractable, such models typically either focus on a subset of commodities, or they model only broad aggregates. And they usually ignore uncertainty and the efficiency of risk allocation. This has two important implications. First, evaluating empirically the efficiency of risk allocation remains quite challenging. Given the difficulty of the task, the best work has focused on specific applications. Reviewing this work is the topic of Chapter 12. Second, if the fastest computers cannot evaluate the efficiency of allocation in complex economies, then how do decision-makers deal with this issue? They try to simplify the decision rules so that they can become manageable. This will depend in part on the institutional environment. For example, *specialization* as well as *decentralization* can contribute to reducing the number of decisions made by any particular decision-maker. As such, they can facilitate the processing of information relevant for each decision, thus allowing reasonably refined decision rules. However, decentralization may not be appropriate in the presence of economies of scale (e.g., national defense). Decentralization also raises the issue of coordination across decision-makers when the decisions of each agent have external effects on other agents. Finally, simpler decision rules may still imply significant loss of information, which can have adverse effects on efficiency (see following). This suggests that, while both contracts and policy rules play an important role in resource allocation, neither is likely to be sufficient to implement efficiency.

THE ROLE OF MARKETS

In this section, we examine the role of markets in supporting an efficient allocation. Our starting point is the maximal allocation given in (4). We have seen that it provides an intuitive and convenient framework to characterize Pareto efficiency. Equation (4) maximizes aggregate benefit subject to feasibility constraints. This constrained optimization problem can be alternatively analyzed using a Lagrange approach (see Appendix B). Denote by $p_{ri}^e = p_{ri}(e)$ $= (p_{ri}(e_1), \ldots, p_{ri}(e_s))'$, and by $p_{ci}^e = p_{ci}(e) = (p_{ci}(e_1), \ldots, p_{ci}(e_s))'$, the Lagrange multipliers associated with the feasibility constraints (2a) and (2b), respectively, $i = 1, \ldots, n$. Consider the Lagrangean

$$L(z^e, p^e, U) = B(q^e, y^e, U) + \sum_{i=1}^{n} p_{ri}^{e\,\prime} \cdot \left[x_i^e - h_i^e - \sum_{j=1}^{n} t_{ij}^e \right] + \sum_{i=1}^{n} p_{ci}^{e\,\prime} \cdot \left[\sum_{j=1}^{n} t_{ji}^e - y_i^e \right],$$

(5)

where $p^e = (p_{r1}^e, \ldots, p_{rn}^e; p_{c1}^e, \ldots, p_{cn}^e)'$. Under some regularity conditions, the optimization problem (4) can be written as the saddle point problem

$$V(U) = \text{Min}_p \, \text{Max}_z \{ L(z^e, p^e, U) : p^e \geq 0, z^e \text{ is feasible} \}.$$

(6)

where the Lagrangean L is maximized with respect to the allocation $z^e = (q^e, h^e, x^e, y^e, t^e)$, while it is minimized with respect to prices $p^e \geq 0$. The Lagrange multipliers p^e have the standard interpretation of measuring the shadow price of the corresponding constraints. Thus, $p_r^e = (p_{r_1}^e, \ldots, p_{rm}^e)'$ measures the shadow prices of resource scarcity for producing private goods, while $p_c^e = (p_{c_1}^e, \ldots, p_{cn}^e)'$ measures the shadow price of resource scarcity for consuming private goods. When normalized such that they $p_{pi}^e{}' g^e = p_{ci}^e{}' g^e = 1$ (where g^e denotes one unit of sure money), they become *the state-dependent prices for the m private goods.*

There is a close relationship between (4) and (6). The solution to (6) always identifies a solution to the maximization problem in (4). But some regularity conditions are needed in order for expression (4) to imply (6). They include the convexity of the feasible set (see Appendix B, and Takayama 1985, p. 75). These regularity conditions are satisfied in situations exhibiting "diminishing marginal values" (which rules out the presence of increasing returns to scale). For simplicity, we will assume below that these conditions are satisfied and that (4) and (6) provide equivalent representations of the maximal allocation $z^{e^*}(U)$. It means that, in situations where $U = (U_1, \ldots, U_n)$ is chosen such that the distributable surplus is zero, $V(U) = 0$, then the saddle-point problem (6) characterizes a Pareto efficient allocation.

Note that the maximization in (6) implies

$$W(p_c^e, q^e, U) = \mathrm{Max}_y \{ B(q^e, y^e, U) - \sum_{i=1}^{n} p_{ci}^e{}' y_i^e : y^e \geq 0 \}, \tag{7a}$$

$$\pi_r(p_r^e, q^e) = \mathrm{Max}_x \left\{ \sum_{i=1}^{n} p_{ri}^e{}' x_i^e : x^e \text{ is feasible} \right\}, \tag{7b}$$

$$\pi_t(p_r^e, p_c^e, q^e) = \mathrm{Max}_{h,t} \left\{ \sum_{i=1}^{n} \sum_{j=1}^{n} (p_{cj}^e - p_{ri}^e)' t_{ij}^e - \sum_{i=1}^{n} p_{ri}^e{}' h_i^e : (h^e, t^e) \text{ are feasible} \right\}, \tag{7c}$$

$$N(p_r^e, p_c^e, U) = \mathrm{Max}_q \{ W(p_c^e, q^e, U) + \pi_r(p_r^e, q^e) + \pi_t(p_r^e, p_c^e, q^e) : q^e \text{ is feasible} \}. \tag{7d}$$

Equations (7a)–(7d) provide some nice intuition about the characterization of efficiency. Equation (7a) states that efficient consumption decisions y^e are the ones that *maximize aggregate net consumer benefit*, defined as aggregate benefit $B(q^e, y^e, U)$ minus consumer expenditures, $\sum_{i=1}^{n} p_{ci}^e{}' y_i^e$. Then, $W(p_c^e, q^e, U)$ in (7a) is a measure of aggregate net consumer benefit. Equation (7b) shows that efficient production decisions x^e are the ones that *maximize aggregate production profit*, $\sum_{i=1}^{n} p_{ri}^e{}' x_i^e$, where $p_{ri}^e{}' x_i^e$ is the production profit generated by the i-th individual (recall that outputs are defined as positive while inputs are negative). Then, $\pi_r(p_r^e, q^e)$ in (7b) measures aggregate production profit. Equation (7c) states that efficient trade decisions (t^e, h^e) maximize *aggregate trade profit*, defined as aggregate revenue from trade activities $\sum_{i=1}^{n} \sum_{j=1}^{n} (p_{cj}^e - p_{ri}^e)' \, t_{ij}^e$ minus the cost of exchange $\sum_{i=1}^{n} p_{ri}^{e\prime} h_i^e$. Then, $\pi_t(p_r^e, p_c^e, q^e)$ in (7c) is a measure of aggregate trade profit. Finally, equation (7d) shows that efficient public goods q^e are the ones that maximize aggregate net consumer benefit $W(p_c^e, q^e, U)$ plus aggregate profit from production activities $\pi_r(p_r^e, q^e)$, as well as trade activities $\pi_t(p_r^e, p_c^e, q^e)$. Then, $N(p_r^e, p_c^e, U)$ in (10) is a measure of aggregate net benefit from consumption, production and trade activities.

If we make the intuitive assumption that each individual trading with himself/herself (as denoted by t_{ii}^e) is costless, then (6) implies that, at the optimum, consumer prices p_c^e and producer prices p_r^e are identical: $p_c^e = p_r^e$. Indeed, as reflected in equation (7c), any differences between producer prices and consumer prices would be arbitraged away. This implies that each individual faces unique prices for the private goods.

Finally, given equations (7a)–(7d), the minimization in (6) implies

$$V(U) = Min_p\{N(p_r^e, p_c^e, U): p^e \geq 0\}. \tag{8}$$

The minimization problem in (8) guarantees that prices are consistent with the feasibility constraints (2a) and (2b). This guarantees nonnegative aggregate excess demand for the private goods. In the case where the distributable surplus is zero, $V(U) = 0$, it follows that the shadow prices p^e given by (8) would support an efficient allocation. To the extent that p^e represents market prices, this would imply that a *market economy can support a Pareto efficient allocation*.

The issue of whether a market economy does support an efficient allocation centers on the economic incentives associated with (7a)–(7d). Equations (7a)–(7d) imply that decisions are made so as to maximize aggregate net benefit and aggregate profit. As previously discussed, in complex economies, this maximization can be quite complex, and there is typically no practical way of solving the associated maximization problems. This focuses the attention on the following question: Is it possible for a *decentralized market exchange* to be Pareto efficient?

With respect to private goods, the answer is yes, for competitive markets in the absence of externalities. To see that, consider the case where there is no externality for producers. This means that the production possibilities of each individual are not directly affected by others' production decisions. In other words, the *i*-th individual production technology is independent of other individuals. It follows that (7b) becomes

$$\pi_{ri}(p_{ri}^e, q^e) = \text{Max}_x \{p_{ri}^{e\,\prime} x_i^e : x_i^e \text{ is feasible}\}, \tag{7b$'$}$$

where $\pi_r(p_r^e, q^e) = \sum_{i=1}^n \pi_{ri}(p_{ri}^e, q^e)$. Equation (7b') states *individual rationality for production decisions* under competitive markets: the i-th individual chooses the private production goods x_i^e to *maximize individual profit*, p_{ri}^e, x_i^e, taking market prices p_{ri}^e as given. This means that, in the absence of externalities, production decisions can efficiently be decentralized. Then, the aggregate production profit $\pi_r(p_r^e, q^e)$ becomes simply the sum of the individual profits $\pi_{ri}(p_{ri}^e, q^e)$ across all individuals.

In addition, using (3b), note that (7a) can be alternatively written as

$$W_i(p_{ci}^e, q^e, U_i) = \text{Max}_y \{b_i(q^e, y_i^e, U_i) - p_{ci}^{e\,\prime} y_i^e : y_i^e \geq 0\}, \, i = 1, \ldots, n, \tag{7a$'$}$$

where $W(p_c^e, q^e, U) = \sum_{i=1}^n W_i(p_{ci}^e, q^e, U_i)$. Equation (7a') states the *individual rationality of private consumption decisions*: the i-th individual chooses the private consumption goods y_i^e to maximize his/her benefit $b_i(q^e, y_i^e, Ui)$ net of consumer expenditures, $p_{ci}^{e\,\prime} y_i^e$, taking prices p_{ci}^e as given. This means that consumption decisions can be efficiently decentralized. And the aggregate consumer net benefit $W(p_c^e, q^e, U)$ is simply the sum of the individual benefits $W_i(p_{ci}^e, q^e, U_i)$ across all individuals.

This gives the following key result:

In the absence of externalities, a competitive market economy where production and consumption decisions of private goods are decentralized can support a Pareto efficient allocation.

A similar result would apply to the efficiency of decentralized trade decisions under competitive markets in the absence of externalities in trade (from 7c). This is a remarkable statement. It shows that, under some conditions, decentralized private decision-making under competitive market prices generates an efficient allocation. Here, competitive markets mean that individuals take the market prices p^e as given. And decentralized private decision-making means that the i-th individual chooses his/her consumption goods y_i^e and production decision x_i^e based only on competitive prices p^e, his/her own preferences, and his/her own production technology. This greatly simplifies the decision-making process. Indeed, for each individual, the competitive market prices p^e provide all the necessary information about resource scarcity in the rest of the economy. This is Adam Smith's "invisible hand," where market prices help guide individual decisions toward an efficient outcome. The great virtue of competitive markets is their ability to support both decentralized decision-making and a Pareto efficient allocation.

However, such a property applies only to the allocation of private goods and in the absence of externalities. From (7d), it is clear that the allocation of public goods cannot be easily decentralized. It means that public centralized institutions (e.g., government) are needed to choose the public goods q^e in an efficient way.

What about externalities? Note that (7b) differs from (7b') in the presence of production externalities. The reason is profit maximizing input-output choices in (7b') would fail to consider external production effects across individuals. This suggests that decentralized decisions would fail to generate an efficient allocation in the presence of externalities. And the associated market equilibrium would generate inefficient prices that do not satisfy (8). One possible solution would be to develop a fiscal policy imposing Pigouvian taxes that would bridge the gap between market prices and efficient prices (the latter ones given by equation (8)). An alternative solution would be government regulations that would stipulate that individuals make efficient decisions. But these centralized solutions can be difficult to implement; identifying the efficient prices or efficient quantities requires finding a solution to the saddle-point problem (6). As discussed above, in complex economies, this is typically intractable. Alternative solutions would be to develop some more decentralized schemes. For example, when the externality takes place between two firms, the merging of the two firms would solve the problem. Another possibility would be the Coasian solution: to develop a contract between the two firms so as to specify that production decisions are consistent with (7b). But these decentralized solutions are likely to be practical only if the externality is "local" and involves few individuals. This suggests the presence of significant complementarities between markets, contracts, and government in generating efficient resource allocation.

Finally, equation (7c) establishes that, under prices (p_r^e, p_c^e, q^e), efficient exchange exhausts all profit opportunities. It applies to commodity markets, as well as risk markets under transaction cost. Note that it applies as well in the absence of transaction costs. In this case, it is always efficient to choose $h^e = 0$, and equation (7c) implies that $\pi_t(p_r^e, p_c^e, q^e) = 0$. Indeed, with $h^e = 0$, a positive (negative) profit $\pi_t(p_r^e, p_c^e, q^e)$ would provide an incentive to exchange more (less), implying that a nonzero profit cannot hold at equilibrium. Thus, in the absence of transaction costs, the zero-profit condition, $\pi_t(p_r^e, p_c^e, q^e) = 0$, necessarily applies. This has been called the *no-arbitrage condition*. This condition has been found to be useful in the analysis of asset pricing in finance. Under *arbitrage pricing*, given the price of a subset of assets, the equilibrium price of all other assets whose payoffs can be duplicated by this subset must be consistent with the no-arbitrage condition. This has been used extensively in the pricing of options, warrants, and other derivative securities—financial securities whose payoffs depend on the prices of other securities (see Hull 2002). However, note that arbitrage pricing applies only in the absence of transaction costs. Indeed, in the presence of transaction cost, the maximized profit $\pi_t(p_r^e, p_c^e, q^e)$ in equation (7c) can be nonzero.

THE ROLE OF TRANSACTION COST

Our analysis incorporates transaction costs in economic analysis. Indeed, we consider the case where resources h^e are used in the exchange process. They include transportation activities, information acquisition, etc. Transaction costs are given by the term $[\sum_{i=1}^{n} p_{ri}^{e\prime} h_i^e]$ in equation (5) or (7c). Since transaction costs are subtracted from aggregate net benefit in (5), they contribute to reducing the aggregate distributable surplus $V(U)$ and to an inward shift in the Pareto utility frontier. Alternatively, reducing transaction costs (e.g., due to improvements in infrastructure and information technology) would improve efficiency, contributing to an increase in distributable surplus $V(U)$ and an outward shift in the Pareto utility frontier. In general, lower transaction costs stimulate exchange, thus generating increased gains from trade. These gains can be measured by the associated increase in aggregate distributable surplus. This suggests that private management and/or public policy that reduce transaction costs can contribute to significant efficiency gains.

To obtain additional insights in the role of transaction costs, define the transaction cost function $C(p_r^e, t^e) = \text{Min}_h \{ \sum_{i=1}^{n} p_{ri}^{e\prime} h_i^e : (h^e, t^e) \text{ are feasible} \}$. Assume that the function $C(p_r^e, t^e)$ is differentiable in t^e. Then, consider the optimization in (7c) with respect to $t_{ijk}(e_s) \geq 0$, the quantity of the k-th commodity exchanged between individuals i and j under state s. It implies the familiar Kuhn–Tucker conditions:

$$p_{jk}(e_s) - p_{ik}(e_s) - \partial C / \partial t_{ijk}(e_s) \leq 0 \ for \ t_{ijk}(e_s) \geq 0, \tag{9a}$$

and

$$[q_{jk}(e_s) - q_{ik}(e_s) - \partial C / \partial t_{ijk}(e_s)] \cdot t_{ijk}(e_s) = 0. \tag{9b}$$

In the context of a market equilibrium, equation (9a) implies that $[p_{jk}(e_s) - p_{ik}(e_s)] \leq \partial C / \partial t_{ijk}(e_s)$, i.e., that the price difference for commodity k between individuals i and j $[q_{jk}(e_s) - q_{ik}(e_s)]$ cannot exceed the marginal transaction cost $\partial C / \partial t_{ijk}(e_s)$ under state s. And when trade takes place between individuals i and agent j for the k-th commodity (with $t_{ijk}(e_s) > 0$), then (9a) and (9b) imply that $[p_{jk}(e_s) - q_{ik}(e_s)] = \partial C / \partial t_{ijk}(e_s)$. In this case, the price difference $[q_{jk}(e_s) - q_{ik}(e_s)]$ must equal the marginal transaction cost $\partial C / \partial t_{ijk}(e_s)$ under state s. This is the first-order condition for profit maximizing trade. It follows that, in the absence of transaction costs where $\partial C / \partial t_{ijk}(e_s) = 0$, the *law of one price* applies since $p_{jk}(e_s) = p_{ik}(e_s)$. Alternatively, when $\partial C / \partial t_{ijk} > 0$, transaction costs create a price wedge between $q_{jk}(e_s)$ and $q_{ik}(e_s)$. In such a situation, the law of one price clearly fails to apply. This implies "local markets" where participants in each market are endogenously determined (depending on transaction technology and price differences). This can also imply thin markets, when the number of market participants is small. This is relevant in risk markets (e.g., the case of insurance contracts). And when transaction costs are "high enough" so that $\partial C/\partial t_{ijk}(e_s) > [p_{jk}(e_s) - p_{ik}(e_s)]$ for some i and j satisfying $[q_{jk}(e_s) - q_{ik}(e_s)] \geq 0$, then the incentive to trade disappears as (9b) implies $t_{ijk}(e_s) = 0$. Then, under state s, the k-th commodity becomes nontraded between individuals i and j. If this happens for all states, this implies the *absence of state-dependent exchange* for the k-th commodity. This illustrates well the adverse effects of transaction costs on market activities. It means that high transaction costs contribute to the *incompleteness of markets* in general.

Note that markets for many state-contingent goods are notoriously absent. For example, there is no market for purchasing an umbrella only when it rains, for purchasing a car only when it does not have a flat tire, or for producing corn only when it rains. Thus, *risk markets are typically incomplete*. This can be explained in part by their high transaction costs. In the absence of many risk markets, the associated risks must be managed in other ways (either privately, through contracts, or through government policy). However, risk markets do exist for some important commodities. An important example is insurance, which involves state-dependent payments contingent on the occurrence of a specific event (e.g., if a house is destroyed by fire). Our analysis stresses that low transaction costs (including low information cost) is critical in the proper functioning of risk markets. And the lowering of transaction costs (e.g., due to improved information technology) can contribute to the creation and development of risk markets. This is well illustrated by the growth and development of financial markets over the last decades. This means that, even if incomplete, risk markets do play an important role in the efficiency of risk allocation.

THE ROLE OF UNCERTAINTY

As discussed in Chapters 4 and 10, risk can affect individual welfare in two ways: (1) because of the implicit cost of risk under risk aversion, and (2) because of information under learning. We show below that similar arguments apply to the efficiency evaluation of risk.

RISK AVERSION

In Chapter 4, we defined the implicit cost of private risk bearing by the Arrow–Pratt risk premium. Although the analysis was presented using the expected utility model, we explore briefly how to extend it in the context of state-dependent preferences. The uncertainty is represented by the states $e = (e_1, \ldots, e_s)$. Let the i-th individual have preferences represented by the ex-ante utility function $u_i(z^e)$, where $z^e = (z_1(e_1), \ldots, z_1(e_s); z_2(e_1), \ldots, z_2(e_s); \ldots)$, $z_k(e_s)$ being the k-th decision made under state e_s. Assume that the *i*-th individual assesses the uncertainty through a subjective probability distribution of the states: $Pr(e_1, i), \ldots, Pr(e_s, i)$. Consider the state-independent commodities $E_i(z^e) = (E_i(z_1(e)), \ldots, E_i(z_1(e)); E_i(z_2(e)), \ldots, E_i(z_2(e_s))\ldots)$, where $E_i(z_k(e)) = \sum_{s=1}^{s} Pr(e_s, i)z_k(e_s)$ denotes the expected value of $z_k(e)$. Using the individual benefit function $b_i(z^e, U_i)$ defined in equation (3a), define the *risk premium R* as

$$R_i = b_i(E_i(z^e), u_i(z^e)).$$

It means that R is the ex-ante amount of money the *i*-th individual is willing to pay to eliminate risk exposure by replacing the state-dependent commodities z^e with its state-independent counterpart $E_i(z^e)$. It measures the implicit cost of private risk bearing for the *i*-th individual. This generalizes the Arrow–Pratt risk premium discussed in Chapter 4 in two directions: (1) it allows for multiple sources of uncertainty, and (2) it applies under general state-dependent preferences.

As in Chapter 4, the nature of risk preferences can be evaluated depending on the sign of the risk premium. The *i*-th individual is said to be risk averse, risk neutral, or risk loving depending upon whether $R_i > 0$, $= 0 \ or < 0$, respectively. From Jensen's inequality in Chapter 4, $R_i \geq 0$, $= 0 \ or \leq 0$ when $b_i(z^e, \cdot)$ is concave, linear, or convex in z^e. This means that risk aversion is associated with the concavity of the benefit function $b_i(z^e, \cdot)$, i.e., with the presence of "diminishing marginal benefits" (see Luenberger 1995; Chambers and Quiggin; Chavas and Bouamra-Mechemache 2002). This establishes a useful linkage between the intuitive concept of "diminishing marginal values" and the prevalence of risk aversion. It also indicates that the aggregate benefit function $B(\cdot)$ used to evaluate efficiency (see equations (3b), (4), and (5)) has an implicit risk component. Under risk aversion, the implicit cost of private risk bearing R_i is positive and private risk exposure tends to reduce individual benefit. Private risk exposure reduces aggregate benefit and aggregate distributable surplus in (4) or (5), and contributes to an inward shift in the Pareto utility frontier. This means that, under risk aversion, private risk exposure can contribute to inefficiency. In general, the social cost of private risk bearing can be measured by the aggregate risk premium $\sum_{i=1}^{n} R_i$, which is positive under risk aversion. This makes it clear that risk management is an integral part of efficient resource allocation. Under risk aversion, reducing private risk exposure can be done in a variety of ways: through private management (e.g., diversification strategies), through markets (e.g., insurance markets), through contracts (e.g., sharecropping contracts), as well as through policy (e.g., government policy establishing a "social safety net"). Either by reducing private risk exposure or by transferring risk toward individuals who are less risk averse, such schemes can help reduce the aggregate risk premium $\sum_{i=1}^{n} R_i$, thus increase aggregate benefit and aggregate distributable surplus in (4) or (5). As such, they contribute to an outward shift in the Pareto utility frontier and an improvement in efficiency.

THE VALUE OF INFORMATION

We have represented the quality of information by the information structure P supporting all decisions made by all individuals. As reflected in equation (1), this information structure imposes restrictions on the decisions rules $z(e)$. As previously discussed, better information implies fewer restrictions in (1), while poorer information implies additional restrictions. This is intuitive; better information means more refined decision rules.

First, consider the simple case where information is costless. This means that more refined information structures P can be obtained without the use of resources. Under information structure P, denote the distributable surplus in (4) by $V(U, P)$. Since better information means fewer restrictions in (1), improving information tends to expand the feasible set in (4), thus increasing the distributable surplus $V(U, P)$ and generating an outward shift in the Pareto utility frontier. This generates the following key result:

Better costless information contributes to improved efficiency.

It means that, under costless information, more information is always desirable in the sense that it contributes to more refined state-dependent decision rules that contribute to improving the efficiency of resource allocation under risk. Alternatively, the inability to use information would necessarily reduce efficiency.

Define two extreme information structures: P^- corresponding to no information (where all decisions are chosen ex-ante and are constrained to be the same in all states), and P^+ corresponding to perfect information (where all decisions are made ex-post as (1) imposes no restriction). Then, through equation (1), P^- would be the most restrictive in (4), while P^+ would be the least restrictive. For any information structure P, this gives the general result:

$$V(U, P^-) \leq V(U, P) \leq V(U, P^+).$$

It states that the distributable surplus $V(U, P)$ is bounded between the distributable surplus under no information $V(U, P^-)$ and the distributable surplus under perfect information $V(U, P^+)$. It suggests that $V(U, P) - V(U, P^-) \geq 0$ can provide a general measure of the value of (costless) information under P. And with $V(U, P^+)$ as an upper bound, it implies that, if information were free to obtain, any information structure short of perfect information would typically be inefficient. While interesting, this intuitive result does not appear particularly realistic. It suggests a need to explore in more depth the role of information cost.

When information is costly, obtaining improved information makes use of resources. In this case, the cost of information is the opportunity cost of resources used in the learning process. One interesting possibility is the case where perfect information P^+ may not be feasible. This would happen when current resources available are not sufficient to obtain perfect information. This is a scenario of *bounded rationality*, when there are severe limitations to obtaining and processing information under a complex economic environment (e.g., due a very large number of states). Then, in the quest for perfect information, information gathering activities could increase up to a point where there is no resource left for other activities. In addition, even if enough resources could be found to generate new information, the decision-makers' ability to process this information may be constrained by the capacity of their brain to retain it and use it in an effective manner. Under such scenarios, bounded rationality implies that perfect information P^+ is not feasible. In this context, economic institutions and decision-making processes must function under imperfect information.

This raises the question, how much information should be used under costly information? Our analysis of Pareto efficiency provides the answer. The efficient choice of information would the information structure P^* that solves the maximization problem in (4), subject to a zero aggregate distributable surplus, $V(U) = 0$. It corresponds to using an information structure P^* that maximizes aggregate benefits, and then redistributing the surplus entirely to the n agents. This involves trading off the benefits of better information (generating more refined state-dependent decision rules) with its cost (as measured by the opportunity cost of the information gathering activities). In situations where the benefits of new information are larger than their cost, then the information is worth getting. Alternatively, if the cost of new information is larger than its benefits, neglecting this information would be efficient. This means that efficient decision rules would not depend on such information. It suggests that information cost can help explain why both contracts and risk markets are typically incomplete. Incomplete contracts mean that some ex-post contingencies were not anticipated ex-ante, raising the potential for ex-post disputes among the interested parties. Such disputes are often settled through ex-post bargaining. Also, the courts provide a formal framework for settling disputes when private bargaining fails.

This stresses the importance of information in risk management. In this context, efficient risk management is closely associated with an efficient management of information. In general, improved information management tries to increase distributable surplus and generate an outward shift in the

Pareto utility frontier. The efficiency gains can come from two sources: (1) lower information cost by reducing resources used in information acquisition, (2) and better information which contributes to improved efficiency through the use of more refined state-dependent decision rules. Note that this latter effect would apply to production, consumption as well as exchange activities. Then, more refined information would contribute to more refined contracts as well and stimulate the development of state-contingent exchange. Alternatively, poorer information would generate less refined state-dependent decision rules, i.e., less refined contracts and fewer state-dependent exchanges. This can provide useful insights into *organizational efficiency* as alternative forms of organizations (e.g., firms) can process information differently, thus influencing the efficiency of resource allocation and risk distribution (e.g., the efficiency of contractual arrangements).

The linkages between information and exchange are worth stressing. From equation (1), it is clear that refined state-dependent decisions are possible only under refined information. Equation (1) implies that no agent can implement a trade that depends on information not available to him/her. There can be no markets for contracts that depend on information that is not available to someone in the economy. More generally, net trade between two groups of agents can at most depend on the information that is common to both groups. Since risk markets/contracts require state-dependent decisions, their development requires the interested parties to be well informed. In addition, because common information is needed to trade state-dependent contracts, heterogeneity of information across agents has additional adverse effects on such markets/contracts. In extreme cases, imperfect and *asymmetric information* can contribute to the disappearance of all risk markets (with efficient exchange becoming state-independent; see Radner 1968). This indicates the importance of both the amount and distribution of information in the development of risk markets as well as contracts. In general, poor and asymmetric information can contribute to contract and market failure. If the relevant information is the individual's private situation and preferences, this is called a problem of *adverse selection* (e.g., the case of eligibility criteria in an insurance contract). Alternatively, if the relevant information is the individual's actions, this is called a problem of *moral hazard* (e.g., the case of monetary rewards that depend on the individuals' effort). These issues are discussed in more details in Chapter 12.

There are scenarios under which centralized management of information can be efficient. They include situations where there are economies of scale in obtaining information and where information is a public good or involves significant externalities. In this context, a decentralized decision-making process would typically fail to be efficient without appropriate policy intervention. This suggests a role for government to generate the associated public goods, or to intervene in the management of the information externalities (whether they are positive or negative). It could involve public institutions, regulations, and/or Pigouvian taxes inducing each agent to choose efficient bundles. Examples include national defense (where information involves strong economies of scale), basic research (generating public goods), and pollution (generating significant externalities).

But there are also many scenarios suggesting decentralized management of information. They can be motivated in part by the bounded rationality of centralized decision-makers. In situations where the number of agents is large, the economic environment is complex (with a large number of states), and there is significant heterogeneity across agents, one can expect that centralized decision-makers face severe limitations in obtaining information. This would provide an incentive to decentralize the decision-making process. Again, the optimal form of economic organization would involve tradeoffs between information costs and the benefits of using more refined decision rules. When the benefits of information tend to be "local" and the costs of information are relatively low, decentralized decision-making can be efficient. This applies to production, consumption as well as exchange activities. In the context of exchange, both transaction costs and information costs need to be relatively low to motivate any transaction between agents. If such costs are low enough to motivate a transaction, two possible mechanisms are relevant: a market mechanism and contracts. Market mechanisms tend to arise when the number of potential market participants interested in exchanging standard commodities is relatively large. Alternatively, contracts develop when the number of parties involved is small and/or the object of exchange is nonstandard (as defined by quality, timing, etc.). In either case, good ability to obtain and process information seems crucial to support active risk markets and generate efficient risk allocation. Then, more refined state-contingent decision rules as well as risk redistribution away from the more risk averse individuals can generate significant efficiency gains.

PROBLEMS

Note: An asterisk (*) indicates that the problem has an accompanying Excel file on the Web page http://www.aae.wisc.edu/chavas/risk.htm.

*1. Consider a public choice concerning the design and financing of a project involving two individuals, $i = 1, 2$. The project consists in a public good x that affects the welfare of each individual and that generates uncertain returns that are redistributed to the two individuals. The investment cost is $[2\ x]$ while the investment gross return is $[(8x - .4x^2)e/10]$ where e is a discrete random variable that can take any of 10 possible values, $e_j = j, j = 1, 2, \ldots, 10$.

Each individual behaves in a way consistent with the expected utility hypothesis with a utility function $U_i(w_i, x, e) = -\exp(-w_i) - a_i \exp(-xe_j)$, $i = 1, 2$. The initial wealth w_i for the ith individual is: $w_1 = 1$ and $w_2 = 0$. The preference parameter a_i is: $a_1 = 2$ and $a_2 = 1$. The ith individual's subjective probability of state j is $p_{ij} = .1$; $i = 1, 2$; $j = 1, 2, \ldots, 10$.

    a. Characterize a Pareto optimal design of the project, assuming that both x and the transfers t can be state-dependent.

    b. Obtain numerical solutions to a Pareto optimal project.

       1. Evaluate the utility frontier $u_1 = f(u_2)$.

       2. What is the optimal investment x? Does it vary with e? Does it vary with (u_1, u_2)?

       3. What are the optimal transfers t for the two individuals? Evaluate the transfers as a function of "net return." How do your findings vary with (u_1, u_2)?

       Interpret your results.

    c. Assume that x is chosen ex-ante. How does that affect your answers in question b? Interpret.

    d. Assume now that the quality of public information deteriorates. It is no longer possible to distinguish between the four states $\{1, 2, 3, 4, 5\}$ or between the four states $\{6, 7, 8, 9, 10\}$. How does that affect your answers in question b? Interpret.

    e. Assume that the subjective riskiness facing individual 2 increases, the probabilities p_{2j} now being equal to $\{p_{2j}\} = (.19, .19, .1, .01, .01, .01, .01, .1, .19, .19)$. (Assume that p_{1j} remains unchanged and that all states e are observable for public decision-making.) How does the higher risk affect your results in question b? Interpret your findings.

2. Show that, under constant absolute risk aversion for all agents, production and investment decisions are independent of the distribution of wealth.

3. Show that, under an efficient allocation and competitive markets, there does not exist a contract that can increase aggregate profit. Explore the implications for insurance contracts.

Chapter 12

Contract and Policy Design Under Risk: Applications

In Chapter 11, we presented a general analysis of the economic efficiency of risk allocation. We showed that efficient risk allocations have two objectives: (1) to reduce private risk exposure and redistribute the risk away from risk-averse individuals, and (2) to improve the quality of the information available in the decision-making process. However, the implementation of these objectives can be complex. This chapter focuses on some applications. Specific applications lead to more specific efficient decision rules. This provides additional insights on the economics of contract and policy design under imperfect information.

RISK SHARING

A generic issue in risk allocation is how to redistribute risk within a group of individuals. Here, we consider the case where the risk is associated with the outcome of a public project. The public project involves an ex-ante investment x that generates an uncertain net monetary return $\pi(x, e)$, where e is a random variable representing the uncertainty. The questions are: (1) How much to invest? and (2) How to redistribute the benefits of the public investment under uncertainty?

Assume that there are n individuals involved. Denote by $t_i^e = t_i(e)$ the decision rule giving the net payment made to the i-th individual when the random variable takes the value e. Feasibility implies that

$$\sum_{i=1}^{n} t_i(e) \leq \pi(x, e).$$

The ex-ante utility function of the i-th individual is $u_i(t_i^e)$, $i = 1, \ldots, n$. This means that the only benefit of the public investment x comes from the redistribution of the net return $\pi(x, e)$ among the n individuals. The i-th individual benefit function is $b_i(t_i^e, U_i)$, which satisfies

$$u_i(t_i^e - b_i) = U_i, i = 1, \ldots, n. \tag{1}$$

From Chapter 11, an efficient allocation satisfies

$$0 = V(U) = \text{Max} \left\{ \sum_{i=1}^{n} b_i(t_i^e, U_i): \sum_{i=1}^{n} t_i(e) \le \pi(x, e) \right\}. \tag{2}$$

where $U = (U_1, \ldots, U_n)$. This identifies efficient allocations that maximize aggregate benefit $\sum_{i=1}^{n} b_i(t_i^e, U_i)$, and completely redistribute the resulting surplus $V(U)$ among the n individuals.

To obtain more specific results, consider the situation where the random variable e has a probability distribution that is common knowledge. Let $\mu = E(e)$ denote the mean of e, and $\sigma^2 = \text{Var}(e)$ denote the variance of e. Assume that the net return from public investment takes the specific form: $\pi(x, e) = x \cdot e$. Assume that the payment to the i-th individual uses a *linear decision rule*: $t_i(e) = \alpha_i + \beta_i \pi(x, e) = \alpha_i + \beta_i \cdot x \cdot e$, where α_i and β_i are parameters to be chosen ex-ante, $i = 1, \ldots, n$. Here the α_i's can be interpreted as lump sum transfers, while β_i measures the proportion of net return π that is redistributed to the i-th individual. Finally, assume that the i-th individual has a mean variance preference function $u_i(t_i^e) = E(t_i^e) - \frac{1}{2} r_i \cdot \text{Var}(t_i^e)$, where $r_i > 0$ is a risk-aversion parameter. This means that $[E(t_i^e) - \frac{1}{2} r_i \cdot \text{Var}(t_i^e)]$ is the certainty equivalent, and $R_i = [\frac{1}{2} r_i \cdot \text{Var}(t_i^e)]$ is the i-th individual risk premium (see Chapter 3). As seen in Chapter 3, this is consistent with the expected utility model under constant absolute risk aversion (CARA) where r_i is the absolute risk aversion coefficient. With $r_i > 0$, each individual is risk averse and exhibits a positive risk premium, $R_i > 0$.

From equation (1), the i-th individual benefit function b_i satisfies $E(t_i^e) - \frac{1}{2} r_i \cdot \text{Var}(t_i^e) - b_i = U_i$, implying that

$$b_i = E(t_i^e) - \frac{1}{2} r_i \cdot \text{Var}(t_i^e) - U_i, i = 1, \ldots, n. \tag{3a}$$

This makes it clear that the risk premium $R_i = [\frac{1}{2} r_i \cdot \text{Var}(t_i^e)]$ is the implicit cost of private risk bearing: it is measured in monetary units and contributes to reducing the individual benefit function b_i in (3a). Under a linear decision rule, we have $E(t_i^e) = \alpha_i + \beta_i \cdot x \cdot \mu$, and $\text{Var}(t_i^e) = \beta_i^2 \cdot x^2 \cdot \sigma^2$. Then, the i-th individual benefit (3a) becomes

$$b_i = \alpha_i + \beta_i \cdot x \cdot \mu - \frac{1}{2} r_i \cdot \beta_i^2 \cdot x^2 \cdot \sigma^2 - U_i, i = 1, \ldots, n. \tag{3b}$$

The efficient allocation given in (2) becomes

$$0 = V(U) = \text{Max}\left\{\sum_{i=1}^{n}[\alpha_i + \beta_i \cdot x \cdot \mu - 1/2\, r_i \cdot \beta_i^2 \cdot x^2 \cdot \sigma^2 - U_i]:\right.$$

$$\left.\sum_{i=1}^{n}[\alpha_i + \beta_i \cdot x \cdot e] \leq x \cdot e\right\}. \tag{4}$$

This is a constrained optimization problem. Note that, under efficiency, the constraint is always binding (if not, the public project would generate a monetary surplus that can be redistributed to some individual, making him/her better off). Thus, the constraint becomes $\sum_{i=1}^{n}\alpha_i + (-1 + \sum_{i=1}^{n}\beta_i) \cdot (x \cdot e) = 0$. This can hold for all e only if

$$\sum_{i=1}^{n}\beta_i = 1, \tag{5a}$$

and

$$\sum_{i=1}^{n}\alpha_i = 0. \tag{5b}$$

Note from (3b) that the marginal benefit with respect to β_i is: $\partial b_i/\partial \beta_i = x \cdot \mu - r_i \cdot \beta_i \cdot x^2 \cdot \sigma^2$. Given $r_i > 0$ and $x > 0$, the proportion β_i maximizing aggregate benefit satisfies the first-order condition: $\mu = r_i \cdot \beta_i \cdot x \cdot \sigma^2$, yielding

$$\beta_i = \mu/[r_i \cdot x \cdot \sigma^2]. \tag{5c}$$

Substituting (5c) into (5a) implies $\left[\sum_{i=1}^{n}(1/ri)\right] \cdot \mu/[x \cdot \sigma^2] = 1$, giving the optimal investment

$$x^* = \left[\sum_{i=1}^{n}(1/r_i)\right] \cdot \mu/(\sigma^2). \tag{6a}$$

Substituting (6a) into (5c) yields the optimal proportion

$$\beta_i^* = (1/r_i)/\left[\sum_{i=1}^{n}(1/r_i)\right]. \tag{6b}$$

Finally, given $t_i(e) = \alpha_i + \beta_i \cdot x \cdot e$, the optimal payment to the i-th individual is

$$t_i(e)^* = \alpha_i^* + \beta_i \cdot \mu/(r_i \cdot \sigma^2) \cdot x \cdot e, \tag{6c}$$

for any α_i^* satisfying $\sum_{i=1}^{n} \alpha_i^* = 0$ in (5b). Equation (6) characterizes the Pareto efficient allocation of resources under risk. It includes the optimal investment x^* in (6a), the optimal proportions β_i^*'s in (6b), and the optimal individual payments $t_i(e)^*$ in (6c). And the surplus is entirely redistributed (with $V(U) = 0$) when U satisfies $U_i = \alpha_i^* + \beta_i^* \cdot x \cdot \mu - \frac{1}{2} r_i \cdot \beta_i^{*2} \cdot x^{*2} \cdot \sigma^2$, $i = 1, \ldots, n$. Note that changes in α's satisfying (5b) amount to lump sum transfers. Then, moving along the Pareto utility frontier simply involves income transfers among the n individuals through the α's. These transfers have no effect on the optimal decision rules in (6a)–(6b). This corresponds to a case of "zero income effects," where efficient decision rules can be evaluated independently on income distribution.

The Pareto efficient policies (6a)–(6c) provide useful and intuitive information about efficient behavior under risk. First, consider the properties of the optimal provision of the public good x^* in (6a):

- $\partial x^* / \partial \mu > 0$,
- $\partial x^* / \partial \sigma^2 < 0$,
- $\partial x^* / \partial r_i < 0$, $i = 1, \ldots, n$.

This indicates that higher expected returns (μ) have a *positive effect* on public investment x. It also shows that both higher risk (σ^2) and higher degree of risk aversion (r_i) by any individual has a *negative influence* on public investment x. These effects are due to risk aversion. Decreasing public investment is an efficient way to reduce the aggregate cost of risk (as measured by the aggregate risk premium ($\sum_{i=1}^{n} R_i = \sum_{i=1}^{n} 1/2 \, r_i \cdot \beta_i^2 \cdot x^2 \cdot \sigma^2$) in response to an increase in risk σ^2 or in risk aversion r_i.

Second, consider the properties of the optimal transfers $t_i(e)^*$ in (6c).

- $\partial t_i(e)^* / \partial \mu > 0$,
- $\partial t_i(e)^* / \partial e > 0$,
- $\partial t_i(e)^* / \partial \sigma^2 < 0$,
- $\partial t_i(e)^* / \partial r_j < 0$, *for $j = i$,*
  - $= 0$ *for $j \neq i$, $i = 1, \ldots, n$.*

This shows that a higher expected return (μ) as well as a higher realized value of the random variable e tend to *increase* the transfers toward any member of the group. It also indicates that a higher risk (σ^2) *decreases* the payments toward all individuals. Finally, it shows that a higher degree of risk aversion by the i-th individual (r_i) *decreases* the transfer payment to this individual, but leaves the payments to other members of the group unaffected. This decreased payment toward the i-th individual reduces his/her private risk exposure, which is an efficient way of reducing the aggregate cost of risk.

INSURANCE

Consider a group of n agents, $i = 1, \ldots, n$, where $i = 1$ represents an insurance firm, and $i = 2, \ldots, n$, denotes a set of $(n - 1)$ individuals interested in insurance coverage. Each agent is facing a stochastic return $\pi_i(e)$, where e is a random variable, $i = 1, \ldots, n$. Under the expected utility model, the objective function of the i-th agent is given by

$$E_i u_i[t_i(e) + \pi_i(e)],$$

where E_i is the expectation operator based on the subjective probability distribution of e by the i-th individual, and $t_i(e)$ is the payment received by the i-th individual under state e. From Chapter 4, this objective function can be equivalently written in terms of the certainty equivalent

$$E_i[t_i(e)] + E_i[\pi_i(e)] - R_i, \; i = 1, \ldots, n,$$

where R_i is the Arrow–Pratt risk premium for the i-th individual: $R_i = 0$ under risk neutrality, and $R_i > 0$ under risk aversion. The problem is to design an efficient insurance contract between the insurance firm and the $(n - 1)$ individuals.

The associated benefit function b_i for the i-th individual satisfies $E_i u_i[t_i(e) + \pi_i(e) - b_i] = U_i$, or $E_i[t_i(e)] + E_i[\pi_i(e)] - R_i - b_i = u_i^{-1}(U_i)$. This implies the following individual benefit

$$b_i(t_i(e)) = E_i[t_i(e)] + E_i[\pi_i(e)] - R_i - u_i^{-1}(U_i), \; i = 1, \ldots, n.$$

Again, this shows that the risk premium R_i is the implicit cost of private risk bearing: it is measured in monetary units and contributes to reducing the individual benefit function $b_i(\cdot)$. Then, from Chapter 11, the efficient insurance scheme is given by

$$0 = V(U) = \text{Max} \left\{ \sum_{i=1}^{n} \{ E_i[t_i(e)] + E_i[\pi_i(e)] - R_i - u_i^{-1}(U_i) \} \right\}. \quad (7)$$

This means that efficient transfers $t(e)$ maximize aggregate benefit $\sum_{i=1}^{n} b_i$, while the resulting surplus $V(U)$ is completely redistributed among the n individuals.

Consider the following situation:

- There is no asymmetric information within the group.
- The insurance firm is risk neutral ($R_i = 0$).
- The insured individuals are risk averse ($R_i \geq 0$, with $R_i = 0$ if and only if the i-th individual faces no risk, $i = 2, \ldots, n$).

Then, the *efficient transfer* (or the efficient insurance contract) is of the form:

$t_i(e)^* = K_i - \pi_i(e)$ for some (non-random) constant K_i, $i = 2, \ldots, n$,

$$t_1(e)^* = -\sum_{i=2}^{n} t_i(e)^* = \sum_{i=2}^{n} [\pi_i(e) - K_i].$$

To see that, note that the above decision rule implies that $[t_i(e)^* + \pi_i(e)] = K_i$. Since K_i is nonrandom, this means that the i-th individual faces no risk and thus that his/her risk premium is zero: $R_i = 0$ for $i = 2, \ldots, n$. And $R_1 = 0$ because the insurance firm is risk neutral. Then it is sufficient to note that any other transfer rule would imply $R_i > 0$ for some $i \geq 2$, thus increasing the aggregate risk premium $\sum_{i=1}^{n} R_i$ and reducing aggregate benefit in (7). Also, note that the surplus is entirely redistributed (with $V(U) = 0$) when U satisfies $u_i^{-1}(U_i) = E_i[t_i(e)] + E_i[\pi_i(e)] - R_i$, $i = 1, \ldots, n$. And changes in the K's are equivalent to lump sum transfers between the n agents, generating moves along the Pareto utility frontier.

Thus, in the *absence of asymmetric information*, the optimal transfer is as follows:

- The risk neutral insurance firm bears *all* the risks;
- The optimal insurance contract *eliminates all private risk-bearing* by the risk-averse insured individuals.

This reflects the main benefit of insurance: redistributing the risk away from the (more) risk-averse individuals. This lowers the social cost of risk and improves the efficiency of risk allocation.

THE PRINCIPAL–AGENT MODEL

In general, risk transfers are decided jointly with other allocation decisions. The jointness of these decisions under imperfect information has generated much interest. The related economic issues have been presented in the simple context of two individuals: $n = 2$. When one individual is called "the principal" and the other "the agent," this generates the classical principal–agent model (see Shavell 1979; Holmstrom 1979).

Let individual 1 be "the principal" and individual 2 be "the agent." Let e be a random variable representing uncertainty facing the two individuals. Assume that the principal designs a contract for the agent to choose an ex-ante "effort level" z generating a stochastic monetary return $\pi(z, e)$ to be shared between the two parties. The return is shared such that, under state e, the agent receives $t_2(e)$ and the principal receives $t_1(e) = [\pi(z, e) - t_2(e)]$. The issue is how to make efficient decisions for effort z and payment $t_2(e)$. Under the expected utility model, assume that the objective function of the principal is $E_1 u_1[\pi(z, e) - t_2(e)]$, while the objective function of the agent is $E_2 u_2(t_2(e)) - v(z)$, where E_i is the expectation operator based on the information available to the i-th individual, $i = 1, 2$. The term $v(z)$ reflects the utility cost of effort for the agent. Throughout, we assume nonsatiation where the marginal utility of income is positive: $\partial u_1 / \partial \pi > 0$ and $\partial u_2 / \partial t_2 > 0$. As seen in Chapter 11, efficiency in the principal–agent model can be represented as follows:

$$\text{Max}\{E_1 u_1[\pi(z, e) - t_2(e)] : E_2 u_2(t_2(e)) - v(z) \geq U_2, z \text{ is feasible}\}, \quad (8)$$

where U_2 is the reservation utility for the agent. The constraint $E_2 u_2(t_2(e)) - v(z) \geq U_2$ is called the *participation constraint* or the *individual rationality constraint*. It states that if U_2 represents the utility received by the agent in the absence of contract, then the agent would not agree with a contract generating utility less than U_2. From Chapter 3, note that expression (8) can be equivalently expressed in terms of the corresponding certainty equivalents:

$$\text{Max}\{E_1[\pi(z, e) - t_2(e)] - R_1 : E_2[t_2(e)] - R_2 \geq u_2^{-1}[U_2 + v(z)], z \text{ is feasible}\}, \quad (8')$$

where R_i is the risk premium measuring the implicit cost of private risk bearing the i-th individual, $i = 1, 2$.

THE OPTIMAL CONTRACT WHEN EFFORT IS OBSERVABLE

We first consider the case of *symmetric information*, where the principal and the agent have access to the same information. This implies that *the effort level z chosen by the agent is observable by the principal*. It means that the principal can include the effort level in the terms of the contract. The efficient contract then corresponds to the optimal solution $(t_2(e)^*, z^*)$ of the constrained optimization problem (8). The associated Lagrangean is $L = E_1 u_1[\pi(z, e) - t_2(e)] + \lambda[E_2 u_2(t_2(e)) - v(z) - U_2]$, where $\lambda \geq 0$ is the Lagrange multiplier associated with the participation constraint (see Appendix B). Under efficiency, one expects the participation constraint to be binding. To see that, simply note that a nonbinding constraint (where $\lambda = 0$) always implies an inefficient contract since the principal could be made better off by reducing the payment $t_2(e)$. As a result, the associated Lagrange multiplier λ is necessarily positive at the optimum: $\lambda^* > 0$. Under differentiability, the first-order necessary conditions for an interior solution $(t_2(e)^*, z^*)$ to (8) are:

$$\partial u_1 / \partial \pi = \lambda \, \partial u_2 / \partial t_2(e), \quad (9a)$$

$$E_1[(\partial u_1/\partial \pi)(\partial \pi/\partial z)] = \lambda \, \partial v/\partial z, \tag{9b}$$

$$E_2 u_2(t_2(e)) - v(z) = U_2. \tag{9c}$$

Equation (9a) can be alternatively written as

$$[\partial u_1/\partial \pi]/[\partial u_2/\partial t_2(e)] = \lambda. \tag{9a'}$$

The left-hand side in (9a') is the ratio of marginal utility of the principal to the marginal utility of the agent. It measures the marginal rate of substitution from transferring \$1 from the agent to the principal under state e. Then, equation (9a') states that at the optimal $t_2(e)^*$, *the ratio of the marginal utilities of the principal and the agent are constant for all states e.* This is the condition characterizing *efficient risk distribution between the two parties.* In addition, equation (9a') identifies the Lagrange multiplier $\lambda^* > 0$ as measuring the marginal rate of substitution from transferring \$1 from the agent to the principal *under any state.* Equation (9b) states that, at the optimum effort z^*, the marginal value of effort, $E_1[(\partial u_1/\partial \pi)(\partial \pi/\partial z)]$, equals its marginal cost, $\lambda \partial v/\partial z$, all being expressed in terms of the utility of the principal. Finally, equation (9c) simply reflects that the participation constraint is binding.

To better understand the implications of (9a') for risk allocation, it will be useful to consider alternative situations. First, if *the principal is risk neutral,* $u_1(\pi - t_2)$ is linear in π and $\partial u_1/\partial \pi$ is a constant for all e. Then at the optimum, equation (9a') implies that $\partial u_2/\partial t_2(e)$ must also be a constant for all states e. If the agent is risk averse (with $\partial^2 u_2/\partial t_2^2 < 0$), equation (9a') can hold only if $t_2(e)$ is a constant. This means that, under an efficient contract, *the risk-averse agent must receive a payment $t_2(e)$ that is independent of the state e: $t_2(e)^* = K_1$,* where K_1 is a nonstochastic constant. This corresponds to a *standard wage contract* where the agent receives a fixed amount K_1 from the principal who is the residual claimant (receiving $\pi(z^*, e) - K_1$ under state e). Thus, when effort is observable, efficiency in risk allocation implies that *a risk-neutral principal must bear all the risk, completely insuring the risk-averse agent.* This is an intuitive result. Indeed, from (8'), the risk premium for a risk-neutral principal is always zero ($R_1 = 0$), while the risk premium for a risk-averse agent is nonnegative ($R_2 \geq 0$) and equals zero if and only if the agent faces no risk. Thus, the contract where $t_2(e)^* = K_1$ is the only situation where $R_1 = R_2 = 0$, i.e. where the total cost of risk bearing is zero. This is the situation where all the observable risk is efficiently transferred to the risk-neutral principal.

Second, consider the opposite situation where *the agent is risk neutral.* Then, $u_2(t_2)$ is linear in t_2 and $\partial u_2/\partial t_2(e)$ is a constant for all e. Then at the optimum, equation (9a') implies that $\partial u_1/\partial \pi$ must also be a constant for all states e. If the principal is risk averse (with $\partial^2 u_1/\partial \pi^2 < 0$), equation (9a') can hold only if $\pi(z, e) - t_2(e)$ is a constant. This means that, under an efficient contract, *the risk-averse principal must receive a payoff $\pi(z, e) - t_2(e)$ that is independent of the state e*: $\pi(z^*, e) - t_2(e)^* = K_2$, where K_2 is a nonstochastic constant. The agent would then receive $t_2(e)^* = \pi(z^*, e) - K_2$. This corresponds to a *franchise contract* where the agent pays a fixed amount K_2 to the principal and keeps the rest: $\pi(z^*, e) - K_2$ under state e. Since the agent becomes the residual claimant, this can also be interpreted as the agent buying the activity (the firm) from the principal. Thus, when effort is observable, efficiency in risk allocation implies that *a risk-neutral agent must bear all the risk, completely insuring the risk-averse principal*. Again, this is an intuitive result. Indeed, from (8'), the risk premium for a risk-neutral agent is always zero ($R_2 = 0$), while the risk premium for a risk-averse principal is non-negative ($R_1 \geq 0$) and equals zero if and only if the principal faces no risk. Thus, the contract where $t_2(e)^* = \pi(z^*, e) - K_2$ is the only situation where $R_1 = R_2 = 0$, i.e. where the total cost of risk bearing is zero. This is the situation where all the observable risk is efficiently transferred to the risk-neutral agent.

Third, consider the situation where *both principal and agent are risk averse*. From equation (8'), the risk premium R_i is nonnegative in general and strictly positive when the i-th individual faces some risk, $i = 1, 2$. It means that it is no longer possible to design a risk-sharing scheme that would reduce both R_1 and R_2 down to zero. Then, efficient risk sharing will take place when the aggregate cost of risk bearing ($R_1 + R_2$) is minimized. This typically means that *both the principal and the agent accept part of the risk*. To illustrate, consider the simple case where z^* is fixed, and the risk premiums take the form $R_1 = r_1 \text{Var}[\pi(z^*, e) - t_2(e)]$ *and* $R_2 = r_2 \text{Var}[t_2(e)]$, $r_i > 0$ being the coefficient of risk aversion of the i-th individual (see Chapter 6). Assume that $t_2(e) = \alpha + \beta\pi(z^*, e)$ where β *measures the proportion of the risky payoff received by the agent*. Then, $R_1 = r_1(1 - \beta)^2 \text{Var}(\pi)$, $R_2 = r_2\beta^2 \text{Var}(\pi)$, *and* $(R_1 + R_2) = [r_1(1-\beta)^2 + r_2\beta^2]\text{Var}(\pi)$. Then, the value of β that minimizes $(R_1 + R_2)$ is $\beta^* = r_1/(r_1 + r_2)$. This implies $\partial\beta^*/\partial r_1 > 0$ and $\partial\beta^*/\partial r_2 < 0$, with $0 < \beta^* < 1$. Thus, *the proportion of risk shared with the agent increases with the risk aversion of the principal ($\partial\beta^*/\partial r_1 > 0$), and decreases with the risk aversion of the agent ($\partial\beta^*/\partial r_2 < 0$)*. Intuitively, this illustrates that it is efficient to shift the risk toward the individual who is less risk averse. Note that this includes the situations discussed above as special cases: as $r_1 \to 0$, $\beta^* \to 0$ as the risk-neutral principal absorbs all the risk; and as $r_2 \to 0$, $\beta^* \to 1$ as the risk-neutral agent absorbs all the risk.

The Optimal Contract When Effort is not Observable

We just analyzed efficient contract design under symmetric information, where effort was observable by the principal. We now introduce *asymmetric information* between the two parties. The main issue is, how does asymmetric information affect the design of an efficient contract? In the case where the principal has more information than the agent, then the analysis just presented applies—the principal can use his/her superior information to design an efficient contract. But the situation becomes more complex when *the agent has more information than the principal*. Indeed, the contract written by the principal can only depend on the information available to the principal. This allows the agent to take advantage of his/her better information. We want to investigate how this affects optimal contracts.

We start our analysis focusing on a particular type of asymmetric information: when *the principal cannot observe the agent's behavior*. In the context of the principal–agent model, this means that the principal does not observe the effort level z chosen by the agent. It implies that the *effort level cannot be specified in the terms of the contract*. Intuitively, when effort is costly, this gives an incentive for the agent to apply little effort, which may be detrimental to the efficiency of resource allocation. This type of asymmetric information problem is known as *moral hazard*. Below, we study the optimal contract under asymmetric information with respect to effort.

Without observing the agent's effort, the principal cannot force the agent to choose a particular effort level. Then, the only option is for the principal to choose a payment scheme that *induces* the agent to choose the efficient level of effort. When effort z is not specified in the contract, the agent chooses z according to the optimization problem

$$z \text{ solves Max}_z\{E_2u_2(t_2(e)) - v(z): \ z \text{ is feasible}\}. \tag{10}$$

This condition is called the *incentive compatibility constraint*. For a given payment scheme $t_2(e)$, it states that, since effort is not verifiable, the agent chooses the level of effort that maximizes his/her objective function. Without observing z, the principal takes the incentive compatibility constraint as given. After adding this constraint to the optimization problem (8), the efficient contract under moral hazard can be represented as

$$\text{Max}\{E_1u_1[\pi(z, e) - t_2(e)]: E_2u_2(t_2(e)) - v(z) \geq U_2;$$
$$z \text{ solves Max}_z\{E_2u_2(t_2(e)) - v(z): \ z \text{ is feasible}\}\}. \tag{11}$$

This is the standard formulation of the *principal–agent model under moral hazard*. It provides a formal framework to analyze efficient contract design under asymmetric information about the agent's behavior. Comparing (8) to

(11), asymmetric information about effort has added the incentive compatibility constraint (10). Since adding a constraint cannot increase the value of the objective function in a maximization problem, it follows that *introducing asymmetric information and moral hazard tends to make the principal worse off*. This is just another statement that the (gross) value of information is nonnegative (see Chapter 11).

The Case of a Risk-Neutral Agent:

Note that when the incentive compatibility constraint is nonbinding in (11), then moral hazard creates no welfare loss, and the optimal contract is the one obtained under symmetric information (as previously discussed). This happens if the *agent is risk neutral*, in which case the efficient contract stipulates a payment scheme $t_2(e)^* = \pi(z^*, e) - K_2$, where K_2 is a nonstochastic constant. As seen above, this corresponds to a *franchise contract* where the agent pays a fixed amount K_2 to the principal and is the residual claimant receiving $\pi(z^*, e) - K_2$. In this case, note that the optimal contract obtained in (8) under symmetric information always satisfies the incentive compatibility constraint (10). Thus, *when the agent is risk neutral, it remains efficient to shift all the risk to the agent, whether or not there is asymmetric information about effort*.

The Case of a Risk-Averse Agent:

In situations where *the agent is risk averse*, asymmetric information about the agent's effort tends to have adverse welfare effects. When the incentive compatibility constraint (10) becomes binding, the optimal contract differs from the symmetric information case. Unfortunately, when binding, the incentive compatibility constraint can be difficult to evaluate in general.

For the purpose of illustration, it will be convenient to focus on the simple case where the agent is risk averse ($R_2 \geq 0$ with $R_2 = 0$ if and only if the agent faces no risk), the *principal is risk neutral*($R_1 = 0$), and the agent chooses between *two levels of effort*, high effort z_H and low effort z_L. Assume that the utility-cost of effort satisfies $v(z_H) > v(z_L)$. It means that any fixed payment scheme would only get the agent to choose the low level of effort z_L. If the principal prefers low level of effort z_L, the incentive compatibility constraint is always satisfied, and the contract obtained under symmetric information remains efficient. The problem becomes of interest when the principal prefers high effort to low effort (e.g., when the risky propect $\pi(z_H, e)$ exhibits first-order stochastic dominance over $\pi(z_L, e)$; see Chapter 5). We focus on this situation below. Consider the case where e is a discrete random variable satisfying $Pr_{H_s} = \text{Prob}(\pi(z_H, e_s))$ and $Pr_{Ls} = \text{Prob}(\pi(z_L, e_s))$, $s = 1, \ldots, S$. In order to induce the agent to choose a high level of effort, the contact must involve a state-dependent transfer $t_2(e)$, which induces the agent to choose z_H. This is reflected by the incentive compatibility constraint (10), which takes the form:

$$\sum_{s=1}^{S} Pr_{Hs}u_2(t_2(e_s)) - v(z_H)] \geq \sum_{s=1}^{S} Pr_{Ls}u_2(t_2(e_s)) - v(z_L)],$$

or

$$\sum_{s=1}^{S} [Pr_{Hs} - Pr_{Ls}]u_2(t_2(e_s)) \geq v(z_H)] - v(z_L). \qquad (12)$$

Equation (12) is intuitive: it states that the expected utility gain from choosing high effort must be at least as large as the associated increase in cost.

We have seen above that, under symmetric information and a risk-neutral principal, it is optimal for the principal to bear all the risk, corresponding to $t_2(e_s) = K_1$, where K_1 is a nonstochastic constant. Note that this implies that the left-hand side in (12) is zero (since $\sum_{s=1}^{S} Pr_{Hs} = \sum_{s=1}^{s} Pr_{Ls} = 1$). But this is inconsistent with (12) (since $v(z_H) > v(z_L)$ means that the right-hand side in (12) is positive). Thus, the optimal contract obtained under symmetric information never satisfies the incentive compatibility constraint. This means that, under this scenario, *the incentive compatibility constraint (12) is always binding, and the optimal contract under moral hazard necessarily differs from the one obtained under symmetric information.*

For a risk-neutral principal who prefers z_H, the Lagrangean associated with the optimization problem (11) is $L = \sum_{s=1}^{S} Pr_{Hs}[\pi(z_H, e_s) - t_2(e_s)] + \lambda [\sum_{s=1}^{S} Pr_{Hs}u_2(t_2(e_s)) - v(z) - U_2] + \gamma [\sum_{s=1}^{S} [Pr_{Hs} - Pr_{Ls}]u_2(t_2(e)) - v(z_H)] + v(z_L)]$, where $\lambda \geq 0$ and $\gamma \geq 0$ are Lagrange multipliers associated with the participation constraint and the incentive compatibility constraint, respectively. Under differentiability, the first-order necessary condition with respect to $t_2(e)$ is

$$-Pr_{Hs} + \lambda Pr_{Hs}\partial u_2/\partial t_2(e_s) + \gamma [Pr_{Hs} - Pr_{Ls}]\partial u_2/\partial t_2(e_s) = 0,$$

or

$$1/[\partial u_2/\partial t_2(e_s)] = \lambda + \gamma [1 - (Pr_{Ls}/Pr_{Hs})], \qquad (13)$$

for $s = 1, \ldots, S$. Note that $\gamma > 0$ since we have just seen that the incentive compatibility constraint is necessarily binding. With $\gamma > 0$, equation (13) implies that $\partial u_2/\partial t_2(e_s)$ increases with the *likelihood ratio* (Pr_{Ls}/Pr_{Hs}), $s = 1, \ldots, S$. Given a risk-averse agent, $\partial^2 u_2/\partial t_2(e_s)^2 < 0$ and $\partial u_2/\partial t_2$ is a decreasing function of t_2. It follows from (13) that *the efficient payment*

$t_2(e_s)^*$ *must be a decreasing function of the likelihood ratio*(Pr_{Ls}/Pr_{Hs}), $s = 1, \ldots, S$. It means that, for a given state e_s, the smaller likelihood ratio (Pr_{Ls}/Pr_{Hs}), the larger the probability that the effort was z_H (as opposed to z_L), the larger the payment $t_2(e_s)^*$, $s = 1, \ldots, S$. This is intuitive: *Under moral hazard, the optimal payment to the agent is larger (smaller) in states that are more (less) likely to be associated with the desired high effort.* It provides an incentive for the agent to exert high effort. Interestingly, this does not necessarily link the payment $t_2(e_s)^*$ to the payoff $\pi(z, e_s)$. Rather, it uses observations on $\pi(z, e_s)$ as an information device on the agent's behavior. See Macho-Stadler and Pérez-Castrillo 1997, or Salanié 1999 for additional discussion.

In summary, under moral hazard and a risk-averse agent, the efficient contract has the following characteristics:

- at least *some risk will be faced by the principal* (otherwise, the benefits of risk sharing with the risk-averse agent would not be obtained)
- if the incentive compatibility constraint is binding, then *some risk will be faced by the agent*. To see that, assume the contrary where the agent faces no risk and receives a nonstochastic payment K. Then, the agent would receive utility $u_2(K) - v(z)$, and would choose z so as to minimize the cost of effort $v(z)$. When the incentive compatibility constraint is binding, the principal would prefer a different choice for z, implying that the effort provided by the agent is not optimal. This means that a fixed payment K to the agent cannot be efficient. Under this scenario, in contrast with the symmetric information case, it is efficient for the risk-averse agent to face some risk. Obviously, this optimal risk exposure cannot be motivated by concerns about the private cost of risk bearing. Rather, it is motivated as an incentive for the agent to behave more efficiently. For example, in the context of insurance, a complete redistribution of risk away from the agent would mean that the agent no longer has private incentives to reduce the risk being insured (e.g., by providing "appropriate effort" to prevent fire under fire insurance). In this case, it is efficient to shift some of the risk to the agent. This provides an *incentive effect* for effort z, attempting to correct for the existence of moral hazard in contract under asymmetric information.

Some Examples:

The usefulness of the previous analysis is illustrated next in a few examples.

Example 1: *Liability Rules* between an individual or a firm (the agent) and society, typically represented by a government agency (the principal). Dealing with an accident that can happen with some positive probability, there are two broad categories of liability rules:

- *strict liability*, where the agent pays a fee but only if the accident occurs.
- *negligence*, where the agent pays a fee, depending on whether the firm has been negligent or not.

The above results suggest that *strict liability rules are appropriate if the firm is risk neutral.* Alternatively, *negligence standards are appropriate if the firm is risk averse.*

Example 2: *Moral hazard and insurance*, where the agent is the insured individual and the principal is the insurance firm. In the context of asymmetric information, our results suggest that, if the agent is risk averse, moral hazard can imply that he/she must bear some of the risk. Then, in an efficient insurance contract under asymmetric information, the insurance coverage should not shift all the risk away from the agent and should include a *deductible*.

Example 3: *Sharecropping*, where the principal is the landlord, and the agent is the tenant. Then, if the tenant is risk neutral, a *cash rent* contract would be efficient. Alternatively, if the principal and the agent are both risk averse, then some form of *sharecropping* would be efficient. In this case, both risk-sharing and incentive issues would motivate the design of a sharecropping contract (see Stiglitz 1974).

ADVERSE SELECTION

We have just analyzed the efficiency of contract design when there is asymmetric information about individual behavior. Here, we investigate the implications of another form of asymmetric information, when "the principal" chooses a decision rule affecting the welfare of other individuals without being able to observe some of the characteristics of these individuals. To illustrate, consider a competitive insurance industry composed of risk-neutral insurance firms. There are two types of potentially insurable individuals:

- *type a*: "low risk" individuals facing a prospect of loss $\pi_a(e) > 0$,
- *type b*: "high risk" individuals facing a prospect of loss $\pi_b(e) > 0$,

with $E(\pi_a) < E(\pi_b)$.

Assume that all individuals behave in way consistent with the expected utility model and have the same risk-averse preferences $U(-\pi)$, implying

$$EU(-\pi_a) = U(E(-\pi_a) - R_a), \text{ for individuals of "type a"}$$

and

$$EU(-\pi_b) = U(E(-\pi_b) - R_b), \text{ for individuals of "type b"}$$

where $R_a > 0$ and $R_b > 0$ are the risk premium.

The insurance firms know that there are percent individuals of type a, and $(1 - \alpha)$ percent individuals of type b, but they *do not know the type of each individual*. This is a situation of *asymmetric information*, not about the actions of individuals but about their "type."

Under competition, the insurance firms may want to offer an insurance contract for the loss π, with premium set equal to the expected value of the loss among all individuals:

$$\alpha E(\pi_a) + (1 - \alpha)E(\pi_b).$$

Type b individuals would always accept this contract since

$$U[- E(\pi_b) - R_b] = EU(- \pi_b) < U[- \alpha E(\pi_a) - (1 - \alpha)E(\pi_b)]$$

or

$$0 > \alpha[E(\pi_a) - E(\pi_b)] < R_b > 0.$$

However, type a individuals would *not accept this contract if*:

$$U[- E(\pi_a) - R_a] = EU(- \pi_a) > U[= \alpha E(\pi_a) - (1 - \alpha)E(\pi_b)]$$

or

$$(1 - \alpha)[E(\pi_b) - E(\pi_a)] > R_a.$$

In this case, "low risk" individuals would *self-select* and would not purchase a contract. The insurance firms would face higher losses than anticipated (because only "high-risk" individuals would purchase the contract). As a result, the proposed contract *cannot be an equilibrium contract*. Thus, under asymmetric information, low-risk individuals may not be able to obtain an equilibrium insurance contract, resulting in a *market failure*. This has been called a problem of *adverse selection*.

Other examples of adverse selection can be found in product quality (when the buyer has less information about product quality than the seller), labor market (when the worker knows his/her innate abilities better than the employer), credit market (when the creditor has better information than the bank about ability to repay a loan), etc.

In general, asymmetric information about individual characteristics is a concern when it restricts the terms of contracts. As discussed in Chapter 11, designing contracts under poor information implies a reduction in the efficiency of resource allocation. Thus, asymmetric information is in general a source of inefficiency. And as just illustrated, it can contribute to market failures. In extreme cases, it can lead to the disappearance of markets. However, this is not always the case. Even though asymmetric information reduces efficiency, sometimes it is possible to develop contracts that can discriminate among individual types. The idea is to try to develop a menu of contracts such that each contract is designed for an individual type, and each individual has an incentive to purchase only the contract designed for his/her type. When this is possible, then a price discrimination scheme among the different contracts may be an effective way of dealing with information asymmetry (see Rothschild and Stiglitz 1970, Macho-Stadler and Pérez-Castrillo 1997, or Salanié 1999 for additional discussion).

THE ROLE OF ASYMMETRIC INFORMATION

We saw in Chapter 11 that asymmetric information contributes to inefficiency in resource allocation in two ways: (1) it implies less refined decision rules by the poorly informed individuals, and (2) it has adverse effects on exchange, meaning that it contributes to both incomplete markets and incomplete contracts and reduces the gains from trade. We have seen two situations pointing out the adverse effects of asymmetric information: moral hazard (associated with the decisions made by "more-informed" individuals) and adverse selection (associated with self-selection of individuals with "hidden characteristics"). Since there is typically much heterogeneity among individuals and in their access to information, this suggests that asymmetric information issues are generic in evaluating the efficiency of resource allocation. This stresses that information generates *external effects* that need to be addressed in contract and policy design.

How can asymmetric information be efficiently managed? Note that this is an issue only in situations where information is costly (otherwise the less-informed individuals could always obtain additional information). One option is to invest in information-gathering activities to help better inform the decision-making process. Under costly information, this would take place up to the point where the marginal benefit equals the marginal cost of the additional information.

An alternative involves contract or policy rules designed such that the better-informed individuals are willing to reveal their information to the principal. There is extensive literature on this topic, broadly called *mechanism design*. The scheme is to design a contract involving *informational rents* paid to the well-informed agents, rents that provide them with an incentive to reveal what they know. This is often seen as an effective decentralized way of dealing with asymmetric information issues. It can lead to price discrimination schemes (or nonlinear pricing) where different bundles are priced in such a way that the well-informed buyers reveal their information through their purchase decision. Finally, in cases where the informational rent is large (i.e., when the incentive effects dominate possible risk-sharing benefits), it would be efficient to make the better-informed individual face all risk and be the "residual claimant".

Another way involves "signaling." Consider a well-informed agent adversely affected by an adverse selection problem. Then, this agent can send a signal observed by the principal that may influence the principal's beliefs about the agent's identity. To the extent that the signal is credible, it can help deal with asymmetric information issues (see Macho-Stadler and Pérez-Castrillo 1997, and Salanié 1999 for a discussion). An example is the case of education used as a signal in the labor market for the underlying unknown ability of individuals. Finally, another way to deal with asymmetric information problems involves interlinkage of contracts and transactions (e.g., credit contract and land contract); it may help reduce transaction costs and decrease moral hazard problems.

This discussion stresses the importance of information and information management. While good information is crucial in efficient resource allocation, its distribution across individuals often involves external effects that can be difficult to manage. In complex economies, bounded rationality means that centralized management of information can be difficult and often inefficient. But decentralized management of information externalities is also difficult. Given the discussion presented in Chapter 11, efficient contracts, efficient policy, and efficient forms of economic organizations typically depend on individual abilities to obtain and process information, and on associated transaction costs.

PROBLEMS

1. A principal contracts an agent to carry out a specific task under uncertainty. The agent chooses a level of effort z, generating the payoff π. The probability function of the payoff (conditional on z) is $f(\pi, z)$. Risk preferences are represented by the utility function $U_p(\pi - t)$ for the principal, and $U_a = u(t, z)$ for the agent, where t denotes the payment made by the principal to the agent.
   a. Evaluate the efficient contract.
   b. What is the optimal contract if the principal is risk neutral?
2. A worker can exert two levels of effort, high effort z_H and low effort z_L, which induce a production error with probability 0.25 and 0.75, respectively. His utility function is $U(t, z) = 100 - 10/t - v(z)$, where t denotes the payment received and $v(z) = 2$ when $z = z_H$, and 0 when $z = z_L$. The product obtained is worth 20 if there are no errors and 0 otherwise. The principal is risk neutral, and the worker has reservation utility equal to 0.
   a. Find the optimal contract and the optimal effort under symmetric information.

b. Now assume that production errors are observable by the principal, but effort is not. Then, under asymmetric information, find the optimal contract and the effort that the principal desires.

3. Consider a contract between a risk-neutral principal and a risk-averse agent, where the agent effort is not observable. The utility function of the agent is $u(t, z) = t^{1/2} - z^2$, where t is the payment to agent and z is the effort level. The agent can choose between low effort $z_L = 0$ and high effort $z_H = 3$. His reservation utility is 21. The risky payoff π can vary from 0, to 1000 to 2500, with associated probabilities:

probability	$\pi = 0$	$\pi = 1000$	$\pi = 2500$
z_L	0.4	0.4	0.2
z_H	0.2	0.4	0.4

a. What is the efficient contract under symmetric information?
b. Under moral hazard, what is the optimal contract?
c. What is the optimal contract if the agent is risk neutral?

Chapter 13

Price Stabilization

Competitive market equilibrium plays a crucial role in economic analysis. It focuses on the role of competitive markets and competitive prices in resource allocation. One key result obtained in Chapter 11 is the following:

In the presence of complete competitive markets and in the absence of externalities, a market economy can generate a Pareto efficient allocation of resources.

This result has sometimes been used to argue in favor of a market economy and against the involvement of government in economic policy. In this context, in order to justify government policy, it becomes necessary to identify the presence of market failures. Market failures can take many forms (e.g., noncompetitive markets, externalities, the presence of public goods). This section focuses on a particular form of market failure: the fact that risk markets are typically *incomplete* under uncertainty.

Indeed, under uncertainty and in the absence of externalities, we saw in Chapter 11 that competitive market equilibrium is Pareto efficient *if there exists a competitive market for each possible state of nature*. This is the assumption of *perfect contingent claim markets*. The problem is that, although many markets exist in the real world, they clearly do not cover *all possible states of nature*. For example, there is no market that would trade on whether the growing season will be good for farmers ten years from now. Thus, we are in a typical situation of *incomplete risk markets*. This suggests that incomplete contingent claim markets can generate inefficient resource allocation. In this case, nonmarket institutions (including government) could possibly help improve the efficiency of resource allocation. But are there scenarios under which a market economy may still be efficient in the presence of incomplete risk markets?

We consider a simple static competitive market under uncertainty. Competitive prices are determined by the market equilibrium condition equating supply and demand. Uncertainty can influence both the supply function and the demand function.

REVIEW OF CONSUMER THEORY

Consumer theory consists in the following problem. Maximize consumer preferences represented by the direct utility function $U(y)$ subject to a budget constraint:

$$V(p, I) = \text{Max}_y\{U(y): p'y = I\}$$

where y is a vector of consumer goods, p is the vector of market prices for y, $(p'\, y)$ denotes consumer expenditures, $I > 0$ denotes consumer income, and $V(p, I)$ is the indirect utility function. Denote the Marshallian demand by $y^*(p, I)$, the optimal choice function for y in the above optimization. Some key results of consumer theory are as follows:

$\partial V/\partial I > 0$ is the marginal utility of income (assumed to be positive),

$$\partial V/\partial p = -y^*(\partial V/\partial I), \quad (Roy's\ identity). \tag{1}$$

CONSUMER BENEFITS FROM STABILIZATION

Assume that a consumer faces some uncertainty represented by the random variable e (e.g., price uncertainty or preference uncertainty). Assume that e is *known at the time of the consumer decision y, but not known before it*. The indirect utility function then takes the form $V(e, I)$. Let $\mu = E(e)$ denote the mean of e and $\sigma^2 = \text{Var}(e) > 0$ denote the variance of e. Under the expected utility model, the consumer welfare is evaluated ex-ante as represented by the function $EV(e, I)$, where E is the expectation operator.

The question is, what is the consumer's willingness-to-pay to stabilize e to its mean μ? This willingness-to-pay is the sure amount of money B that satisfies:

$$EV(e, I) = V(\mu, I - B), \tag{2}$$

where B is the maximum amount of money the consumer would be willing to give up ex-ante to replace e by its mean μ.

A useful local approximation of B can be obtained as follows. Take a second-order Taylor series approximation of $EV(e, I)$ with respect to e in the neighborhood of μ:

$$EV(e, I) \approx E\{V(\mu, I) + (\partial V(\mu, I)/\partial\mu)[e - \mu] + 1/2(\partial^2 V(\mu, I)/\partial\mu^2)[e - \mu]^2\}$$
$$\approx V(\mu, I) + 1/2(\partial^2 V(\mu, I)/\partial\mu^2)\sigma^2.$$

Similarly, taking a first-order Taylor series expansion of $V(\mu, I - B)$ with respect to μ in the neighborhood of $B = 0$ gives

$$V(\mu, I - B) \approx V(\mu, I) - B \cdot [\partial V(\mu, I)/\partial I].$$

Combining these two results and using the definition of B in (2) yields

$$-B(\partial V(\mu, I)/\partial I) \simeq 1/2(\partial^2 V(\mu, I)/\partial\mu^2)\sigma^2,$$

or

$$B \approx -1/2\sigma^2[\partial^2 V(\mu, I)/\partial\mu^2]/[\partial V(\mu, I)/\partial I]. \qquad (3)$$

Given $\sigma^2 > 0$ and $[\partial V(\mu, I)/\partial I] > 0$ by assumption, it follows that

$$B >, =, < 0 \ as \ [\partial^2 V(\mu, I)/\partial\mu^2] <, =, > 0.$$

Thus, *the consumer benefits (loses) from stabilizing the risk e to its mean μ if the indirect utility function V is concave (convex) in e.*

CONSUMER BENEFITS FROM PRICE STABILIZATION

Let $e = p$, where e is the price of some commodity y. We have just shown that the consumer benefits (loses) from price stabilization if the indirect utility function V is concave (convex) in the price p. Thus, we need to investigate the concavity/convexity property of the indirect utility function V with respect to the price p.

Following Turnovsky et al., differentiating Roy's identity (1) with respect to I and p gives:

$$\partial^2 V/\partial I\partial p = -(\partial^2 V/\partial I^2)y^* - (\partial V/\partial I)(\partial y^*/\partial I)$$

and

$$\partial^2 V/\partial p^2 = -(\partial^2 V/\partial I\partial p)y^* - (\partial V/\partial I)(\partial y^*/\partial p)$$
$$= [(\partial^2 V/\partial I^2)y^* + (\partial V/\partial I)(\partial y^*/\partial I)]y^* - (\partial V/\partial I)(\partial y^*/\partial p).$$

It follows that

$$(\partial^2 V/\partial p^2)/(\partial V/\partial I) = [(\partial^2 V/\partial I^2)/(\partial V/\partial I)]y^{*2}+(\partial y^*/\partial I)y^* - (\partial y^*/\partial p)$$
$$= (y/p)[(\partial^2 V/\partial I^2)/(\partial V/\partial I)I](py/I)+(\partial y^*/\partial I)(I/y)(py)/I$$
$$-(\partial y^*/\partial p)(p/y)$$
$$= (y/p)[-\bar{r}(py/I)+(\partial \ln y^*/\partial \ln I)(py/I)-(\partial \ln y^*/\partial \ln p)]$$

where $\bar{r} = -I[(\partial^2 V/\partial I^2)/(\partial V/\partial I)]$ is the *relative risk-aversion coefficient* (see Chapter 4). But we know from (3) that $B \approx -\sigma^2(\partial^2 V/\partial p^2)/(\partial V/\partial I)$ = sign$[-(\partial^2 V/\partial p^2)/(\partial V/\partial I)]$. This gives

$$B > (<)0 \text{ as } (\partial \ln y^*/\partial \ln I) < (>) \bar{r} + (\partial \ln y^*/\partial \ln p)/(py/I).$$

It shows that the consumer may either benefit or lose from price stabilization depending on the relative risk-aversion coefficient , on the price elasticity of demand $[\partial \ln y^*/\partial \ln p]$, and on the income elasticity of demand $[\partial \ln y^*/\partial \ln I]$. It implies that the *consumer benefits from price stabilization increase with a higher degree of risk aversion, with a lower income elasticity and a more inelastic demand.*

Example: Consider the case of price stabilization policies commonly found in agriculture. Some "typical" estimates for food demand are: $\bar{r} = 1$; $[\partial \ln y^*/\partial \ln p] = -0.2$; $[\partial \ln y^*/\partial \ln I] = .6$; and $[py/I] = 0.3$. In this case, the above derivations yield $B < 0$, implying that consumers would obtain *no direct benefits* from agricultural price stabilization policy. However, it should be kept in mind that the previous arguments are developed in a partial equilibrium framework and that they do not consider the possible benefits of risk sharing and risk redistribution between producers and consumers. These issues are explored next.

THE EFFICIENCY OF MARKET EQUILIBRIUM UNDER RISK

Following Newbery and Stiglitz (1981), consider a competitive commodity market model with one representative producer and one representative consumer. The producer faces uncertain output price p, and uncertain production $y = f(x, e)$ where y denotes output, x is a vector of inputs, and e represents production uncertainty (e.g., due to weather). We assume that there exists no contingent claim market on the random variable e. In the context of agriculture, this can reflect the widespread failure of insurance markets against agricultural production risk. Under the expected utility model, the producer makes the supply decision $y^s = f(x^s, e)$, where x^s is the input choice that maximizes the expected utility $EU(p\,f(x, e), x)$.

The consumer purchases the output y at price p, exhibits an indirect utility function $V(p, I)$, and generates the demand $y^d(p, I)$ for y.

In this context, market equilibrium corresponds to:

$$y^s = y^d.$$

We want to focus on the efficiency of risk allocation. To simplify the analysis, we want to eliminate the possibility of information externalities (which could be another source of possible inefficiency). As a result, we assume that expectations are *rational*. In other words, we assume that the subjective probability function of p for both the producer and the consumer is the same as the equilibrium probability function p^e defined implicitly as

$$y^s = f(x^s, e) = y^d(p^e, I).$$

Under such conditions, is the market a locat on efficient? The key result is the following (see Newbery and Stiglitz (1981), sections 15.3, 15.4):

Given risk and a risk-averse producer and the absence of risk markets, a competitive commodity market allocation is Pareto efficient if and only if

$$V(p, I) = -k \ln(p) + b\,h(I).$$

To obtain this result, use Roy's identity (1) for the previous utility function to obtain the corresponding demand function

$$y^d = -(\partial V/\partial p)/(\partial V/\partial I) = -k/(p\,b\,\partial h/\partial I).$$

This implies that

$$\partial \ln(y^d)/\partial \ln(p) = -1,$$

i.e., a *unitary price elasticity of demand*. In this case, note that $[py^d] = -k/(b\partial h/\partial I)$, which is nonrandom. Thus, given a unitary price elasticity of demand, the *uncertainty of production revenue is eliminated* for the producer.

Also, note that the previous utility function implies that $\partial V/\partial I = b \cdot \partial h/\partial I =$ nonrandom. In this case, the consumer is risk neutral with respect to income and thus has *no incentive to share risk*. Thus, if risk markets existed, they would generate no efficiency gains. Alternatively, the absence of risk markets has no adverse effects on efficiency. This shows that the previous utility function corresponds to a situation where a competitive market generates a Pareto efficient allocation of risk between the producer and the consumer.

To summarize, the previous result shows that, given a risk-averse producer, a unitary elasticity of demand preserves the efficiency of market equilibrium under risk. Alternatively, whenever the price elasticity of demand is not unitary, the allocation of resources generated by a competitive commodity market equilibrium would in general be inefficient.

This raises the question, what happens if we consider many producers where each faces a different production uncertainty? In this case, the previous result does not hold. The reason is that revenue uncertainty can never be totally eliminated. If the producers are risk averse, there are some incentives for redistributing risk toward the less risk-averse individuals. In the absence of risk markets, competitive commodity market equilibrium would always be inefficient. Alternatively stated, competitive market equilibrium would then be efficient only if all producers are risk neutral (see Newbery and Stiglitz 1981, section 15.8).

It is useful to apply these results to economic policies attempting to stabilize prices in the agricultural sector. In general, the empirical evidence is that:

1. farmers tend to be risk averse;
2. the demand for food is price inelastic.

This suggests that, in the absence of complete contingent claim markets, *market allocation in agriculture is likely inefficient*. This raises the following questions:

- How to improve the allocation of resources in agriculture under risk?
- What is the role of markets versus nonmarket institutions (e.g., contracts or government policy) in the management of risk in agriculture?

The extensive involvement of government policy and the growing use of contracts can possibly be interpreted as an institutional response to market failures in agriculture. However, there are also significant opportunities for government failures. Weighing one kind of failure against another has generated much debate about the efficiency (or inefficiency) of agricultural policies around the world. Unfortunately, the empirical evidence supporting each argument is sometimes difficult to develop, due to the complexity of conducting applied policy analysis under incomplete risk markets.

Finally, note that the previous analysis has implications for the *economic efficiency of free trade*. In particular, under incomplete markets, it is not true in general that free trade always generates a Pareto efficient resource allocation (see Newbery and Stiglitz 1981, Chapter 23). As an example, consider two agricultural regions, each growing a risky agricultural crop and a safe crop. The representative farmer in each region is assumed to be risk averse. The output of the risky crop in the two regions is negatively correlated. Assume that each region faces a unitary price elasticity of demand for the risky crop. In the absence of trade, because of the unitary elasticity of demand, price variations provide perfect income insurance for the farmer in each region. With the opening of trade, because of the negative correlation between output in the two regions, price variations no longer offset output variations in each country, implying an increased risk of growing the risky crop. This makes the risk-averse farmers worse off and induces them to shift away from the risky crop, raising its average price. If the farmers are sufficiently risk averse and if the consumers are not very risk averse, then both producers and consumers could be made worse off by opening trade. In this case, free trade would be Pareto inferior under incomplete risk markets.

Of course, such a result is not general. For example, there are many situations where opening trade under incomplete risk markets is efficiency enhancing. The problem is one of second-best allocations. In the presence of multiple sources of market failures, a partial move toward market liberalization is not always improving efficiency. The previous example is an illustration of such a situation. This makes the analysis of contract and policy design in a "second-best world" more difficult. Indeed, the many possible sources of inefficiency can interact with each other in complex ways. As a result, policy and efficiency analysis in a second-best world remain quite challenging.

Appendix A: Probability and Statistics

INTRODUCTION

The concepts of chance and uncertainty are as old as civilization. People have always had to cope with weather uncertainty, health hazards, food insecurity, and other risky aspects of their environment. As a result, they have devised risk-management schemes that reduce uncertainty and improve the chances for their own survival. Interestingly, early risk-management strategies were developed without formal logical structures. An example is the decision rule: Do not all put your eggs in the same basket. This simple decision rule does not require any specific assessment of risk. This indicates that modern probability and statistics are not absolutely necessary for risk management. Yet, in many situations, there is much to gain from imposing some structure on what is not known. This includes gambling games.

Games of chance have a long history. Gambling with dice has been popular for many centuries. The precursors of dice have been found in Egypt and elsewhere by 3500 B.C. Interestingly, because they are relatively simple, gambling games provided the impetus for the development of probability theory in the sixteenth and seventeenth century. Girolamo Cardano (1501–1576) and Galileo Galilei (1564–1642) calculated numerical probabilities for certain dice combinations. Blaise Pascal (1623–1662) and Pierre Fermat (1601–1665) started the mathematical theory of probability by deriving the probabilities for certain gambling problems involving dice. Since then the theory of probability has been developed and refined, with applications to engineering, science, and management.

The main motivation for probability theory is to impose a structure on what is not known. While this may appear to be an impossible task, it has two significant payoffs. First, it provides a framework for an empirical assessment of what we do not know. Second, it helps us represent learning as we get more information about our physical, economic, and social environments. Over the last two centuries, humans have accumulated a massive amount of information, which contributed to rapid scientific progress in science and engineering. It seems fair to say that probability theory stimulated this considerable learning.

Following, we summarize the basic structure of probability theory. To be useful, the theory has to be applicable to a wide variety of situations. This means that it has to be general enough to cover any situation where something is not perfectly known. As a result, the language of probability theory is somewhat abstract. It may be useful to keep specific examples in mind to help motivate the theoretical arguments (e.g., the outcome of tossing a coin, or your income next year). The first step is to identify the situation of interest. It involves identifying a decision-maker facing an uncertain situation at a given time. The task at hand is to impose a mathematical structure on this uncertain situation—structure that will eventually prove useful in the analysis of this situation and/or the associated decisions made.

Define the sample space, denoted by S, as the set of all possible occurrences in the situation of interest. The elements of the sample space are called events. Thus any event A is always a subset of the sample space S: $A \in S$. The union of two events A_1 and A_2 (denoted by $A_1 \cup A_2$) consists of all events that belong to either A_1 or A_2. The intersection of two events A_1 and A_2 (denoted by $A_1 \cap A_2$) consists of all events that belong to both A_1 and A_2. Two events A_1 and A_2 are disjoint or mutually exclusive if they have no outcome in common, i.e., if their intersection is empty and satisfies $A_1 \cap A_2 = \varnothing$ (where $\varnothing$ denotes the empty set). Finally, events in a collection of events are said to be disjoint if no two events in the collection have any outcome in common.

AXIOMS OF PROBABILITY

For any event A in a sample space S, the probability that event A will occur is given by $Pr(A)$ satisfying:

Axiom 1. $Pr(A) \geq 0$ for any $A \in S$
Axiom 2. $Pr(S) = 1$
Axiom 3. if A_1, A_2, A_3, ..., is a disjoint sequence of events in S, then

$$Pr(A_1 \cup A_2 \cup A_3 \cup \ldots) = Pr(A_1) + Pr(A_2) + Pr(A_3) + \ldots$$

Axiom 1 states that probabilities are always nonnegative. Axiom 2 indicates that if an event is certain to occur, then its probability is 1 (which can be interpreted to mean 100 percent chance of occurrence). Axiom 3 assumes that probabilities of disjoint events are additive (which may appear less intuitive). This provides a formal mathematical definition of probabilities: For a given sample space S, any function $Pr(A)$ satisfying Axioms 1, 2, and 3 is a probability function.

RANDOM VARIABLES

Often, it is convenient to represent our physical and socioeconomic environment using real measurements. Examples include rainfall, temperature, prices, quantities, income, etc. Under situations of uncertainty (where an individual does not have perfect information about the occurrences in his/her environment), it means that the real value taken by our measurements are not known ahead of time. This motivates the use of random variables. Given a sample space S, a *random variable* is a function $X(s)$ that assigns a real number $X \in R$ to each possible outcome $s \in S$, where R denotes the real line. Some random variables can take continuous values (e.g., the temperature outside your home tomorrow at 7 A.M., as measured in degree Celsius or in degree Fahrenheit). They are called continuous random variables. But some can take only discrete values (e.g., the number of heads obtained after tossing a coin ten times), in which case they are called discrete random variables.

DISTRIBUTION FUNCTION FOR A RANDOM VARIABLE

When X is a random variable, let B be some subset of the real line. For a given sample space S, denote by $Pr(X \in B)$ the probability that the value of X will belong to the subset B. Then, this probability can be written as $Pr(X \in B) = Pr\{s\colon X(s) \in B\}$.

The distribution function for a random variable X is the function $F(t) = Pr(X \leq t)$, where t is a real number. The distribution function has the following properties:

- $F(t)$ is nondecreasing and continuous from the right,
- $F(-\infty) = 0$,
- $F(+\infty) = 1$.

It means that, in general, $0 \leq F(t) \leq 1$ for any t. In addition, for any $t_1 < t_2$, $Pr(t_1 < X \leq t_2) = F(t_2) - F(t_1)$.

PROBABILITY FUNCTION FOR A RANDOM VARIABLE

First consider the case where X is a *discrete* random variable, i.e., a random variable that can take a countable number of discrete values: x_1, x_2, x_3, ... Then the probability function for X is $f(x)$ defined as

$$f(x) = Pr(X = x).$$

For any point x that is not one of the possible values of X, it means that $f(x) = 0$. Also, $\sum_{i \geq 1} f(x_i) = 1$. Finally, with B being some subset of the real line, the probability of B is given by

$$Pr(X \in B) = \Sigma_{i \geq 1}[f(x_i): x_i \in B)].$$

When X is a *continuous* random variable, the above characterization changes. The probability of a continuous random variable X is defined by the function $f(x)$ that satisfies

$$Pr(X \in B) = \int_{x \in B} f(x)dx.$$

In the continuous case, the probability that X will belong to a subset B of the real line is found by integrating (instead of summing) the probability function f(x) over that subset. In general, $f(x) \geq 0$, and $\int_{x \in R} f(x)dx = 1$. And at points where f(x) is continuous, then

$$f(x) = \partial F(x)/\partial x,$$

showing that the probability function is equal to the derivative of the corresponding distribution function.

Note that with continuous random variables, the probability of any point on the real line is 0: $Pr(X = x) = 0$ (otherwise $\int_{x \in R} f(x)dx = 1$ would not hold). This has two implications. First, the probability function of a continuous random variable is *not unique* (since we can always change $f(x)$ at a number of points without affecting its properties). Second, for a continuous random variable, $f(x)$ *cannot* be interpreted to be the probability of being at point x (even though $Pr(x \in B) = \int_{x \in B} f(x)dx$ remains valid).

MULTIVARIATE JOINT DISTRIBUTION

Typically, our uncertain environment is complex and involves more than a single random variable (e.g., weather, income, health, etc.). To represent such situations, consider the case of n random variables, where $X = (X_1, X_2, ..., X_n)'$ taking real values $x = (x_1, ..., x_n)$ in R^n, where X_i denotes the i-th random variable, $i = 1, \ldots, n$. Then the probability concepts presented in the univariate case can be readily extended to the multivariate case. The *joint distribution function* for X evaluated at $x = (x_1, \ldots, x_n) \in R^n$ is defined as

$$F_n(x) = Pr(X_1 \le x_1, \ X_2 \le x_2, \ldots, \ X_n \le x_n).$$

This multivariate extension holds in the continuous as well as the discrete case.

We need to distinguish between continuous and discrete random variables to address multivariate probability function. For *discrete* random variables, the *joint probability function* $f_n(x)$ is defined as $f_n(x_1, \ldots, x_n) = Pr(X_1 = x_1, \ldots, X_n = x_n)$. If $x = (x_1, \ldots, x_n)$ is not one of the possible values for X, then $f_n(x_1, \ldots, x_n) = 0$. Also, for any subset B of R^n, $Pr(X \in B) = \sum_{x \in B} f_n(x_1, \ldots, x_n)$. Finally, $f_n(x_1, \ldots, x_n) \ge 0$, and $F_n(t_1, \ldots, t_n) = \sum_{x \le t} f_n(x_1, \ldots, x_n)$.

For *continuous* random variables, the *joint probability function* of x is the function $f_n(x_1, \ldots, x_n)$ satisfying

$$Pr[(X_1, \ldots, X_n) \in B] = \int_B \ldots \int f_n(x_1, \ldots, x_n) dx_1 \ldots dx_n,$$

where $B \in R^n$. Again, $f_n(x_1, \ldots, x_n) \ge 0$, and $F_n(t_1, \ldots, t_n) = \int_{x \le t} \ldots \int_{x \le t} f_n(x) dx_1 \ldots dx_n$. Finally, if $f_n(x)$ is continuous, then $f_n(x_1, \ldots, x_n) = \partial^n F(x_1, \ldots, x_n) / \partial x_1 \ldots \partial x_n$.

In the case of mixed variables where some are discrete while others are continuous, things become more complex. In this situation, the joint probability function $f_n(x)$ still exists. And its basic property holds: The probability that X belongs to a certain region $B \in R^n$ is obtained by summing the values of $f_n(x)$ over the discrete random variables while integrating $f_n(x)$ over the continuous random variables.

MARGINAL DISTRIBUTIONS

When facing n random variables, it is often of interest to focus our attention on a subset of them. The probabilities facing this subset can be characterized using marginal distribution functions. Let $X = (X_1, X_2, \ldots, X_n)$. Given $1 \le k < n$, the *marginal distribution function* of the subset of random variables $(X_1, X_2, \ldots, X_k)$ evaluated at $(x_1, \ldots, x_k) \in R^k$ is defined as

$$F_k(x_1, \ldots, x_k) = F_n(x_1, \ldots, x_k, \infty, \ldots, \infty).$$

Consider the case where $f_n(x_1, \ldots, x_n)$ is the joint probability function of x. In situations where x involves *discrete* random variables, the *marginal probability function* of $(X_1, \ldots, X_k)$ evaluated at $(x_1, \ldots, x_k) \in R^k$ is

$$f_k(x_1, \ldots, x_k) = \sum_{X_{k+1}} \ldots \sum_{x_n} f_n(x_1, \ldots, x_n).$$

And in the case where the random variables x are continuous, the *marginal probability function* of $(X_1, \ldots, X_k)$ evaluated at $(x_1, \ldots, x_k) \in R^k$ is defined as

$$f_k(x_1, \ldots, x_k) = \int_R \ldots \int_R f_n(x_1, \ldots, x_n)dx_{k+1} \ldots dx_n.$$

Note that when $k = 1$, the marginal distribution function $F_1(x_1)$ behaves just like a standard univariate distribution function. And the marginal probability function $f_1(x_1)$ behaves just like a standard univariate probability function: it satisfies $f_1(x_1) \geq 0$ and $F_1(t_1) = \int_{X_1 \leq t_1} f_1(x_1)dx_1$.

INDEPENDENCE

Let $F_i(x_i)$ and $f_i(x_i)$ denote, respectively, the marginal distribution and marginal probability function of the random variable X_i, $i = 1, \ldots, n$. Then, the n random variables $(X_1, X_2, \ldots, X_n)$ are said to be *mutually independent* if

$$F_n(x_1, x_2, \ldots, x_n) = F_1(x_1)F_2(x_2) \ldots F_n(x_n),$$

or if

$$f_n(x_1, x_2, \ldots, x_n) = f_1(x_1)f_2(x_2) \ldots f_n(x_n),$$

for all points $(x_1, \ldots, x_n) \in R^n$. These apply for discrete as well as continuous random variables.

CONDITIONAL PROBABILITY

Let $f(x, y)$ be the joint probability function for two sets of random variables $X = (X_1, \ldots, X_n)$ taking real values $x = (x_1, \ldots, x_n)$ in R^n, and $Y = (Y_1, \ldots, Y_m)$ taking real values $y = (y_1, \ldots, y_m)$ in R^m. Then, $g_x(x) = [\int_R \ldots \int_R f(x, y)dy_1 \ldots dy_m]$ is the marginal probability function for X evaluated at x, and $g_y(y) = [\int_R \ldots \int_R f(x, y)dx_1 \ldots dx_n]$ is the marginal probability function for Y evaluated at y.

When $g_y(y) > 0$, the *conditional probability function of X given $Y = y$* is defined as

$$h_x(x|y) = f(x, y)/g_y(y).$$

Similarly, when $g_x(x) > 0$, the *conditional probability function of Y given $X = x$* is defined as

$$h_y(y|x) = f(x, y)/g_x(x).$$

These definitions apply to continuous as well as discrete random variables. Note that conditional probabilities behave just like probability functions. For example, they satisfy $h_x(x|y) \geq 0$, and $[\int_R \dots \int_R h_x(x|y) dx_1 \dots dx_n] = 1$.

BAYES' THEOREM

Again consider the situation involving two sets of random variables $X = (X_1, \dots, X_n)$ and $Y = (Y_1, \dots, Y_m)$. Assume that $g_x(x) > 0$. Then, in the continuous case,

$$h_y(y|x) = \frac{h_x(x|y)g_y(y)}{\int_R \dots \int_R h_x(x|y)g_y(y) dy_1 \dots dy_m},$$

while in the discrete case,

$$h_y(y|x) = \frac{h_x(x|y)g_y(y)}{\sum_y h_x(x|y)g_y(y)}.$$

These equalities constitute Bayes' theorem. As a proof, consider the discrete case. The definitions of marginal and conditional probabilities imply that

$$h_y(y|x) = f(x, y)/g_x(x) = \frac{f(x, y)}{\sum_y f(x, y)} = \frac{h_x(x|y)g_y(y)}{\sum_y h_x(x|y)g_y(y)},$$

which gives the desired result.

Bayes' theorem provides simple updating of probabilities about the random variables Y given new information obtained by observing the random variables X. In the case where observing $X = x$ corresponds to *sample information*, $g_y(y)$ is called the *prior probability* of the random variables Y, $h_x(x|y)$ is called the *likelihood function of the sample*, and $h_y(y|x)$ is called the *posterior probability* of Y given $X = x$. This shows that the likelihood function of the sample $h_x(x|y)$ provides all the information required to update the prior probability function for Y, $g_y(y)$, into its posterior probability $h_x(x|y)$ after the random variables X are observed to take the value x. Note that Bayes' theorem follows directly from the axioms of probability. As such, it provides a powerful and convenient framework to represent learning.

EXPECTATION

Consider a real function $r(X)$ of a random variable X. X being a random variable, it follows that $r(X)$ is also a random variable. Let $f(x)$ be the probability function of X. The *expected value* of the function $r(X)$ is defined as

$$E[r(X)] = \int_R r(x)f(x)dx, \text{ in the continuous case,}$$

or

$$E[r(x)] = \sum_x r(x)f(x), \text{ in the discrete case,}$$

where E denotes the "expectation operator."

First, consider the case where $r(x) = x^k$, $k = 1, 2, \ldots$. Then the *k-th moment* of the random variable X is denoted by m_k and defined as $m_k = E(x^k)$, $k = 1, 2, \ldots$. When $k = 1$, then $m_1 = E(x)$ defines the *mean (or average) of X*, a common measure of location for X. When $k = 2$, then $m_2 = E(x^2)$ is the second moment of X. When $k = 3$, then $m_3 = E(x^3)$ is the third moment of X. And so on . . . . Note that moments are meaningful only if they are finite. A moment is said to exist if and only if it is finite. If the random variable X is bounded, then all its moments always exist (i.e., they are all finite). In the case where the random variable X is unbounded, then its moments may or may not exist.

Second, consider the case where $r(x) = [x - m_1]^k$, $k = 2, 3, \ldots$. Then the *k-th central moment* of the random variable X is denoted by M_k and defined as $M_k = E[(x - m_1)^k]$, $k = 1, 2, \ldots$. When $k = 2$, then $M_2 = E[(x - m_1)^2] \geq 0$ defines the *variance of X*, a common measure of the spread or dispersion of X. The *standard deviation of X* is defined as the positive square root of the variance: $(M_2)^{1/2}$. When $m_1 > 0$, an alternative relative measure of dispersion is the *coefficient of variation*: $(M_2)^{1/2}/m_1$. When $k = 3$, then $M_3 = E[(x - m_1)^3]$ is the *third central moment* of X. It is often used to characterize possible asymmetries in the probability function $f(x)$. For a probability function that is symmetric with respect to its mean (e.g., the normal distribution), the odd central moments of the corresponding random variable are all zero: $M_3 = M_5 = \ldots = 0$. Alternatively, $M_3 \neq 0$ identifies asymmetry in the probability function $f(x)$. More specifically, $M_3 > 0$ (< 0) corresponds to positive (negative) *skewness*, the upper tail of $f(x)$ being thicker (thinner) than its lower tail. The extent of the asymmetry can be investigated using the *relative skewness*: $M_3/(M_2)^{1.5}$. When $k = 4$, then $M_4 = E[(x - m_1)^4] \geq 0$ is the *fourth central moment* of X. It is often used to evaluate the thickness in the tails of the probability function $f(x)$. For the normal distribution, $M_4 = 3(M_2)^2$. The extent of tail thickness is often investigated using the *relative kurtosis*: $M_4/(M_2)^2$. Distributions with a relative kurtosis greater than 3 are said to be leptokurtic: They have "fat tails" relative to the normal distribution.

Given that X has mean $m_1 = E(X)$, its variance (or second central moment) is often denoted by $\text{Var}(X) = M_2 = E[(X - m_1)^2]$. For any random variable X, a general relationship between the second moment, $m_2 = E(X^2)$, and its variance $\text{Var}(X)$ is

$$\text{Var}(X) = E[(X - m_1)^2] = E(X^2 + m_1^2 - 2Xm_1)$$
$$= m_2 - m_1^2.$$

The *covariance* between two random variables X and Y is defined as $\text{Cov}(X, Y) = E[(X - E(X))(Y - E(Y))]$. It can alternatively be expressed as

$$\text{Cov}(X, Y) = E[XY - XE(Y) - YE(X) + E(X)E(Y)]$$
$$= E(XY) - E(X)E(Y).$$

The *correlation coefficient* between two random variables X and Y is defined as

$$\rho(X, Y) = \text{Cov}(X, Y)/[(\text{Var}(X)\text{Var}(Y)]^{1/2}.$$

The correlation coefficient ρ is always bounded between -1 and $+1$. When $\rho = 0$, the random variables X and Y are uncorrelated. The independence of the random variables X and Y is a sufficient (but not necessary) condition for them to be uncorrelated.

Let $X = (X_1, X_2, \ldots, X_n)'$ be a set of n random variables. Denote the mean of X by the $(n \times 1)$ vector $E(X) = \mu = (\mu_1, \mu_2, \ldots, \mu_n)'$, where $\mu_i = E(X_i)$, $i = 1, \ldots, n$. Let $\sigma_{ii} = \text{Var}(X_i)$ be the variance of X_i, and $\sigma_{ij} = \text{Cov}(X_i, X_j)$ be the covariance between X_i and X_j. Denote the variance of X by the $(n \times n)$ matrix $\text{Var}(X) = \Sigma =$

$$\begin{bmatrix} \sigma_{11} & \sigma_{12} & \cdots & \sigma_{1n} \\ \sigma_{21} & \sigma_{22} & \cdots & \sigma_{2n} \\ \vdots & \vdots & \ddots & \vdots \\ \sigma_{n1} & \sigma_{n2} & \cdots & \sigma_{nn} \end{bmatrix}.$$

The variance-covariance matrix Σ is symmetric (meaning that $\sigma_{ij} = \sigma_{ji}$ for all $i \neq j$) and positive semidefinite (meaning that $u'\Sigma u \geq 0$ for all $(n \times 1)$ vectors $u \in R^n$).

Consider two sets of random variables: $X = (X_1, \ldots, X_n)$, and $Y = (Y_1, \ldots, Y_m)$. Assume that the following linear relationship exists between X and Y

$$Y_i = \Sigma_j A_{ij} X_j + b_i, \; i = 1, \ldots, n,$$

or

$$Y = AX + b,$$

where $A = \{A_{ij}\}$ is a $(m \times n)$ matrix of constants, and $b = (b_1, \ldots, b_m)'$ is a $(m \times 1)$ vector of constants. Then,

$$E(Y) = AE(X) + b = A\mu + b$$
$$\text{Var}(Y) = A\text{Var}(X)A' = A\Sigma A'.$$

When $m = n = 1$, it follows that $\text{Var}(Y) = A^2\text{Var}(X)$. In the case where $Y = A_1X_1 + A_2X_2 + b$ (i.e., with $m = 1, n = 2$, and $A = [A_1, A_2]$), we obtain

$$E(Y) = A_1E(X_1) + A_2E(X_2) + b = A_1\mu_1 + A_2\mu_2 + b$$
$$\text{Var}(Y) = A_1^2\text{Var}(X_1) + A_2^2\text{Var}(X_2) + 2A_1A_2\text{Cov}(X_1, X_2)$$
$$= A_1^2\sigma_{11} + A_2^2\sigma_{22} + 2A_1A_2\sigma_{12}.$$

If the random variables X_1 and X_2 are independently distributed with finite variances, then $\text{Cov}(X_1, X_2) = 0$, implying that $\text{Var}(A_1X_1 + A_2X_2)$ $= A_1^2\text{Var}(X_1) + A_2^2\text{Var}(X_2)$.

CHEBYSCHEV INEQUALITY

For any random variable X with a finite variance $\text{Var}(X)$

$$Pr[|X - E(X)| \geq t] \leq \text{Var}(X)/t^2.$$

Note that this Chebyschev inequality is quite general. It applies to any probability distribution that has a finite variance.

MOMENT GENERATING FUNCTION

Define the function $G(t) = E(e^{tx})$. The function $G(t)$ is called the moment generating function due the following property:

If m_r is finite, then $[\partial^r G(t)/\partial t^r]|_{t=0} = E(x^r) = m_r, r = 1, 2, 3, \ldots$

(To show this, consider a Taylor series expansion of e^{tx} evaluated at $tx = 0$: $G(t) = E[1 + tx + (tx)^2/2! + (tx)^3/3! + \ldots]$. Evaluating the derivatives of this expression with respect to t at $t = 0$ gives the desired result.)

CONDITIONAL EXPECTATION

Let $f(x, y)$ be a joint probability function for the random variables (X, Y), $g_y(y)$ be the marginal probability function of Y, and $h_x(x|y) = f(x, y)/g_y(y)$ be the conditional probability of X given $Y = y$. The conditional expectation of a random variable X given $Y = y$ is the expectation based on the conditional probability $h_x(x|y)$. The unconditional expectation $E_{x,y}$ of some function $r(X, Y)$ is given by applying iterative expectations

$$E_{x,y}r(X, Y) = E_y[E_{x|y}r(X, Y)].$$

where $E_{x|y}$ is the conditional expectation operator and E_y is the expectation based on the marginal probability of y. To see that, note the following relationships applied to discrete random variables

$$\begin{aligned} E_{x,y}r(x,y) &= \Sigma_{x,y}r(x,y)f(x,y) \\ &= \Sigma_{x,y}r(x,y)h_x(x|y)g_y(y) \\ &= \Sigma_y[\Sigma_x r(x,y)h_x(x|y)]g_y(y) \\ &= E_y[E_{x|y}r(x,y)]. \end{aligned}$$

CONJUGATE DISTRIBUTIONS

In a Bayesian framework, a distribution is conjugate if, for some likelihood function, the prior and posterior distributions belong to the same family. An example is given by the unknown mean of a random sample from a normal distribution.

SOME SPECIAL DISCRETE DISTRIBUTIONS

	Probability function f(x)	Moment generating function G(t)	Mean E(X)	Variance Var(X)
Binomial	$\dfrac{n!}{x!(n-x)!}p^x(1-p)^{n-x}$ for $0<p<1$, $x=0,1,,\ldots,n$	$[pe^t + (1-p)]^n$	np	$np(1-p)$
Bernoulli (= **binomial** with n = 1)	$p^x(1-p)^{1-x}$ for $0 < p < 1, x = 0,1$		p	$p(1-p)$
Negative binomial	$\dfrac{(r+x-1)!}{x!(r-1)!}p^r(1-p)^x$ for $0<p<1$, $x=0,1,,\ldots,n$	$[p/(1-(1-p)e^t)]^r$ for $[(1-p)e^t] < 1$	$r(1-p)/p$	$r(1-p)/p^2$
Geometric (= **negative binomial** with r = 1)	$p(1-p)^x$ for $0<p<1$, $x=0,1,,\ldots,n$		$(1-p)/p$	$(1-p)/p^2$
Poisson	$e^{-\lambda}\lambda^x/x!$ for $\lambda>0, x=0,1,2,\ldots$	$\exp[\lambda(e^t-1)]$	λ	λ
Uniform	$1/n$ for $n=$ integer, $x=1,2,\ldots,n$		$(n+1)/2$	$(n^2-1)/12$

SOME SPECIAL CONTINUOUS DISTRIBUTIONS

	Probability function $f(x)$	Moment generating function $G(t)$	Mean $E(X)$	Variance $Var(X)$
Beta	$\dfrac{\Gamma(\alpha+\beta)}{\Gamma(\alpha)\Gamma(\beta)}x^{\alpha-1}(1-x)^{\beta-1}$ for $0 < x < 1$		$\alpha/(\alpha+\beta)$	$\alpha\beta/[(\alpha+\beta)^2(\alpha+\beta+1)]$
Uniform	$1/(b-a)$ for $a < x < b$		$(b+a)/2$	$(b-a)^2/12$
Normal	$\dfrac{1}{\sqrt{2\pi\sigma^2}}\exp[-(x-\mu)^2/(2\sigma^2)]$ for $\sigma > 0$	$\exp[\mu t + \sigma^2 t^2/2]$	μ	σ^2
Gamma	$\dfrac{\beta^\alpha}{\Gamma(\alpha)}x^{\alpha-1}e^{-\beta x}$ for $\alpha>0, \beta>0, x>0$	$[\beta/(\beta-t)]^\alpha$ for $t < \beta$	α/β	α/β^2
Exponential (= gamma with $\alpha = 1$)	$\beta e^{-\beta x}$ for $\beta > 0, x > 0$	$[\beta/(\beta-t)]$ for $t < \beta$	$1/\beta$	$1/\beta^2$
Chi square (= gamma with $\alpha = k/2$, $\beta = 1/2$)	$\dfrac{1}{2^{k/2}\Gamma(k/2)}x^{(k/2)-1}e^{-x/2}$ for $k =$ positive integer, $x > 0$	$[1/(1-2t)]^{k/2}$ for $t < 1/2$	k	$2k$
Pareto	$\alpha k^\alpha/x^{\alpha+1}$		$\alpha k/(\alpha-1)$ for $\alpha > 1$	$\alpha k^2/[(\alpha-2)(\alpha-1)^2]$ for $\alpha > 2$
Lognormal	$\dfrac{1}{x\sqrt{2\pi\sigma^2}}\exp[-(\ln(x)-\mu)^2/(2\sigma^2)]$ for $\sigma > 0, x > 0$		$\exp(\mu + \sigma^2/2)$	$[\exp(\sigma^2) - 1]\exp(2\mu + \sigma^2)$

Note: $n! = n(n-1)(n-2)\ldots 1$.

$$\Gamma(\alpha) = \int_0^\infty y^{\alpha-1}e^{-y}dy = 1 \text{ if } \alpha = 1 = (\alpha-1)! \text{ if } \alpha \text{ is an integer.}$$

Appendix B: Optimization

INTRODUCTION

The concept of optimization is central to economic analysis and efficiency. Economic rationality means that economic agents do the best they can to improve their welfare. This is represented by an optimization problem: Decisions are made so that each agent maximizes his/her objective function subject to constraints imposed by the economic environment. The objective function is a utility function representing the agent's preferences. The agent can be a household making consumption decisions or a firm making production and investment decisions. Under uncertainty, the utility function reflects risk preferences. In this context, the analysis of economic decisions involves maximization problems subject to feasibility constraints. Below, we review standard tools of analysis based on optimization methods. These tools are used throughout this book to generate useful insights into decision-making under uncertainty and the efficiency of risk allocation.

PRELIMINARIES

Consider a *function* $f(x)$, where $x = (x_1, \ldots, x_n)$ is an n-vector of real numbers. This means that for each x, there exists a unique real number given by $f(x)$. The function f is said to be *concave* if, for any x^a and x^b and any α, $0 \le \alpha \le 1$,

$$f(\alpha x^a + (1 - \alpha)x^b) \ge \alpha f(x^a) + (1 - \alpha)f(x^b).$$

This is illustrated in Figure B.1.

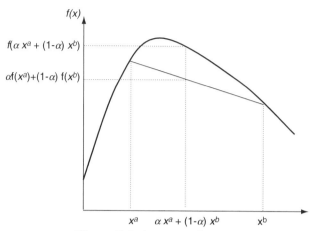

Figure B.1 A concave function

When the function f is differentiable, let $f'(x) \equiv \partial f/\partial x$ denote the first derivative of f, and let $f''(x) \equiv \partial^2 f/\partial x^2$ denote the second derivative of f. The first derivative $f'(x)$ measures the marginal value or local slope of the function at point x. The second derivative $f''(x)$ reflects the marginal change in the slope at point x. When $f(x)$ is differentiable and $n = 1$, the function $f(x)$ is concave if and only if $f''(x) \leq 0$ for all x. Thus, concavity of $f(x)$ is equivalent to diminishing marginal values for the function $f(x)$ at all points. This is illustrated in Figure B.2.

Finally, consider a set of real numbers, denoted by X. The set X is said to be *convex* if for every x^a and x^b in X and every number α, $0 < \alpha < 1$, the point $[\alpha x^a + (1 - \alpha)x^b]$ is also in X. Geometrically, this means that a set is convex if every point on the line segment joining any two points in the set is also in the set. This is illustrated in Figure B.3.

UNCONSTRAINED OPTIMIZATION

Consider an economic agent facing the maximization problem:

$$V(\alpha) = \text{Max}_x f(x, \ \alpha), \tag{1}$$

where $f(x, \ \alpha)$ is the objective function, $x = (x_1, \ \ldots, \ x_n)$ is a vector of n-real numbers representing n decision variables, and $\alpha = (\alpha_1, \ \ldots, \ \alpha_m)$ is a m-vector of parameters. The parameters α are real numbers representing all variables that are *not* decision variables. They include variables representing the economic environment of the decision-maker. The solution of the

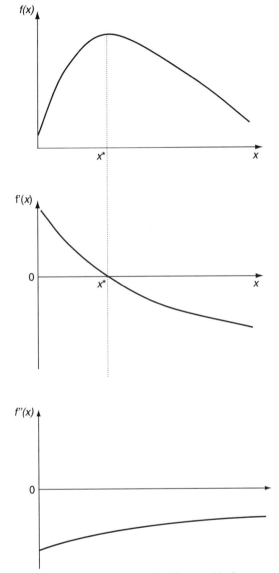

Figure B.2 A concave and differentiable function

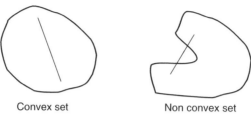

Convex set   Non convex set
Figure B.3 Convexity of sets

maximization problem (1) typically depends on the parameters α. This solution is denoted by the *decision rule* $x^*(\alpha)$, giving the optimal decision for a given economic environment α. By definition, this decision rule satisfies $f(x^*(\alpha),\ \alpha) \geq f(x,\ \alpha)$ for all x: it generates the highest possible value of the objective function for a given α. $V(\alpha)$ in (1) is called the *indirect objective function*. For a given α, it is the value of the objective function evaluated at the optimum $x^*(\alpha)$, with $V(\alpha) \equiv f(x^*(\alpha),\ \alpha)$.

Much economic analysis focuses on the properties of the decision rule $x^*(\alpha)$. This decision rule summarizes how economic choices optimally adjust to changes in the decision-maker's economic environment. We need to gain insights into the properties of $x^*(\alpha)$. Analyzing such properties is particularly convenient using calculus, i.e., assuming differentiability. Thus, below, we assume that the objective function $f(x,\ \alpha)$ is differentiable in $(x,\ \alpha)$.

First, the optimal decision $x^*(\alpha)$ associated with (1) must satisfy the following condition

$$\frac{\partial f}{\partial x}(x^*(\alpha),\ \alpha) = 0. \tag{2}$$

Equation (2) is called the *first-order necessary condition*. It is first order since it involves the first derivative of the objective function, $\partial f/\partial x$ or f''. And it is necessary in the sense that it always characterizes the optimal solution of an unconstrained optimization problem. This can be seen in Figure B.2, where $f''(x) > 0$ means that x is "too small," $f''(x) < 0$ means that x is "too large," and indeed $f''(x) = 0$ holds at $x = x^*$. When $n > 1$, equation (2) constitutes a system of n equations: $\partial f/\partial x_1 = 0, \ldots, \partial f/\partial x_n = 0$. Under some regularity conditions, this system of equation can be solved for the n optimal decisions: $x^*(\alpha) = (x_1^*(\alpha), \ldots, x_n^*(\alpha))$. Then, the first-order conditions (2) provide a formal way of identifying the optimal decision rule $x^*(\alpha)$. However, solving a system of (possibly nonlinear) equations can be difficult. One way around this difficulty is again to rely on calculus. Evaluated at $x^*(\alpha)$, differentiating equation (2) with respect to α and using the chain rule yields

$$\partial^2 f/\partial x \partial \alpha + (\partial^2 f/\partial x^2)(\partial x^*/\partial \alpha) = 0, \tag{3a}$$

where $\partial^2 f / \partial x \partial \alpha = \begin{bmatrix} \partial^2 f / \partial x_1 \partial \alpha_1 & \cdots & \partial^2 f / \partial x_1 \partial \alpha_m \\ \vdots & \ddots & \vdots \\ \partial^2 f / \partial x_n \partial \alpha_1 & \cdots & \partial^2 f / \partial x_n \partial \alpha_m \end{bmatrix}$ is a $n \times m$ matrix,

$$\partial^2 f / \partial x^2 = \begin{bmatrix} \partial^2 f / \partial x_1^2 & \cdots & \partial^2 f / \partial x_1 \partial x_n \\ \vdots & \ddots & \vdots \\ \partial^2 f / \partial x_n \partial x_1 & \cdots & \partial^2 f / \partial x_n^2 \end{bmatrix}$$ is a $n \times n$ matrix, and

$$\partial x^* / \partial \alpha = \begin{bmatrix} \partial x_1^* / \partial x_1 & \cdots & \partial x_1^* / \partial \alpha_m \\ \vdots & \ddots & \vdots \\ \partial x_n^* / \partial \alpha_1 & \cdots & \partial x_n^* / \partial \alpha_m \end{bmatrix}$$ is a $n \times m$ matrix. In the case

where the matrix $f'' \equiv \partial^2 f / \partial x^2$ is invertible, equation (3a) implies

$$\partial x^* / \partial \alpha = -[\partial^2 f / \partial x^2]^{-1} \partial^2 f / \partial x \partial \alpha. \tag{3b}$$

The term $\partial x^* / \partial \alpha$ measures the optimal response of $x^*(\alpha)$ to a small change in α. Thus expression (3b) provides the basis for *comparative statics analysis*, showing how small changes in the economic environment affect optimal decisions. Under differentiability and the invertibility of $\partial^2 f / \partial x^2$, this provides a generic approach to analyzing the properties of the optimal decision rules $x^*(\alpha)$.

Finally, noting that $V(\alpha) \equiv f(x^*(\alpha), \alpha)$, differentiating the indirect objective function with respect to α and using the chain rule gives $\partial V / \partial \alpha = \partial f / \partial \alpha + (\partial f / \partial x)(\partial x^* / \partial \alpha)$. Using the first-order condition (2), this yields the *envelope theorem*:

$$\partial V / \partial \alpha = \partial f / \partial \alpha,$$

where $\partial f / \partial \alpha$ is evaluated at $x^*(\alpha)$. The envelope theorem states that the derivative of the indirect objective function with respect to α is equal to the derivative of the direct objective function with respect to α, evaluated at $x^*(\alpha)$. In other words, the two functions $V(\alpha)$ and $f(\alpha, x)$ are tangent to each other with respect to α in the neighborhood of the optimal choice $x^*(\alpha)$.

CONSTRAINED OPTIMIZATION

Often, decision-makers face constraints from their economic environment. These constraints can be technological, legal, financial, or institutional. To

the extent that these constraints affect decisions, they need to be incorpor-
ated in the optimization problem. On that basis, as a generalization of (1),
consider the constrained maximization problem

$$V(\alpha) = \text{Max}_x \{ f(x, \alpha): \ h(x, \alpha) \geq 0 \}, \tag{4}$$

where $h(x, \alpha) = (h_1(x, \alpha), \ldots, h_K(x, \alpha))$ are K functions representing K
constraints facing the decision-maker: $h_1(x, \alpha) \geq 0, \ldots, h_K(x, \alpha) \geq 0$. Equation (4) is a standard constrained optimization problem, where $f(x, \alpha)$ is the
objective function, $h(x, \alpha) \geq 0$ is a set of K inequality constraints,
$x = (x_1, \ldots, x_n)$ is an n-vector of decisions, and $\alpha = (\alpha_1, \ldots, \alpha_m)$ is an
m-vector of parameters reflecting the economic environment of the decision
maker. Again, let $x^*(\alpha)$ denote the optimal decision rule in (4), i.e., the
decision rule that satisfies $f(x^*(\alpha), \alpha) \geq f(x)$ for all feasible x where
$h(x, \alpha) \geq 0$. And $V(\alpha)$ is the indirect objective function satisfying
$V(\alpha) = f(x^*(\alpha), \alpha)$.

The first question is, can we generalize the above results (2)–(3) to
accommodate the constraints in (4)? Under some regularity conditions, the
answer is yes. This is done using the *Lagrangean approach*. The Lagrangean
approach defines K Lagrange multipliers $\lambda_1, \ldots, \lambda_K$.

Associating each Lagrange multiplier with one of the K constraints,
define the Lagrangean function as

$$L(x, \lambda, \alpha) = f(x, \alpha) + \sum_{k=1}^{K} \lambda_k \, h_k(x, \alpha). \tag{5}$$

The properties of the Lagrangean function $L(x, \lambda, \alpha)$ in (5) are closely
linked with the constrained optimization problem (4). First, under differentiability, consider the set of first-order conditions (also called the Kuhn–
Tucker conditions):

$$\frac{\partial L}{\partial x}(x^*(\alpha), \ \lambda^*(\alpha), \ \alpha) = 0, \tag{6a}$$

$$\frac{\partial L}{\partial \lambda}(x^*(\alpha), \ \lambda^*(\alpha), \ \alpha) \geq 0, \tag{6b}$$

$$\lambda^*(\alpha) \geq 0, \tag{6c}$$

$$\lambda_k^*(\alpha)\left[\frac{\partial L}{\partial \lambda_k}(x^*(\alpha), \ \lambda^*(\alpha), \ \alpha)\right] = 0, \ k = 1, \ldots, K. \tag{6d}$$

For given parameters α, equations (6a)–(6d) involve $x^*(\alpha)$ as well as the
Lagrange multipliers $\lambda^*(\alpha)$. When they exist, these Lagrange multipliers have

an intuitive interpretation: $\lambda_k^*(\alpha)$ measures the marginal effect on the objective function of relaxing the k-th constraint, $k = 1, \ldots, K$. This provides useful information on the effects of the constraints on the welfare of the decision-maker. However, there are some (rather rare) situations where the Lagrange multipliers do not exist, in which case the Lagrangean approach fails. Yet, Lagrange multipliers have been shown to exist under fairly general regularity conditions. These regularity conditions are called *constraint qualifications* related to the binding constraints (i.e., constraints satisfying $h_k(x^*(\alpha), \alpha) = 0$). The constraint qualifications are satisfied either if there exists a feasible point x where the constraints are nonbinding (Slater's condition), or if the binding constraints are linearly independent (the rank condition) (see Takayama 1985). Under either condition, the Lagrangean approach applies and equations (6a)–(6d) become *necessary first-order conditions* (in a way similar to (2)). Then, equation (6a) states that, at the optimum, $x^*(\alpha)$ must correspond to a zero marginal value of the Lagrangean function with respect to x. Noting that $\partial L/\partial \lambda_k = h_k(x, \alpha)$ from (5), equation (6b) simply imposes the feasibility constraints: $h_k(x, \alpha) \geq 0$, $k = 1, \ldots, K$. Equation (6c) shows that, under inequality constraints, the Lagrange multipliers (measuring the marginal value of the constraints) are nonnegative. Finally, equation (6d) is called the "complementary slackness condition." It means that $\lambda_k^*(\alpha) > 0$ implies that the corresponding constraint must be binding (i.e., $h_k(x^*(\alpha), \alpha) = 0$). Alternatively, a nonbinding constraint (with $h_k(x^*(\alpha), \alpha) > 0$) must necessarily be associated with a zero Lagrange multiplier ($\lambda_k^*(\alpha) = 0$). Note that this implies that $L(x^*(\alpha), \lambda^*(\alpha), \alpha) = V(\alpha)$. It means that, at the optimum, the Lagrangean $L(x^*(\alpha), \lambda^*(\alpha), \alpha)$ is equal to the indirect objective function $V(\alpha)$.

In the special case where all constraints are binding, equations (6a)–(6d) reduce to the following:

$$\frac{\partial L}{\partial x}(x^*(\alpha), \lambda^*(\alpha), \alpha) = 0, \tag{7a}$$

$$\frac{\partial L}{\partial \lambda}(x^*(\alpha), \lambda^*(\alpha), \alpha) = 0. \tag{7b}$$

Then, under the constraint qualification, the first-order necessary conditions (7a)–(7b) become a system of $(n + K)$ equations: $\partial L/\partial x_i = 0$, $i = 1, \ldots, n$, and $\partial L/\partial \lambda_k = 0$, $k = 1, \ldots, K$. This system of equations can be solved for $x^*(\alpha)$ and $\lambda^*(\alpha)$. This provides a formal way of identifying the optimal decision rule $x^*(\alpha)$ along with the marginal value of the constraints $\lambda^*(\alpha)$. And as presented in (3a)–(3b) above, differentiating (7a)–(7b) with respect to α can provide a basis for conducting comparative statics analysis in constrained optimization.

Under differentiability and when all constraints are binding, note that differentiating $V(\alpha) = L(x^*(\alpha),\ \lambda^*(\alpha),\ \alpha)$ with respect to α gives

$$\partial V/\partial\alpha = (\partial L/\partial x)(\partial x^*/\partial\alpha) + (\partial L/\partial\lambda)(\partial\lambda^*/\partial\alpha) + \partial L/\partial\alpha.$$

Using (7a) and (7b), this gives the *envelope theorem*

$$\partial V/\partial\alpha = \partial L/\partial\alpha,$$

where $\partial L/\partial\alpha$ is evaluated at $(x^*(\alpha),\ \lambda^*(\alpha))$. In the context of a constrained optimization problem, the envelope theorem states that the derivative of the indirect objective function with respect to α is equal to the derivative of the Lagrangean with respect to α, evaluated at $(x^*(\alpha),\ \lambda^*(\alpha))$. In other words, the two functions $V(\alpha)$ and $L(x,\ \lambda,\ \alpha)$ are tangent to each other with respect to α in the neighborhood of the optimal choice $(x^*(\alpha),\ \lambda^*(\alpha))$.

While the Kuhn–Tucker conditions (6a)–(6d) rely on differentiability, note that the Lagrangean approach can still apply without differentiability. To see that, rewrite the constrained optimization problem (4) as

$$V(\alpha) = \text{Max}_x\{f(x,\ \alpha): h(x,\ \alpha) \geq 0,\ x \text{ is in } X\}, \tag{4'}$$

where we have added X as the feasible set for the choice of x (where X is a subset of n real numbers). Starting from the Lagrangean function $L(x,\ \lambda,\ \alpha)$ in (5), consider the saddle-point problem

$$L(x,\ \lambda^*(\alpha),\ \alpha) \leq L(x^*(\alpha),\ \lambda^*(\alpha),\ \alpha) \leq L(x^*(\alpha),\ \lambda,\ \alpha),$$
$$\text{for all } x \text{ in } X \text{ and } \lambda \geq 0. \tag{8}$$

The pair $(x^*(\alpha),\ \lambda^*(\alpha))$ constitutes a saddle-point of the Lagrangean $L(x,\ \lambda,\ \alpha)$ as $x^*(\alpha)$ maximizes L with respect to x (the first inequality in (8)) while $\lambda^*(\alpha)$ minimizes L with respect to $\lambda \geq 0$ (the second inequality in (8)). Two important results are associated with (8) (see Takayama 1981).

1. The saddle-point theorem: If a saddle-point exists in (8), then $x^*(\alpha)$ is necessarily the optimal decision rule in (4').
2. If Slater's condition holds, the set X is convex, and the functions $f(x,\ \alpha)$ and $h(x,\ \alpha)$ are concave in x, then (4') implies (8).

Since neither result requires differentiability, this indicates that the Lagrangean approach applies outside of the realm of calculus. The first result establishes the power of the Lagrangean approach as a means of investigating constrained optimization problems. However, the second result raises a caution: The Lagrangean approach does not always work. Yet, it presents sufficient conditions for its validity in constrained optimization problems. They include Slater's condition (a constraint qualification discussed above), the convexity of the set X, and the concavity of the functions $f(x, \alpha)$ and $h(x, \alpha)$ in x. Under such circumstances, the Lagrange multipliers $\lambda^*(\alpha)$ exist and the saddle-point problem (8) identifies the optimal decision rule $x^*(\alpha)$. And as a byproduct, $\lambda^*(\alpha)$ in (8) provides a measure of the marginal value of the constraints.

References

Allais, M. "Le Comportement de l'Homme Rationnel Devant le Risque, Critique des Postulats et Axiomes de l'Ecole Américaine" *Econometrica* 21(1953): 503–546.

Antle, John M. "Testing the Stochastic Structure of Production: A Flexible Moment-Based Approach" *Journal of Business and Economic Statistics* 1(1983): 192–201.

——— ."Econometric Estimation of Producers' Risk Attitudes" *American Journal of Agricultural Economics* 69(1987): 509–522.

Antle, John M., and W.J. Goodger. "Measuring Stochastic Technology: The Case of Tulare Milk Production" *American Journal of Agricultural Economics* 66(1984): 342–350.

Arrow, K. *Aspects of the Theory of Risk-Bearing.* Yrjo Jahnsson Saatio, Helsinki, 1965.

Becker, Robert A., and John H. Boyd III. *Capital Theory, Equilibrium Analysis and Recursive Utility.* Blackwell Pub., 1997.

Bertsekas, Dimitri P. *Dynamic Programming and Stochastic Control.* Academic Press, 1976.

Binswanger, Hans P. "Attitudes Toward Risk: Theoretical Implications of an Experiment in Rural India" *Economic Journal* 91(1981): 867–890.

Campbell, John Y., A.W. Lo, and A.C. MacKinlay. *The Econometrics of Financial Markets.* Princeton University Press, Princeton, NJ, 1997.

Chambers, Robert G., and J. Quiggin. *Uncertainty, Production, Choice and Agency.* Cambridge University Press, Cambridge, 2000.

Chavas, Jean-Paul. "The Ricardian Rent and the Allocation of Land under Uncertainty" *European Review of Agricultural Economics* 15(1993): 351–366.

Chavas, Jean-Paul, and M.T. Holt. "Economic Behavior under Uncertainty: A Joint Analysis of Risk Preferences and Technology" *Review of Economics and Statistics* 78(1996): 329–335.

Chavas, Jean-Paul, and A. Thomas. "A Dynamic Analysis of Land Prices" *American Journal of Agricultural Economics* 81(1999): 772–784.

Chavas, Jean-Paul, and Z. Bouamra-Mechemache. "The Significance of Risk under Incomplete Markets" in *A Comprehensive Assessment of the Role of Risk in US Agriculture*. Richard E. Just and Rulon D. Pope, Editors, Kluwer Academic Publishers, Boston, (2002): 213–242.

Chavas, Jean-Paul, and D. Mullarkey. "On the Valuation of Uncertainty in Welfare Analysis" *American Journal of Agricultural Economics* 84(2002): 23–38.

Coase, Ronald. "The Problem of Social Cost" *Journal of Law and Economics* 1(1960): 1–44.

Cochrane, John H. *Asset Pricing*. Princeton University Press, Princeton, 2001.

Deaton, Angus. *Understanding Consumption*. Oxford University Press, 1992.

Debreu, Gerard. *Theory of Value*. Cowles Foundation Monograph #17. Yale University Press, New Haven, 1959.

DeGroot, Morris H. *Optimal Statistical Decisions*. McGraw-Hill, New York, 1970.

Dillon, John L., and P.L. Scandizzo. "Risk Attitudes of Subsistence Farmers in Northeast Brazil: A Sampling Approach" *American Journal of Agricultural Economics* 60(1978): 425–435.

Dixit, Avinash K., and Robert S. Pindyck. *Investment under Uncertainty*. Princeton University Press, 1994.

Drèze, Jacques. *Essays on Economic Decisions under Uncertainty*. Cambridge University Press, New York, 1987.

Duffie, Darrell. *Dynamic Asset Pricing Theory*. Princeton University Press, Princeton, 2001.

Eeckhoudt, Louis, and Christian Gollier. *Risk: Evaluation, Management and Sharing*. Harvester and Wheatsheaf, New York, 1995.

Ellsberg, Daniel. "Risk, Ambiguity and the Savage Axioms" *Quarterly Journal of Economics* 75(1961): 643–669.

Epstein, L., and S. Zin. "Substitution, Risk Aversion, and Temporal Behavior of Consumption and Asset Returns: An Empirical Investigation" *Journal of Political Economy*. 99(1991): 263–286.

Feder, Gershon, R.E. Just, and A. Schmitz. "Futures Markets and the Theory of the Firm under Price Uncertainty" *Quarterly Journal of Economics* 94(1980): 317–328.

Fishburn, Peter C. *The Foundations of Expected Utility*. D. Reidel Pub. Co. Boston, MA, 1982.

Friedman, Milton, and Leonard J. Savage. "The Utility Analysis of Choice Involving Risk." *Journal of Political Economy*, 56 (1948): 279–304.

Gollier, Christian. *The Economics of Risk and Time*. MIT Press, Cambridge, MA, 2001.

Graham, Daniel A. "Public Expenditure under Uncertainty: The Net Benefit Criteria" *American Economic Review* 82(1992): 822–846.

Harless, David W., and C.F. Camerer. "The Predictive Utility of Generalized Expected Utility Theories" *Econometrica* 62(1994): 1,251–1,289.

Hey, John D., and C. Orme. "Investigating Generalizations of Expected Utility Theory Using Experimental Data" *Econometrica* 62(1994): 1,291–1,326.

Hirshleifer, Jack, and John G. Riley. *The Analytics of Uncertainty and Information.* Cambridge University Press, Cambridge, 1992.

Holmstrom, Bengt. "Moral Hazard and Observability" *Bell Journal of Economics* 10(1979): 74–91.

Hull, John. *Options, Futures and Other Derivatives.* Fifth Edition. Prentice Hall, 2002.

Jullien, Bruno, and B. Salanié. "Estimating Preferences under Risk: The Case of Racetrack Bettors" *Journal of Political Economy* 108(2000): 503–530.

Just, Richard E., and Rulon D. Pope. "Stochastic Specification of Production Function and Econometric Implications" *Journal of Econometrics* 7(1978): 67–86.

————. "Production Function Estimation and Related Risk Considerations" *American Journal of Agricultural Economics* 61(1979): 276–284.

Kahneman, Daniel, and A. Tversky. "Prospect Theory: An Analysis of Decision under Risk" *Econometrica* 47(1979): 263–191.

Kimball, Miles S. "Precautionary Saving in the Small and in the Large" *Econometrica* 58(1990): 53–73.

Knight, Frank J. *Risk, Uncertainty and Profit.* Houghton Mifflin, New York, 1921.

Lin, William, G.W. Dean, and C.V. Moore. "An Empirical Test of Utility vs. Profit Maximization in Agricultural Production" *American Journal of Agricultural Economics* 56(1974): 497–508.

Lavalle, Irving H. *Fundamentals of Decision Analysis.* Holt, Rinehart and Winston, New York, 1978.

Luenberger, David G. *Microeconomic Theory.* McGraw-Hill, Inc. New York, 1995.

————. *Investment Science.* Oxford University Press, New York, 1998.

Machina, Mark J. "Expected Utility Analysis without the Independence Axiom" *Econometrica* 50(1982): 277–323.

————. "Temporal Risk and the Nature of Induced Preferences" *Journal of Economic Theory* 33(1984): 199–231.

————. "Choice under Uncertainty: Problems Solved and Unsolved." *Journal of Economic Perspectives* 1(1987): 121–154.

Macho-Stadler, Inés, and David Pérez-Castrillo. *An Introduction to the Economics of Information: Incentives and Contracts.* Oxford University Press, Oxford, 1997.

Magill, Michael, and Martine Quinzii. *Theory of Incomplete Markets.* MIT Press, Cambridge, 1996.

Markowitz, H. "Portfolio Selection" *Journal of Finance.* 6(1952): 77–91.

Menezes, C., G. Geiss, and J. Tessler. "Increasing Downside Risk" *American Economic Review* 70(1980): 921–932.

Menezes, C., and D. Hanson. "On the Theory of Risk Aversion" *International Economic Review.* 11(1970): 481–487.

Meyer, Jack. "Choice among Distributions" *Journal of Economic Theory* 13(1977): 326–336.

————. "Two-Moment Decision Models and Expected Utility" *American Economic Review.* 77(1987): 421–430.

Miller, M.H. "The Modigliani-Miller Propositions after Thirty Years" *Journal of Economic Perspectives.* 2(Fall 1988): 99–120.

Modigliani, F., and M.H. Miller. "The Cost of Capital, Corporation Finance and the Theory of Investment" *American Economic Review.* 48(1958): 261–297.

Moscardi, Edgardo, and A. de Janvry. "Attitudes Towards Risk among Peasants: An Econometric Approach" *American Journal of Agricultural Economics* 59(1977): 710–716.

Mukerji, Sujoy. "Ambiguity Aversion and Incompleteness of Contractual Form" *American Economic Review* 88(1998): 1,207–1,231.

Newbery, D.M.G., and J.E. Stiglitz. *The Theory of Commodity Price Stabilization.* Oxford: Clarendon Press, 1981.

Pratt, John W. "Risk Aversion in the Small and in the Large" *Econometrica* 32(1964): 122–136.

Quiggin, John. "A Theory of Anticipated Utility" *Journal of Economic Behavior and Organization.* 3(1982): 323–343.

————.*Generalized Expected Utility Theory: The Rank-Dependent Model.* Kluwer Academic, Amsterdam, 1992.

Radner, Roy. "Competitive Equilibrium under Uncertainty" *Econometrica* 36(1968): 31–58.

Ross, S. "The Arbitrage Theory of Capital Asset Pricing" *Journal of Economic Theory* 13(1976): 341–360.

Rothschild, Michael, and J. Stiglitz. "Increasing Risk: A Definition" *Journal of Economic Theory* 2(1970): 225–243.

————."Increasing Risk: Its Economic Consequences" *Journal of Economic Theory* 3(1971): 66–84.

————."Equilibrium in Competitive Insurance Markets: An Essay on the Economics of Imperfect Information" *Quarterly Journal of Economics* 90(1976): 629–649.

Salanié, Bernard. *The Economics of Contracts: A Primer.* MIT Press, Cambridge, MA, 1999.

Sandmo, Agnar. "On the Theory of the Competitive Firm under Price Uncertainty" *American Economic Review* 61(1971): 65–73.

Shavell, Steven. "Risk Sharing and Incentives in the Principal and Agent Relationship" *Bell Journal of Economics* 10(1979): 55–73.

Savage, Leonard J. *The Foundations of Statistics.* Wiley, New York, 1954.

Shiha, Amr N., and J.P. Chavas. "Capital Market Segmentation and US Farm Real Estate Pricing" *American Journal of Agricultural Economics* 77(1995): 397–407.

Sharpe, W. "A Simplified Model for Portfolio Analysis" *Management Science.* 9(1963): 227–293.

Smithson, Michael. *Fuzzy Set Analysis for Behavioral and Social Sciences.* Springer-Vrelag, New York, 1987.

Schmeidler, David. "Subjective Probability and Expected Utility without Additivity" *Econometrica* 57(1989): 571–587.

Stiglitz, Joseph E. "Incentives and Risk Sharing in Sharecropping" *Review of Economic Studies* 41(1974): 219–255.

Takayama, Akira. *Mathematical Economics.* Cambridge University Press, Cambridge, 1985.

Turnovsky, Stephen J., H. Shalit, and A. Schmitz. "Consumer's Surplus, Price Instability and Consumer Welfare" *Econometrica* 48(1980): 135–152.

Tversky, Amos, and D. Kahneman. "Advances in Prospects Theory: Cumulative Representation of Uncertainty" *Journal of Risk and Uncertainty* 5(1992): 297–323.

Von Neumann, J., and O. Morgenstern. *Theory of Games and Economic Behavior.* Princeton University Press, Princeton, 1944.

Whitmore, G.A., and M.C. Findlay. *Stochastic Dominance: An Approach to Decision-Making under Risk.* Lexington Books, D.C. Heath and Co., Lexington, MA, 1978.

Yaari, M. "The Dual Theory of Choice under Risk" *Econometrica.* 55(1987): 95–116.

Zadeh, Lofti Asker. *Fuzzy Sets and Applications: Selected Papers.* Wiley, New York, 1987.

Zimmermann, H.J. *Fuzzy Set Theory and its Applications.* KluwerAcademic Pub., Boston, 1985.

Index

A

Active learning, 141, 158–159
  optimal, 158
  specialization, 159
Adverse selection (contract design), 196–198
  asymmetric information, 197
  self-selection, 197
Agriculture (risks)
  DARA, 93
  expected profit maximization model,
    91–92
  expected utility maximization model,
    91–92
  free trade efficiency, 206
  market allocation, 206
  reference lottery usage, 92
  risk behaviors, 91–93
  "safety first" model, 92–93
Allais paradox, 83–85
  independence assumption, 83–85
  indifference curves, 83–85, 85f
Ambiguity theory, 12
  probability theory, 12
Arrow-Pratt coefficient, 36, 38, 65, 69, 88–89,
  108, 154, 187
  Independence assumption, 88–89
  insurance, 187
  mean-variance analysis, 69

risk aversion, 36
risk premiums, 108, 154
stochastic dominance, 65
Asymmetric information, 137, 180, 188, 192,
  197–199
  adverse selection (contract design), 197
  external effects, 198
  informational rents, 198
  insurance, 188
  mechanism design, 198
  optimal contracts, 192
  price discrimination schemes, 198
  resource allocation inefficiencies, 198
  "signaling," 199

B

Bayes theorem, 16–18, 140–141, 215
  learning processes, 17–18, 140–141
  posterior probabilities, 16
  probability theorem, 215
Bayesian analysis (statistics), 11, 16–18
  Bayes theorem, 16
  information analysis, 16
Behaviors (risk), 3
Bid prices, 34, 150
  information, 150
  risk preferences, 34